TRADE ASSOCIATIONS MONOGRAPHS

In addition to the Trade Associations Monographs, the Committee for Economic Development is publishing for the Commission on Money and Credit

THE FEDERAL RESERVE AND THE TREASURY: ANSWERS TO QUESTIONS FROM THE COMMISSION ON MONEY AND CREDIT

and fifty-nine individual essays organized into nine separate volumes, each centered around a particular aspect of monetary and fiscal policy. Their titles and the contributing authors are as follows:

IMPACTS OF MONETARY POLICY

Daniel B. Suits; Robert Eisner and Robert H. Strotz, with a bibliography by G. R. Post; Edwin Kuh and John R. Meyer; Leo Grebler and Sherman J. Maisel; Charlotte DeMonte Phelps; Irwin Friend

STABILIZATION POLICIES

E. Cary Brown, Robert M. Solow, Albert Ando, and John Kareken; Milton Friedman and David Meiselman; Lawrence E. Thompson; Arthur M. Okun; Merton H. Miller; Allan H. Meltzer; Oswald Brownlee and Alfred Conrad

MONETARY MANAGEMENT

Frank M. Tamagna; Warren L. Smith; Clark Warburton; Michael D. Reagan; C. P. Kindleberger; Robert Z. Aliber

FISCAL AND DEBT MANAGEMENT POLICIES

William Fellner; Richard A. Musgrave; James Tobin; James R. Schlesinger; Paul H. Cootner; Irving Auerbach; Ralph K. Huitt; John Lindeman

FEDERAL CREDIT AGENCIES

George F. Break; Jack Guttentag; Ernest Bloch; D. Gale Johnson; Dale E. Hathaway; George S. Tolley; John McCroskey

FEDERAL CREDIT PROGRAMS

Stewart Johnson; Warren A. Law; James W. McKie; D. Gale Johnson; James Gillies; Robert C. Turner and Ross M. Robertson; J. Fred Weston

PRIVATE CAPITAL MARKETS

Irwin Friend; Hyman P. Minsky; Raymond W. Goldsmith

PRIVATE FINANCIAL INSTITUTIONS

Paul M. Horvitz; Deane Carson and Paul Cootner; Victor L. Andrews; Thomas G. Gies, Thomas Mayer, and Edward C. Ettin; Lawrence L. Werboff and Marvin E. Rozen; Fred H. Klopstock; E. Gordon Keith

INFLATION, GROWTH, AND EMPLOYMENT

Joseph E. Conard; Jesse W. Markham; Franklyn D. Holzman; John W. Kendrick; Daniel Creamer; Stanley Lebergott; Lawrence R. Klein and Ronald G. Bodkin; Tibor and Anne Scitovsky

THE CONSUMER FINANCE INDUSTRY

PRENTICE-HALL INTERNATIONAL, INC.
London · Tokyo · Sydney · Paris
PRENTICE-HALL OF CANADA, LTD.
PRENTICE-HALL DE MEXICO, S.A.

National Consumer Finance Association

THE CONSUMER
FINANCE INDUSTRY

A MONOGRAPH
PREPARED FOR THE

Commission on Money and Credit

20554

Prentice-Hall, Inc.

Englewood Cliffs, N.J. | *1962*

Library of Congress Catalog Card No.: 62-15509

Printed in the United States of America
16950-C (paperback); 16951-C (clothbound)

FOREWORD

One facet of the Commission on Money and Credit's investigation was an inquiry into the functioning of our financial system in order to arrive at a judgment of the adequacy of that system and its regulation to serve the needs of a growing economy.

In addition to examining other sources of information and having special studies prepared, the Commission also sought the advice, experience, and opinion of practitioners in the financial area. In this latter connection the National Consumer Finance Association was invited to prepare a monograph on the consumer finance industry.

In soliciting the monograph, the Commission indicated the desirability of having it provide information on the following six topics:

1. The nature of government regulation of consumer finance companies, including tax treatment, and its impact upon the functioning of the industry.
2. The operations and practices of the industry, in terms of flow of funds, portfolio practices, liquidity requirements, and so forth.
3. The role of consumer finance companies in the economy, in terms of their influence upon economic growth, their contribution to economic stability, and their impact upon the allocation of resources.
4. The effects of monetary-debt management policy upon the industry and the role of consumer finance companies in transmitting these policies throughout the economy.
5. The structure and competitive position of consumer finance companies within the industry and vis-à-vis other financial intermediaries.
6. The view of the consumer finance industry regarding possible changes in regulatory or tax provisions.

The National Consumer Finance Association responded willingly to the invitation of the Commission and was most cooperative in working out with the staff of the Commission the scope and detailed outline of the planned monograph. The preparation of the monograph itself was a large task and the finished product was a valuable contribution to the Commission.

In making its request to the NCFA for a monograph on the consumer finance industry, the Commission indicated its desire and expectation to

ix

publish important background and research materials which it used in the course of its work. We are pleased that the Association consented to the inclusion of the monograph among the supporting documents of the Commission and agreed to revise for publication the original paper in order to make this further contribution to the general fund of knowledge on the nature of the consumer finance industry and its role in the economy.

On behalf of the Commission and its staff we would like to express our thanks to the National Consumer Finance Association for the preparation of this study.

BERTRAND FOX
Research Director

ELI SHAPIRO
Deputy Research Director

December 1961

ACKNOWLEDGMENTS

Many individuals deserve personal recognition for contributions to the preparation of this monograph. Initially a consumer finance industry committee, in consultation with members of the research staff of the Commission on Money and Credit, planned the course of the project. Innumerable representatives of the industry gave freely of their time, drawing upon their expert knowledge and experience in order to draft portions of the monograph. Companies in the industry willingly cooperated in supplying information from their accounting and statistical records. The final product was made possible by the wholehearted cooperation of outstanding officials and staffs of consumer finance companies, independent scholars in the field of consumer credit, and the staff of National Consumer Finance Association.

The monograph was put into final form by a three-man editorial committee, each member of which had contributed substantial sections in original draft. This committee consisted of Dr. Paul F. Smith, Family Finance Professor at the Wharton School of Finance and Commerce and the consultant on the preparation of the monograph, Dr. Ernst A. Dauer, Director of Consumer Credit Studies of Household Finance Corporation, and Dr. S. Lees Booth, Director of Research of National Consumer Finance Association.

PAUL L. SELBY
Executive Vice President
National Consumer Finance Association

CONTENTS

List of Charts

List of Tables

List of Appendix Tables

Chapter 1

INTRODUCTION

Purpose and Scope of the Monograph

This monograph is presented to the Commission on Money and Credit as a statement outlining the development of the regulated consumer finance business, its growth, legislative and statutory background, role and function in the national economy, and some of the problems involved in the continuing effort of the industry to achieve and maintain a position of maximum service and usefulness to the consumers of America.

Compiled through the offices of the National Consumer Finance Association, this monograph speaks for the consumer finance business which is engaged in the making of consumer instalment loans under enabling acts and regulatory laws designed to afford protection for both borrower and lender. Such acts and laws have been developed by the states to provide a needed service to their citizens.

Increases in population, population movement, growth in personal incomes, a rising standard of living, increase in home ownership, and suburban living and other factors which have substantially increased the demand for consumer instalment loans are analyzed in this monograph and their relationship with expansion of the business and its capital requirements is set forth.

The structure, function, and operations of the consumer finance business are outlined and its service characteristics are analyzed. This presentation includes a summary of the type and size of operating companies, the number of outlets and their geographic distribution, the number and characteristics of borrowers, the purposes or reasons for borrowing, the loss experience, and the trend toward larger loans.

The following pages concentrate on the consumer finance business from the opening of the first office under an operative small loan law in 1911 to the operation of 12,250 licensed offices in forty-three regulated states as of September 1960. Statistics are presented which show that

1

these consumer finance companies make more loans and serve the financial needs of more American families than any other lending institution, and that they make loan service available to a broad segment of consumers which no other credit institution is able to serve as well. This presentation deals also with the relationship of these offices with other instalment loan offices operating in related fields under consumer discount laws, industrial loan acts, and Morris Plan or certificate plan laws.

This monograph deals also with the problem of financing the consumer finance business itself. To satisfy the increasing demand for consumer services, management must go repeatedly to the general money market for capital and working funds. To compete with others in the demand for these funds, the consumer finance business must operate at a profit sufficient to yield to investors rates of return which are comparable to those offered by other users of investment funds. The monograph discusses the major external factors which affect the profitable operation of the business, including restraints imposed by antiquated laws, discriminatory state and federal tax structures, high cost of money for use in the business, sources of funds, and related leverage factors.

Increasing competition in the instalment loan field is also discussed. Thirty years ago the consumer finance companies in the regulated states had little competition from other institutions in the field of lending. In the great depression of the early thirties the Federal Credit Union Act was added to the state credit union acts of many states. The commercial banks began to experiment with consumer instalment loans during the same decade. Since the end of World War II, the banks and credit unions have found the general area of instalment lending increasingly attractive. In the following pages an effort is made to identify the areas of primary function and the nature of service extended by these competing institutions, and to measure the extent of overlap in their lending services.

The nature, function, and effect of competition among consumer finance companies themselves is also discussed.

The following pages will discuss the role of consumer finance companies in contributing to a balance between production, distribution and consumption, and the implications of consumer credit for economic growth and stability. Although consumer credit shares with all other types of credit the role of adding to the problems of maintaining economic stability, it will be shown that the loans of consumer finance companies fluctuate over a much smaller range than those of other types of credit and that the policies and practices of these companies can help reduce the severity of economic fluctuations.

This monograph will show how restraints imposed by traditional small loan laws should be modified to permit more efficient operation and better service to the public, so that each loan transaction can be tailored to fit the individual family situation. It will be shown how federal controls at the consumer level seriously interfered with freedom of service while Regulation W was in effect, and that such federal controls when applied since the war have been futile and useless as an anti-inflationary control. It will be observed that they also increased costs of operation and seriously interfered with the freedom of choice in millions of individual loan decisions at the critical family level, where individual need and expediency were violated by indiscriminate nationwide application of rigid consumer credit restrictions.

In conclusion, the monograph will summarize the role of consumer finance in today's economy and will support the basic position that, given reasonable freedoms in fair competition, the consumer finance business can apply the experience of the last half century to provide a needed and increasingly important economic service in the coming years.

History of Consumer Finance Companies

Development and Legal Background

The consumer finance business as it exists today has developed from the first consumer credit law, conceived in 1916 to remedy the "loan shark" evil by creating a strictly regulated commercial money-lending business. This remedial law was developed by the Russell Sage Foundation and was called the Uniform Small Loan Law.

To understand the present business and the laws under which it is carried on, it is essential to know something of its genesis.[1]

Usury laws were originally constructed for commercial transactions, requiring loans of large amounts, usually well secured and negotiated between sophisticated parties of fairly equal bargaining power. Under such laws "6 percent per annum" became an ingrained standard measurement of moral and economic rectitude.

Between 1875 and 1915, however, vast changes occurred in our economic and social structure. This period brought the urban movement, the mechanization of industry, the change from a rural nation of small entrepreneurs to an economy based on the mass production system relying on mass consumption; it brought the rise of the wage earner and the decline of the small individual producer.

---

[1] See Louis N. Robinson and Rolf Nugent, *Regulation of the Small Loan Business* (New York: Russell Sage Foundation, 1935); F. B. Hubachek, *Annotations on Small Loan Laws* (New York: Russell Sage Foundation, 1938); George G. Bogert, "The Future of Small Loan Legislation," *University of Chicago Law Review*, December 1944, p. 1; F. B. Hubachek, "The Drift Toward a Consumer Credit Code," *University of Chicago Law Review*, Summer 1949, p. 609; F. B. Hubachek, "The Development of Regulatory Small Loan Laws," *Law and Contemporary Problems*, Winter 1941, p. 108.

Our population became mobile. Apartment dwelling among comparative strangers replaced the tradition of living in a private home among family friends. At the end of this period, for a large part of the population, food, clothing, and shelter could be obtained only by purchase using current wages or savings, whereas before the industrial period such necessities could be produced by the individual, stored as reserves, bartered for, or obtained from friends. There was a thin margin between the average wage earner's family subsistence needs and its available income. Savings were necessarily meager, even for the thrifty.

These changes were gradual but cumulative so that at the turn of the century the mass of our population was dependent on the steady continuation of a cash wage flow. Whenever this flow was interrupted, with or without fault of the worker, or when the family's needs were increased by any emergency, there was nothing for the family to do but suffer, beg, or borrow. The need for cash loans in small amounts was an inevitable result of the industrial revolution—in short, the wage system made such loans an economic necessity.

The laws had lagged far behind reality. To fill an insistent demand based on necessity, the lawful supply for which was barred, the loan shark inevitably arose. Attempts to cure the situation by additional prohibitions and penalties, such as New Jersey's prohibition in 1884 against wage assignments and Missouri's invalidation of the pledge or mortgage of personal property in 1891, only raised the price and forced the business to be carried on with more and more oppression and abuse of borrowers. It became a national vice and a scandal. Millions of wage-earner families were in practical peonage. Ten per cent a month, masked by diverse deceptions and trickery, was a minimum charge exacted on the larger loans of $25 and $50. The average victim had several such loans.

It would be difficult to exaggerate the loan shark evil when the Russell Sage Foundation started its studies in 1908. After long research and experimental legislation, the Foundation concluded that a reliable commercial source for small loans was an economic necessity, to be fostered by law and strictly regulated to protect the borrowers and public. This set the stage for the period of remedial small loan laws.

At that time all debt was frowned on and personal borrowing except for a serious emergency was abhorrent to the conscience of most consumers. The desire of human beings for goods and services past their capacity to pay was deplored and every reasonable obstacle was placed in the way of personal debt except for necessities.

Massachusetts had pioneered the field with the first state small loan law, placed on the books in 1911. Between then and 1916, five more states—Michigan, New Jersey, New York, Ohio, and Pennsylvania—enacted small loan legislation.

In that framework and atmosphere, the first Uniform Small Loan Law was drafted in 1916, the joint product of the Russell Sage Foundation and a few enlightened lenders. Consumer credit at that time was limited to the charge accounts of the carriage trade, rudimentary Morris hypothecated certificate plans, a few scattered credit unions, and a rare instalment sales system such as that of the Singer Sewing Machine Company.

In consequence the model small loan law contained only one permission, the right to charge a commercially practicable rate; but many stringent regulations designed to prevent abuse of the borrower and to deter him from borrowing except after sober forethought.

The most important innovation of these remedial laws was the "all-inclusive rate." Every amount which the lender received, no matter what it was for and whether or not it was part of the "price of money lent," was treated as interest.[2] This had two purposes. First, fees, examination of security, service charges, brokerage, collection costs, tie-in sales, discounts in advance, renewal and extension and delinquency charges, and insurance premiums were favorite devices of the loan shark. Hence, they were all thrown together, bona fide or not, and treated as interest— to be included in one percentage per month maximum figure. Second, this highly overstated rate of charge, in comparison with 6 percent per annum and the understated charge of most lenders, was designed to shock the borrower and deter him from non-necessitous loans.

The use of a per month instead of a per year figure was deliberate and sound. The wage or salary earner lives by the month as a unit of time. His income and principal expenses are by the month, as is his budget.

The rigid restrictions on lenders under these laws were also innovations. Licensed, bonded, unable to make loans except in a registered office or to operate in the same office as another business, required to give itemized receipts and elaborate payment books, subjected to rules and regulations of licensing authorities and expensive periodical examinations, required to keep complicated records in a prescribed manner, subjected to restraints on advertising, denied the right to take certain types of security or to exercise certain legal powers of creditors—these provisions date back to the days when the business was created by statute to cure the loan shark evil, and to discourage borrowing in a period when personal debt was generally deplored.

Today, many of these restraints are as outmoded as the whalebone corset, and even more injurious. They do not permit the adoption of

---

2 All of the costs of verifying the credit worthiness of the consumer-borrower and other related costs as well as the return to the lender for use of his funds, i.e., interest in the economic or commercial sense, were (and still are) included in the all-inclusive rate and referred to as interest.

modern processing and accounting techniques and therefore add to the cost of loans to consumers.

The Uniform Small Loan Law eliminated the loan shark wherever it was enacted. With increasing deviations from the model, laws of this type were enacted by many states, totaling forty-three in 1960. The Uniform Law laid the foundation for the enormous consumer loan and sales finance businesses existing today.

The present consumer finance business has developed under these state small loan laws. The enormous vitality of the business and its necessity in the national economy are proven by its survival and growth under such restraints. The business has held its position against much less-regulated, often unrestrained competition from many other agencies. The national interest would be well served by releasing the industry from restrictions which are now anachronisms.

Growth of the Industry

The consumer finance industry may trace its beginnings to 1911 when the first office was opened under an operative state small loan law in Massachusetts. It was largely based on the findings of Charles W. Wassam and Arthur H. Ham, who as graduate students at Columbia University carried out research projects later published by the Russell Sage Foundation. During the next few years, other states also passed legislation which was operative and more or less effective.

When the Uniform Small Loan Law was agreed upon in 1916, there were six states in which rudimentary small loan laws were in force: Massachusetts, Michigan, New Jersey, New York, Ohio and Pennsylvania.[3] By 1931 there were twenty-two states which had passed statutes containing all of the essential elements of the Uniform Small Loan Laws. As of September 1, 1961, there were thirty-seven states having laws similar to the Uniform Small Loan Law which were reasonably effective. (See Appendix Table A-1.) Most of the others had regulatory statutes of one form or another under which consumer finance companies were permitted to operate.[4]

Impelled by the increasing demand for consumer credit, the industry has grown rapidly over the last several decades. (See Appendix Tables A-2 and A-3.) With the exception of some years during the great depres-

---

[3] The history of the developments during this period are contained in Louis N. Robinson and Rolf Nugent, *op. cit.*, pp. 74-117.

[4] For a detailed discussion of the classification of small loan laws see: Wallace P. Mors, *Small Loan Laws*, Educational Pamphlet No. 2, Western Reserve University, Bureau of Business Research, 1958. Information on statutory small loan rates may be found in *Roster of Consumer Finance Companies* (Washington, D.C.: National Consumer Finance Association), published annually.

sion and during World War II, the number of licensees has increased regularly. During the depression years of the 1930's, the number of licensees in the United States decreased as the level of personal income fell off. (See Chart 1.) After a low point, reached in 1935, the number of licensees began to increase. Not until 1938 did the number of offices once again equal the number operating in 1930. For each of the next few years, until 1941, the number of offices increased substantially. Thereafter, the economics of wartime reduced the number until a wartime low was reached in 1944.

In large measure the cause that led to the closing of hundreds of consumer finance offices in the war years was the manpower shortage. Many young men who operated one or more offices were drafted for military service and sold their businesses to larger companies. These larger companies consolidated the newly purchased offices with others in the same or nearby communities, and also merged many of their own units whose locations were near to each other. Male personnel shortage became so severe that many companies broke tradition to train women as loan office managers. Another factor that worked toward reducing the number of consumer finance offices during the war was the stoppage of the production of consumer durable goods. With these goods not on the market, the demand for consumer credit was reduced accordingly. However, consumer finance companies were affected less by this factor than were many other credit grantors because one of the important uses of credit from consumer finance companies is to meet unexpected or emergency expenses.

Consumer finance offices again began to increase in number during the year 1945 and by 1947 the number in existence was back to the 1941 level. Thereafter, the number has increased steadily each year. By September 1, 1960, there were 12,250 consumer finance offices in operation.[5]

Until 1945 the changes in the volume of loans outstanding at licensed offices of the consumer finance industry followed rather closely the changes in the number of offices. Since World War II, however, the volume of loans outstanding has increased faster than the number of licensed offices, and as a consequence the average volume of loans outstanding per office has increased.

The relationship of the growth in the consumer finance industry to that of personal income is shown graphically in Chart 1. Curtailment of consumer lending during World War II brought a decline in the industry at the very time that personal income was increasing rapidly. Partly reflecting the restoration of the industry to its previous position

[5] For more detail on this historical background, see M. R. Neifeld, *Trends in Consumer Finance* (Easton, Pa.: Mack Publishing Company, 1954).

CHART 1

GROWTH OF PERSONAL INCOME AND OF
THE CONSUMER FINANCE INDUSTRY, 1930-1960

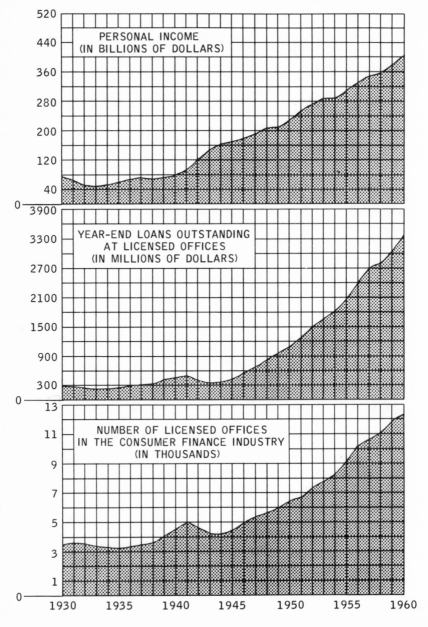

Source: Appendix Table A-2.

8

and partly because of the more widespread acceptance of consumer credit, the consumer finance industry has grown more rapidly than personal income since World War II.

Nature and Types of Consumer Finance Companies and Services Performed

The Nature of the Industry

By way of definition for purposes of this monograph, a consumer finance company is a company engaged in the business of making instalment loans to individuals and families under effective state regulatory and enabling law, commonly called a small loan law. The provisions of the Model Small Loan Law constitute the basis for an effective state small loan law.[6] The "effectiveness" of small loan laws is generally measured in terms of the provisions of the "Uniform Small Loan Law" originally promulgated by the Russell Sage Foundation, or in terms of the "Model Small Loan Law" drawn up by the National Consumer Finance Association in 1948. Most of the companies now operating under licenses are known as consumer finance companies, small loan companies, or personal loan companies.

Some licensed consumer finance companies, when duly authorized by law or regulation, also engage in the sales finance business. There is a trend among sales finance companies to acquire licenses to make cash instalment loans under consumer finance laws.

Many consumer finance companies and sales finance companies provide cash loan service under legal authority other than the Uniform Small Loan Law.[7] Thus, at the end of September 1960, consumer finance companies held $3,460 million in personal instalment cash loans outstanding and sales finance companies held $970 million of the same type of loans, for a total of $4,430 million or 40.5 percent of total personal instalment cash loans outstanding. The remaining volume of this type of loan was held by commercial banks, credit unions, industrial loan companies, dis-

---

[6] The terms "Uniform Small Loan Law" and "Model Small Loan Law" have come to be used interchangeably. Regulatory features consist of provisions with respect to the following:
  1) Licensing by a state supervisory official;
  2) supervision by a state supervisory official having powers to enforce and interpret the law;
  3) authorization of adequate charges to permit a complete service;
  4) limitation of charges;
  5) regulation of contract provisions;
  6) disclosure of terms and status of loan transactions;
  7) prohibition of evasions and subterfuges;
  8) penalties and enforcement powers.
[7] Some laws require the maintenance of separate offices and/or separate corporate entities to provide the cash loan services under different laws.

count companies, and other institutions. There is still a remnant of direct instalment loans made to borrowers in unregulated states by a narrowing fringe of operators with or without legal authorization. For purposes of this monograph, however, we consider that the consumer finance industry comprises only those lenders operating under the Uniform Small Loan Law or some effective adaptation thereof.

An attempt has been made to determine the total number of business entities engaged in the consumer finance industry as defined above. We have identified sixteen corporations, each of which was operating more than 100 offices licensed in states having effective small loan laws at the end of September 1959. Two of them operated more than 500 offices while the other fourteen companies operated from 101 to 500 offices. In addition, 183 companies operated from five to 100 offices, while 3,334 entities operated from one to four offices. Hence, there appears to be something in excess of 3,500 corporations, partnerships, and individual proprietorships operating 11,779 offices engaged in the licensed consumer finance business.

These consumer finance companies are privately owned, free enterprise institutions. Private investors—shareholders—put up the money for the basic capital structure of the business. The companies obtain additional money by borrowing from banks, from insurance companies, and from private investors. In turn, they distribute this money in smaller amounts to individual borrowers on a retail basis.

In the consumer finance business, as in all other successful businesses, charges are based on two factors: the charges to the customer should be commensurate with the service for which he is paying, and the company must charge enough for its services to be able to pay expenses and make a reasonable profit.

Consumer finance companies lend relatively small sums of money to large numbers of people. With an average loan of roughly $330 in 1958, there were about 300 loans in each $100,000 of loans outstanding. This means a lot of time and expense must be devoted to interviewing each applicant and each borrower to decide whether or not he is a good credit risk, and then to keep the records on each loan until the full sum has been paid.

This involves great expense to the lender. Obviously, consumer finance company costs of doing business are higher than if they loaned large sums of money to only a few borrowers. To be able to continue to provide these services, they must charge enough to meet their expenses and to offer an adequate return to capital. A consumer finance company operates as a retail business. Its charge is an all-inclusive charge for complete service. The maximum rate of charge is fixed by the state law and is based upon the cost of doing business in each state. Of necessity, the operating conditions and the rate of charge will vary from state to state as costs vary, but in all states the consumer finance company bears its full share of federal, state, and local taxes to add to the cost of operating the business.

Field of Service

Consumer finance service is available today in most cities and towns throughout the regulated states. The many licensed offices are widely distributed. These companies are engaged in the business of making consumer instalment loans to individuals and families for constructive purposes. The prime consideration in granting a loan is the character of the individual and his capacity to meet his financial obligations. In many cases, however, security in the form of a co-maker or a security lien on household goods or other durable goods is taken as further assurance of the repayment of the loan.

It should be noted here that the last forty-five years have witnessed a tremendous change in the type of loan service extended by the companies and in the objectives and purposes of the loans made. The original concept of the small loan law—in addition to eliminating the loan shark evil—was to create an institution of credit for needy and necessitous families and to provide for them a decent and respectable means of self-help through financial assistance. Through the years the field of regulated lending under law has been extended into more and more states. The consumer finance business, operating within a legal framework, provided the American family with protection and relief from unscrupulous money lenders, made available credit at fair terms, and counseled wise money management and self-discipline. It thus brought a dignified and desirable method of solving the dire emergency problems, and offered the borrower the opportunity to improve his standard of living through the acquisition of time and labor saving devices, educational, and other cultural advantages.

The instalment cash loan has become an important and accepted part of the economic planning for the American family. The typical borrower is a young family whose annual income ranged from $3,000 to $7,500 in 1958. The head of the household may follow any occupation or profession but is most often a skilled or semi-skilled worker. This family borrows to meet unforeseen emergencies, such as medical bills, to consolidate many obligations into a single monthly payment plan, to pay taxes and insurance, to make major purchases, or to take advantage of opportunities for self-improvement.

The consumer finance business has developed skill in adjusting its credit to the borrower's ability to pay. Consumer finance companies provide constructive counseling in the family's financial affairs to the end that the loan granted will help solve a financial problem rather than become an added burden. Financial counseling service has come to be a vital part of this business and is another of the valuable public services it renders. Consumer finance employees are especially trained in this line of work. Such financial counseling service has helped many families learn to budget their incomes wisely, to get the most for their money and to avoid undue indebtedness.

With this type of financial help and with the cash from a consumer instalment loan, a family can meet unexpected needs and emergencies without having to wipe out its carefully acquired savings or sell some of its assets. Generally speaking the monthly payment on loans made by consumer finance companies does not exceed 6 or 8 percent of the monthly income of the borrower. A consumer finance loan, with payments tailored to the individual income pattern, frequently leaves the family in a position to stay in the market for purchasing more than the routine needs for food, clothing, and shelter.

A new appreciation of the value of a good credit rating has developed as one of the incidental results of consumer finance service. Accumulated bills can often be paid with the proceeds of a cash loan, thus combining the burden of accumulated debts into one monthly instalment payment, making possible the liquidation of one debt on a payment schedule within the ability to pay out of current earnings. Thus, delinquency is eliminated and credit standing is maintained or restored.

In many other cases, money borrowed from a consumer finance company is used for the purchase of durable goods, a used car, major home appliances, or furnishings. Savings effected by cash purchase often exceed the cost of the loan and the borrower increases his net worth with each payment. With credit readily available, wise buying on a planned basis is much easier.

The amount of instalment cash loans in the United States has increased steadily for many years. Instalment cash loans do not have the sporadic changes in volume and outstandings which are so characteristic of sales finance operations. The volume of instalment loans has been steadily rising for many years, indicating the importance of regulated borrowing as an adjunct of family living in America.

Chapter 2

PRESENT STRUCTURE
OF THE INDUSTRY

Distribution

Number of Companies and Offices

On September 30, 1959, there were over 3,500 companies operating 11,779 licensed small loan offices in forty-two states having effective small loan laws.[1] The two largest companies in the industry each held over 500 licenses. At the other extreme, there were over 3,300 small organizations, each with less than five offices. (Table 2-1.)

TABLE 2-1
Distribution of Consumer Finance Companies
by Number of Offices, September 30, 1959

Number of Licensed Small Loan Offices	Number of Companies
Over 500	2
301 to 500	2
101 to 300	12
5 to 100	183
Less than 5	3,334
Total	3,533

In arriving at this figure of 3,533 companies in the consumer finance industry, the criterion for a company was that of operation by the same management. Since in this, as in most industries, it is not uncommon to find a parent concern with several subsidiaries, the total number of

---

[1] These figures are from the *Roster of Consumer Finance Companies* which is compiled each year by the National Consumer Finance Association.

entities—corporations, partnerships, and proprietorships—would exceed this figure.

Moreover, if all of the consumer credit offices operated by companies in the consumer finance industry were included in a total figure, the number of offices would far exceed 11,779. Many of these companies operate additional offices in the United States under other legal authority such as sales finance laws and industrial discount laws. Some companies also operate loan offices in Canada and elsewhere.

Thus, the tabular estimates refer only to offices operated under effective small loan laws and to the number of managing companies in the industry.

Offices by States

In 1960, California and Ohio, each with over 1,000 licensed offices, had by far the largest number of licensees under effective small loan laws. At the other extreme were Alaska with fifteen licensees and Tennessee with five. (See the map; Chart 2.) The relationship between the number of small loan licensees and the population of a state is considerably modified by the degree of urbanization and industrialization.

Since the consumer finance business is a retail operation which depends on mass markets, the states having large concentrations of population generally have proportionately larger numbers of small loan licensees. This is especially true where the labor force is predominated by industrial workers whose incomes are moderately high. However, this trend to concentration in industrial centers is considerably modified by institutional and legal factors. In addition, in some parts of the country there is still a remnant of social disapproval of debt, resulting in laws which are calculated to restrict cash lending by setting rates of charge too low to attract adequate capital. Of greater significance is the lag between legislation and economic change. This factor as it affects the various aspects of the consumer finance industry will be discussed later in the monograph.

Asset-Size Classification

The most recent nation-wide survey of the asset-size of consumer finance companies was made by the Federal Reserve System in June 1955.[2] Since that time many changes have occurred in the asset-size of individual companies. In general, the asset-size has increased with the increasing price level as well as with the adoption by more states of higher ceilings on loans made. In terms of an over-all average, the amount

---

[2] See "Survey of Finance Companies, Mid-1955," *Federal Reserve Bulletin* (Washington, D.C.: Board of Governors of the Federal Reserve System), April 1957, pp. 392-408.

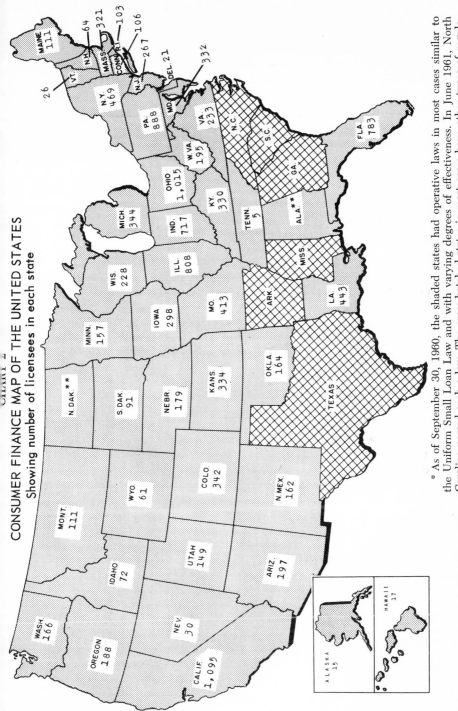

CONSUMER FINANCE MAP OF THE UNITED STATES
Showing number of licensees in each state

MAINE 111
N.H. 64
VT. 26
MASS. 321
CONN. 103
R.I. 106
N.Y. 469
N.J. 267
PA. 888
DEL. 21
MD. 332
W.VA. 195
VA. 233
N.C.
S.C.
GA.
FLA. 783
OHIO 1,015
MICH. 344
IND. 717
KY. 330
TENN. 5
ALA.**
MISS.
LA. 443
ARK.
OKLA. 164
TEXAS
KANS. 334
MO. 413
ILL. 808
IOWA 298
WIS. 228
MINN. 157
N.DAK.**
S.DAK. 91
NEBR. 179
COLO. 342
N.MEX. 162
WYO. 61
UTAH 149
ARIZ. 197
MONT. 111
IDAHO 72
NEV. 30
CALIF. 1,095
WASH. 166
OREGON 188
ALASKA 15
HAWAII 17

* As of September 30, 1960, the shaded states had operative laws in most cases similar to the Uniform Small Loan Law and with varying degrees of effectiveness. In June 1961, North Carolina passed such a law. The cross-hatched states in most cases have other types of regulatory statutes under which consumer finance companies do or may operate.
** The numbers of licensees in Alabama and North Dakota in 1960 are not available.

15

of small loans outstanding per licensee has increased by about 17 percent from about $213,000 in June 1955 to about $250,000 in September 1959.[3] While there undoubtedly have been some shifts in the distribution of consumer finance companies by asset-size classification since 1955, it is probable that the proportions shown in Table 2-2 are still not far from the present situation as long as allowance is made for the increase in the average size of assets per office and per company. Thus, the 1955 survey probably provides a fair approximation of the proportion of large and small companies in the consumer finance industry at the present time. Now, as in 1955, the vast majority of consumer finance companies hold assets of no more than a few hundred thousand dollars, and operate one or two offices. At the other extreme are a few multi-million-dollar companies which operate hundreds of offices in various parts of the country.

Legal and Regulatory Influences of Significance for These Distributions

Licensing Requirements. All of the statutes under which consumer finance companies operate require that each location in which lending activities are conducted be separately and individually licensed. A company operating more than one lending office or branch must obtain a license for each such office or branch.

While the language of such statutes may vary in the different states in minor respects, the following provisions are common among them. (1) Financial responsibility. Over half of such statutes require that a showing must be made that the applicant has available for the operation of such business at the specified location liquid assets of a set minimum amount ranging from $5,000 to $50,000. Thus, even a large company is influenced by the economics of the situation to limit the number and location of its offices, and the entrepreneur whose capital funds are inadequate is discouraged or prevented by this requirement from entering the business. (2) Character and fitness. About 90 percent of these statutes require a finding by the licensing authorities that the financial responsibility, experience, character, and general fitness of the applicant (or the officers and directors thereof) are such as to command the confidence of the public and to warrant the belief that the business will be operated lawfully, honestly, fairly, and efficiently, within the purposes of the statute. (3) Convenience and advantage. About three-fourths of these statutes require a finding by the licensing authorities that allowing the applicant to engage in business at the specified location will promote

---

[3] The June 1955 Federal Reserve survey of consumer finance companies showed an estimated total of 8,830 offices with outstanding loans made under effective small loan laws totaling $1,885 million. In September 1959, there were 11,559 licensees having outstandings of approximately $2,882 million.

TABLE 2-2
Distribution of Consumer Finance Companies by Asset-Size, June 1955

Size of Company (Consumer loans outstanding in thousands of dollars)	Companies		Offices		Total Assets	
	Number	Percent of Total	Number	Percent of Total	(In millions of Dollars)	Percent of Total
25,000 and over	10	0.3	2,560	29.0	1,473	51.0
5,000–24,999	48	1.5	1,586	18.0	555	19.2
1,000–4,999	110	3.5	1,100	12.5	255	8.8
500–999	100	3.1	240	2.7	82	2.8
100–499	1,520	47.8	1,920	21.7	424	14.7
Less than 100	1,390	43.7	1,420	16.1	102	3.5
Total	3,180[a]	100.0	8,830[a]	100.0	2,891	100.0

[a] As reported in *Federal Reserve Bulletin* (April 1957), p. 404, where data were rounded to nearest ten except in the two largest size groups where coverage was complete.

the convenience and advantage of the community in which the licensed office is to be located. A similar finding must be made if, after having obtained a license, the licensee wishes to move its office to a different location.

None of the statutes spells out any tests of what is calculated to "promote the convenience and advantage of the community" or as to what comprises "the community." The result is that there has been no uniformity in the application of this requirement between different states or, in some situations, between different communities or different applicants in the same state.

The practices of the various administrative authorities vary from that of rigid enforcement on the basis of such tests as population, square feet of business space within a defined geographical area, aggregate weekly payroll of the business and industry of the area, number of telephones or electric meters in the community, retail sales, etc., through a strictly arbitrary decision based on no fixed tests, to a complete disregard of the existence of such a requirement.

The "convenience and advantage" licensing provision first appeared in the small loan act of one of the highly industrialized eastern states some thirty years ago. This state had experienced some financial failures among small loan companies which had been organized and rapidly expanded by promoters who foisted worthless securities on the public with the promise of fantastic profits. The introduction of "convenience and advantage" licensing was proposed to help to prevent a recurrence of such experiences.

There are two schools of thought within the consumer finance industry today regarding the propriety of "convenience and advantage" licensing tests.

One school holds that convenience and advantage licensing should remain in regulatory statutes, not only for the purpose for which it originally appeared but also for the protection of the borrowing public, to prevent a saturation of the field with lenders. It is contended by this group that when the consumer finance field becomes saturated with licensees beyond the number necessary to meet the demand of the community, it results in a competitive condition which brings on a laxity in the application of sound credit judgment, a tendency to overload borrowers through multiple loans, and harsh collection practices.

A second school says that convenience and advantage licensing tests have no more place in the consumer finance business than in the retail grocery, drug, or merchandising businesses; that the public is sufficiently educated in the use of credit today that its "convenience and advantage" will best be served by unlimited competition in this field which will give the consumer the same shopping opportunities for cash credit that he has for his other buying; that the character and fitness and financial responsibility tests of the regulatory laws plus the modern statutes controlling the sale of securities are sufficient to prevent frauds on the public; and that adequate loan ceilings coupled with reasonable permissive rates of charge will prevent overloading through multiple loans, as well as discourage the "shoe string" operators, among whom harsh collection practices are most prevalent, from entering the business.

While the lack of uniformity in the interpretation and application of the convenience and advantage test of licensing between the various states and in different communities in the same state, prevents the drawing of any exact conclusions as to its effect upon the distribution of consumer finance offices, it is obvious that any application of such licensing test would be expected to render less effective the normal economic factors which usually determine the number and location of any type of business or financial unit.

Statutory Limitations Upon Licensees. Some of the restrictive provisions of the state regulatory laws have a direct bearing upon the distribution of consumer finance companies.

1) Loan Ceilings—The original draft of the Uniform Small Loan Law prepared in 1916 contained a ceiling of $300 upon the amount of the individual loan permitted to be made by licensees under the Act. Inflation, plus the increased use of consumer cash credit have rendered this ceiling inadequate.

Nevertheless, while the legislatures of most states have given some relief in this respect, the ceilings still range today from $300 to no ceiling. In 1961, twenty-four states with regulatory laws have loan ceilings below $1,000. Seven of these twenty-four states have met the situation by enacting "companion acts" with higher ceilings which acts are commonly referred to by such names as "Consumer Loan Acts," "Industrial Loan Acts," or "Consumer Discount Acts."

The effect of inadequate loan ceilings is to bring about a larger number of licensees in a given area than would otherwise be economically justified.

This is true for two reasons: (1) If a borrower needs $1,000 but the statutory loan ceiling is $500, he must get two loans of $500 each or perhaps three loans, two of $400 each and one of $200. Thus, a false demand for two or three licensees is created where, with an adequate loan ceiling, only one could do the job. If any one licensee can do the whole job, then the borrower is in a better bargaining position, both as to rate and service, and only those licensees who render adequate service will survive. (2) Smaller operators with limited capital tend to flock into areas with low loan ceilings because they are in a better competitive position to bid for a part of a borrower's needs than they would be if they had to meet his full requirements. Also, the small operator with limited capital is attracted by the relatively higher rates permitted on smaller loans.

Asset-size classification is, of course, directly affected by the loan ceiling of a particular state.

2) Rates of Charge—Forty-one states have statutes authorizing rates of charges on loans which scale downward as the amount of the loan made increases. Thus, as the amount of the average loan increases, the rate of return, gross and net, decreases.

The result is that in an economy of rising operating and money costs, the consumer finance company is caught in a squeeze from which it can get no relief except through legislation. In many areas the gross return upon the higher bracket amounts in the larger loans made is less than the aggregate of the per-dollar operating expense, the cost of the money, and taxes, even in the case of the larger companies which are able to borrow capital funds at prime rates. While a number of the larger companies are able and willing to hold on for a period in the hope of ultimate relief, the smaller operators with limited capital cannot survive under such conditions.

Thus, it will be found that smaller companies fail to expand in such areas and eventually either sell out and move to more profitable areas or abandon the business through sale or merger.

Existence of Adequate Enabling Statutes. A number of states do not yet have generally acceptable enabling statutes. A generally acceptable enabling statute is one with a loan ceiling sufficient to meet the needs of the borrowing public and which: (1) authorizes fixed charges on loans adequate to attract capital into the business and at the same time reasonable to the borrower, and (2) contains restrictions and regulations sufficient to assure the protection of the borrower.

While the court decisions interpreting the general usury statutes of a number of states recognize the right of a lender to collect from the borrower, over and above the maximum statutory interest rate, certain reasonable expenses incurred in the making and handling of a loan, the question of what is a "reasonable" expense is generally held to be a question of fact in the case of each individual loan. Thus, a lender who undertakes to make a larger number of small loans in such a legal climate is perpetually vulnerable to attack on the question of whether his service charges are reasonable. For this reason a number of companies in the industry will not risk operation in a state not having a generally acceptable enabling statute.

These conditions account for the fact that some states whose citizens have a genuine need for a consumer finance service and whose general economic conditions are adequate to support a substantial volume of consumer finance lending and a corresponding number of loan outlets have neither. Although some of the larger as well as smaller companies do make loans in such states at rates comparable to those permitted by the statutes of adequately regulated states, such states also contain the remaining hotbeds of so-called "loan shark" lending, involving sums of $50 and less at exorbitant rates of charge. Only a few states presenting this difficulty remain and it is to be expected that eventually there will be none.

The industry, through its national and state trade associations, is carrying on a program of public education designed to create an atmosphere of public understanding and support in which sound enabling statutes can be brought to states not presently having them, and in which such statutes presently in existence can be kept in pace with changing economic conditions and consumer demands.

Competition Within the Industry

Loans

Outlets. Competition for loan outlets is very keen throughout the industry. In states having convenience and advantage licensing restrictions, the number of offices is controlled by state supervisory authorities. The existence of this restriction renders less effective the operation of normal competitive factors.

The number of licensed loan offices in all the states having regulatory licensing statutes increased by 472 from September 1959 to September 1960.

Competitive forces for loan outlets have brought about new trends in the past twenty-five years. Prior to about 1935, consumer finance company lending offices were all located in the heart of the central business districts of the various cities.

This concentration made the establishment of new outlets difficult, both from the standpoint of convenience and advantage licensing, where applicable, and from the point of capturing a share of the market.

Starting about 1935, operators began opening outlets in "neighborhood" areas. These areas are the community business districts which exist adjacent to or within the large cities of the country. A good showing could be made for the need of such outlets under convenience and advantage licensing tests and such outlets also brought a consumer lending service closer to the living and working quarters of the borrowers of the community.

This trend continued, interrupted only by the war years, until 1950 when the immediate potential for this type of expansion was fairly well satisfied. It continues today, however, to a more limited degree, as new population concentrations develop new communities to be served.

Beginning about 1950, and continuing at present, a similar move to develop more outlets started. With the growth of complete shopping centers in suburban areas, consumer lenders are establishing outlets in or adjacent to these centers.

Also, about the same year, the industry began to take note of the fact that increased public demand for consumer credit, coupled with the postwar economic growth of many of the smaller cities and towns throughout the country, made it possible to establish outlets in more of these cities and towns whose residents had previously been forced to commute to the larger adjacent cities to obtain consumer cash credit.

Today, hardly a community of any consequence in the regulated states is without licensed lender services.

Types. For competitive purposes, loans may be broadly classified by purpose, security, and size.

It is generally accepted in the industry that the purpose for which a loan is made has a very strong bearing upon the soundness and collectibility of the loan, and upon the customer good will which produces repeat business. Unless a loan is sought for a constructive purpose which can reasonably be expected to be beneficial to the borrower, the vast majority of the lenders will not make it. Within this general principle, competition is keen.

Contrary to the practice in the early years of consumer lending, very few lenders today limit their activity to secured loans and the unsecured loan is now commonplace. Competition is just as keen for the single signature, or for the husband-and-wife-signature-only loans as for the so-called secured loans. When tangible property is used as security, it frequently has little market value and is "security" largely in a psychological sense. As the size of the loan increases, however, the security factor is given more consideration.

Although the maximum size of loans is set by law in most states, there are two competitive levels determined largely by the resources of the company. The operator with limited capital prefers the smaller average loan with its relatively higher legal rate even though costs are higher per dollar involved. Companies with more money and more mechanization prefer larger loans despite the low rate of gross income on such loans. There appears to be an adequate number of companies in both categories in the industry to produce a keen competition for loans in all legal amounts.

Legal and Regulatory Influences of Significance

There are no legal or regulatory influences which affect competition regarding types of loans. Legal restrictions in this area apply equally to all licensees within the industry. What one licensee can do, so may the other, and what one is prohibited from doing, so are all.

There is, however, a type of self-imposed regulation which is generally followed throughout the industry to prevent overloading of borrowers. This self-regulation is implemented through what is called a Lenders Exchange.

A Lenders Exchange is a voluntary membership organization comprised of the licensed lenders in a given city or trade area. Card files are maintained in an office staffed and supported by the membership showing the names of every applicant of every member. All members clear every application through this Exchange and if the loan is made, the fact is reported to the Exchange.

Thus, upon receiving an application for a loan, a lender may determine whether the applicant has ever applied to or obtained a loan from another lender in the area. If the records indicate a prior application or loan, the lender may contact the other member or members involved to determine whether or not the applicant has a balance or balances outstanding, and the amount or amounts thereof.

Some such Exchanges, by agreement of members, limit the number of loans which will be permitted to be outstanding at one time to one borrower. Others impose no such limits but simply afford lenders the opportunity to evaluate the loan sought by the applicant with the knowledge of his existing loan obligation or obligations.

These Exchanges are prevalent throughout the industry wherever the number of licensees within a given city or trade area is sufficient to warrant the operating expenses. In areas where this is not true, it is the general practice of lenders to make such clearances by direct calls to competitors.

In the area of competition for loan outlets, the legal or regulatory influences of significance have been discussed in Chapter 2.

Competitive Position and Nature of the Competition

Competitive Position vis-à-vis Other Financial Institutions

Essentially all of the financial institutions active and important in the consumer credit field—with the exception of commercial banks—originated as institutions specializing in certain types of consumer credit services. There is no longer the same degree of specialization that once existed. Prior to 1935, the consumer finance companies were practically alone in this field, but since this particular discussion relates to current competitive positions, the period of the last ten years provides the base for this chapter. This period, beginning in 1950, found commercial banks an important factor in the personal instalment loan field. However, our understanding of the competitive position of the various types of institutions is advanced if we recognize that there is still not one consumer credit market but a series of markets, divided in a number of ways.

The estimates prepared and published by the Federal Reserve Board divide the volume of consumer instalment credit outstanding into "major parts"; they also provide figures with respect to the holdings within those major parts of the chief types of financial institutions.

The major parts into which the Federal Reserve Board divides its estimates of outstanding receivables indicate a separation of the total consumer instalment credit market into: (1) credit extended for the purpose of purchasing automobiles; (2) credit extended for the purpose of purchasing other consumer durable goods; (3) credit extended for the repair and modernization of homes; and (4) personal loans.

Each of these areas constitutes a distinct market. Retailers originate credit paper of the first three types, retaining it, or selling it to credit institutions. Cash lending institutions may engage in any one of the four markets in the form of direct loans to consumers. Some banks, for example, make automobile loans directly to consumers; some acquire automobile paper only from dealers; some do both. Some also acquire other types of durable goods paper. Generally speaking, banks do not make loans directly to consumers for the purchase of other types of consumer durable goods when the size of the resulting loan is small, since the legal restriction upon the rates of interest which they may charge results in an inadequate gross income. They will acquire paper covering such durable goods from retailers since they are permitted to charge an adequate rate on such paper. Some banks specialize in the repair and modernization field. Others restrict their activities to the personal instalment cash loan field. Consumer finance company loans are predominantly within the personal loan classification.

The figures released by the Federal Reserve Board cover the entire country. Each individual market, however, has more or less distinct geographic limits since the area served by any one office is restricted to the immediately adjacent territory, which can be conveniently reached by available transportation. Convenience is recognized as an important competitive factor in providing consumer credit service.

The manner in which the various consumer credit institutions share the consumer credit market—i.e., the degree to which each has succeeded in drawing business to itself—is shown in Table 2-3. This table presents the dollar amount, and the percentage distribution of consumer instalment credit outstanding, held on selected dates by the principal consumer credit institutions, both in total and by major parts. September 30, 1950, was the date on which the Federal Reserve Board required reports of all registrants under Regulation W and thus secured a complete census. For September 30, 1958-60, all the figures are as published by the Federal Reserve Board with the exception of the distribution of the

TABLE 2-3
Consumer Instalment Credit Markets by Major Parts, September 30, 1950, and 1958-1960

Holder and Type of Credit	In millions of dollars outstanding				Percentages of each type held by major consumer credit institutions			
	9/30/50	9/30/58	9/30/59	9/30/60	9/30/50	9/30/58	9/30/59	9/30/60
Total Consumer Instalment Credit								
Commercial Banks	5,819	12,633	14,886	16,416	40.3	38.0	39.0	38.6
Sales Finance Companies	3,825	8,891	9,949	11,154	26.5	26.8	26.1	26.2
Consumer Finance Companies	1,192	3,280	3,543	4,111	8.2	9.9	9.3	9.7
Credit Unions	585	2,591	3,130	3,795	4.0	7.8	8.2	8.9
Other Financial Institutions	396	1,444	1,678	1,842	2.7	4.3	4.4	4.3
Total Financial Institutions	11,817	28,839	33,186	37,318	81.8	86.8	87.0	87.8
Retailers	2,635	4,391	4,979	5,199	18.2	13.2	13.0	12.2
Total	14,452	33,230	38,165	42,517	100.0	100.0	100.0	100.0
Retail Automobile Credit								
Commercial Banks	2,519	6,190	7,279	8,091	40.7	42.9	44.3	44.9
Sales Finance Companies	3,034	6,601	7,328	7,832	49.0	45.8	44.6	43.5
Consumer Finance Companies	112	123	125	128	1.8	0.9	0.8	0.7
Credit Unions	154	850	990	1,220	2.5	5.9	6.0	6.8
Other Financial Institutions	86	155	215	231	1.4	1.1	1.3	1.3
Total Financial Institutions	5,905	13,919	15,937	17,502	95.4	96.6	96.9	97.1
Retailers	286	496	506	519	4.6	3.4	3.1	2.9
Total	6,191	14,415	16,443	18,021	100.0	100.0	100.0	100.0
Other Consumer Goods Credit								
Commercial Banks	1,429	2,221	2,557	2,686	31.4	26.9	26.9	25.5
Sales Finance Companies	576	1,551	1,761	2,292	12.7	18.8	18.5	21.7
Consumer Finance Companies	104	325	400	523	2.3	3.9	4.2	5.0
Credit Unions	36	225	270	320	0.8	2.7	2.8	3.0
Other Financial Institutions	52	41	39	42	1.1	0.5	0.4	0.4
Total Financial Institutions	2,197	4,363	5,027	5,863	48.3	52.8	52.9	55.6
Department Stores (Inc. Mail Order)	687	1,543	1,903	2,049	15.1	18.7	20.0	19.4
Furniture Stores	777	1,047	1,118	1,129	17.1	12.7	11.8	10.7
Household Appliance Stores	260	295	299	291	5.7	3.6	3.1	2.8
Other Retailers	625	1,010	1,153	1,211	13.7	12.2	12.1	11.5
Total Retailers	2,349	3,895	4,473	4,680	51.7	47.2	47.1	44.4
Total	4,546	8,258	9,500	10,543	100.0	100.0	100.0	100.0
Repair and Modernization Credit								
Commercial Banks	816	1,659	1,953	2,162	81.9	74.0	73.3	72.0
Sales Finance Companies	65	20	30	60	6.5	0.9	1.1	2.0
Credit Unions	29	115	170	210	2.9	5.1	6.4	7.0
Other Financial Institutions	86	449	511	569	8.6	20.0	19.2	19.0
Total	996	2,243	2,664	3,001	100.0	100.0	100.0	100.0
Personal Loans								
Commercial Banks	1,055	2,563	3,097	3,477	38.8	30.8	32.4	31.7
Sales Finance Companies	150	719	830	970	5.5	8.6	8.7	8.9
Consumer Finance Companies	970	2,832	3,018	3,460	35.6	34.1	31.6	31.6
Credit Unions	366	1,400	1,700	2,040	13.5	16.8	17.8	18.6
Other Financial Institutions	178	800	913	1,005	6.5	9.6	9.5	9.2
Total	2,719	8,314	9,558	10,952	100.0	100.0	100.0	100.0

Sources: *Federal Reserve Bulletin* (October 1951; December 1960; August 1961). Credit union outstandings, by major parts, from "Report on Credit Unions," R. Modley, ed., (Kent. Conn.: Reports, Inc.) Consumer finance company outstandings, by major parts for Board of Governors of the Federal Reserve System, release R&S-2395, dated December 1960.

holdings of credit unions for which the estimate of Dr. Rudolf Modley was used.[4]

The percentage tables confirm the earlier statement that it is necessary to look not at total instalment credit, but rather at the figures for major parts to obtain an understanding of the competitive situation. The most important fact shown is that some change, but not much, occurred over the ten-year period.

Over the ten-year period, the share of total consumer instalment credit held by consumer finance companies increased from 8.2 percent to 9.7 percent. Since about 85 percent of the outstandings of the consumer finance companies are represented by personal instalment cash loans, extended for purposes other than the purchase of goods and services, it is the figure for this "major part" of the consumer instalment credit market which is important.

In looking at the competitive position within the personal instalment cash loan field, it is necessary to combine the published figures for consumer finance companies and sales finance companies. The cash lending subsidiaries of sales finance companies, to which the latter figures apply, are generally licensed under small loan laws and are usually members of the National Consumer Finance Association. The formation of such subsidiaries reflects the desire of the parent companies for diversification of credit activities.

Roughly three-quarters of the personal instalment cash loans are held by consumer finance companies, sales finance company subsidiaries, and commercial banks. Over the ten-year period, the percentage held by commercial banks dropped from 38.8 percent in 1950 to 31.7 percent in 1960. The combined share held by consumer finance companies, sales finance companies, and sales finance company subsidiaries remained virtually unchanged, being 41.1 percent in 1950 and 40.5 percent in 1960. The share held by credit unions has shown a steady increase from year to year. The significant increase shown by miscellaneous financial institutions presumably reflects the growth in loans under laws recently passed in several states, which differ markedly from the provisions of the Uniform Small Loan Law.

Examination of the shifts, from year to year within the period, indicates that a number of different influences have been at work. In certain years, changing money market conditions, and in other years, changes in credit policies have had a marked influence on the competitive position of banks and sales finance companies in the automobile field. The significant growth in the dollar amount of personal loans held by commercial

---

[4] As published in Rudolph Modley, ed., *Report on Credit Unions* (Kent, Connecticut: Reports, Inc.).

banks from 1958 to 1959 (accounting for almost 40 percent of the increase in total personal instalment cash loans in that period) undoubtedly reflects the aggressive promotion by banks of newer forms of personal loans. In 1960, however, the percentage of personal loans held by commercial banks dropped to 31.7 percent from 32.4 percent in 1959, as credit union holdings increased by about the same percentage.

Competition for Consumer Loans

Many of the writings of economists make assumptions relative to the existence of a perfectly competitive market. In his classic article with respect to the nature of competition in the consumer credit field,[5] Professor Theodore O. Yntema pointed out that a perfectly competitive market does not actually exist anywhere in our economic system—and hence does not exist in the consumer credit field. In such a market, every decision to buy or to sell, and from whom to buy or to sell, would be determined by prices. Such a perfectly competitive market would require the following characteristics: (1) a commodity or service which is uniform in type and quality, and (equally important) that this uniformity is recognized by buyers and sellers; (2) a large number of sellers, each independently offering the commodity or service for sale, and a large number of buyers independently bidding for the commodity; (3) all buyers and sellers accurately and fairly completely informed as to the price offered and bid; and (4) buyers and sellers who encounter no obstacles in entering or retiring from the market, such as costs sunk in organization and equipment.

At first blush, it would appear that "money" or the "use of money" is a uniform product or service. However, consumer credit involves not merely the receipt by the consumer of a certain amount of money or its equivalent (i.e., goods or services) and the payment of money at a future date or dates. An integral part of the transaction is confidence on the part of the consumer in the fair dealing of the lender or seller. Every loan represents the result of analysis of the needs and capabilities of the borrower, and a program designed personally for him. Thus, technically, every consumer credit transaction is unique since there are not two borrowers or purchasers whose needs and capabilities are identical.

The principal lenders of cash are consumer finance companies operating (primarily) under small loan laws, commercial (and industrial) banks, credit unions, industrial loan companies, and (in some states) illegal lenders. State or federal laws circumscribe the operations of each

---

[5] Theodore O. Yntema, "The Market for Consumer Credit: A Case in 'Imperfect Competition,'" *Annals of the American Academy of Political and Social Science,* March 1938, pp. 79-81. See also Clyde W. Phelps, "Monopolistic and Imperfect Competition in Consumer Loans," *Journal of Marketing,* April 1944, pp. 382-393.

type of institution. Such restrictions, which vary from state to state,[6] apply to all companies or units of a particular type, but do not apply to the types uniformly.

Small loan laws restrict companies operating under them with respect to the maximum amount of loan, require uniform payments, and limit the term or schedule of loan payments. They prescribe the method of calculating and stating charges. Historically, they have required that rates of charge be calculated, or stated, as a percent per month of unpaid principal balances.[7] They usually regulate advertising and other practices in the interest of protecting the borrower. Small loan laws do not permit the use of real estate mortgages as security, but do permit chattel mortgages.

To a lesser degree, and with infinite variations from state to state, the operations of the other principal types of cash lending institutions are circumscribed by statutes and by applicable regulations. The service offered by any one lender is differentiated from that of others by the legal requirements applicable to its type and by the security requirements, loan policy, and collection policy established by its own management, as well. The product, the credit service, is not uniform or identical.

Commercial banks are restricted in a majority of the states as to the size of consumer instalment loans, and rates of charge. Generally speaking, however, their operating practices are not circumscribed by law to the degree found in small loan laws.

Credit union services are offered only to members of credit unions; the credit union law restricts membership within any single credit union to a more or less homogeneous group of members having a common bond of interest. Credit union laws also restrict the rate of charge, and the amount of loan which may be made to a single borrower.

In sales transactions, in which the consumer acquires not money but goods or services, the retailer is the key figure. The terms of the credit sale may vary greatly with respect to the down payment, cost of the credit service, and the clauses of the contract. The retailer may use down payment and maturity terms, and the rate or amount of the finance charge to attract business, and may vary them when bargaining with an individual purchaser. He may also vary other conditions of the contract. For example, he may not take advantage of repossession clauses.

Generally, the variations described will result from the credit and collection policies of the individual retailer. Until recently, retail policies and practices with respect to credit sales have been circumscribed to only a minor degree by state law. Indiana and Wisconsin adopted retail

---

[6] We are ignoring the question of the areas in which, if any, state or federal laws are supreme in the case of federal credit unions and national banks.

[7] Several recent laws may reflect a trend toward permitting, as an alternate method, charges stated in dollars per $100 of initial loan balance.

instalment sales legislation as early as 1935, and about ten states followed suit in the ensuing fifteen years. Today, there are well over thirty states with retail instalment legislation, much of it adopted since 1956.[8] However, many of these laws apply to automobile transactions only.

Instalment contracts may be retained by the retailer throughout their life or they may be transferred to a credit institution. Credit standards and collection practices, and rates of charge of these credit institutions, are determined by their individual policies—subject to the restrictions imposed by state law. Unlike the situation in the cash lending field where different laws cover different types of lenders, the retail instalment sales laws apply uniformly to all types of financing agencies. Thus, if anything, they tend to promote a degree of uniformity of credit services.

Competition Between Types of Financial Institutions

The devices, techniques, and methods by which consumer credit institutions compete vary from one type to another. In the cash lending field, individual institutions make a direct appeal to the consumer to attract his patronage.

Commercial banks generally stress lowness of rates of charge—a condition which is made possible through specialization in large loans to select risks. Individual banks, though their rates of charge may vary, do not tend to emphasize rate competition among themselves, but only vis-à-vis other types of institutions. The lower rates of charge impose a limit upon the costs which a bank can incur in attracting applicants, in investigating their credit-worthiness, and in servicing and collecting loans. Bank management, aware of the cost limitations and of its responsibilities to depositors, usually sets materially higher credit standards in selecting risks than other consumer credit institutions.

Credit unions generally stress lowness of rates of charge vis-à-vis other institutions. They also stress idealistic or moralistic motives of helpfulness to fellow members. However, a consumer can obtain a loan from a credit union only if he is a member of that credit union; but the same individual who has access to credit union services can utilize the services of a bank, a consumer finance company, or other lending institution, depending upon his ability to meet their credit standards, or upon the degree to which his needs can be served by them.

Consumer finance companies tend to stress the quality, convenience, and availability of their service. They have a unique characteristic which is pertinent to the nature of their credit services. As has been pointed out earlier, the small loan law was enacted for the purpose of providing a legitimate source of cash credit for a substantial body of consumers

---

[8] For summaries of these laws, see Alan S. Jeffrey, "A Summary of State Instalment Sales Laws—1959," *Time Sales Financing* (September 1959), pp. 3 ff.

who were not being served by existing legitimate sources. To be effective, these small loan laws had to provide a rate of charge sufficient to permit an efficient manager of a small loan office to provide a financial counseling service to the potential borrower, to tailor the loan and its terms to fit the borrower's specific needs, and to guide him in the appropriate steps necessary to effect his financial rehabilitation if he is in trouble. Small loan rates of charge are designed to permit the necessary higher costs of these services, of the more complete investigation, and the special services attendant to instalment lending of relatively small sums of money.

Consumer Reaction to Competition

Yntema and Phelps have both pointed out, correctly, that imperfect knowledge on the part of consumers of the variety of services available, and of the prices of those services, is a deterrent to the perfect working of competitive forces. The complexity in the variety of consumer credit service, the infrequency of using those services, and the private nature of most consumer credit transactions tend to prevent consumers from knowing which type of service best fits his needs.[9]

Many consumers set significant values upon convenience, upon continuing relationships with those in whom they have confidence, and upon the environment in which they do business. In general, they tend to seek out the institution whose eligibility requirements they can meet. Often this requires an amount of investigation, to establish credit worthiness, greater than the institutions which charge "low rates," can afford to make.

Although very little published information is available about the characteristics of bank borrowers, it is a generally accepted fact that they tend to be in higher income classes than borrowers from consumer finance companies; they tend also to be in different occupational groups. This situation tends to exist even in those states (for example, Missouri and Rhode Island) where banks are permitted to charge rates on consumer loans comparable to those under which consumer finance companies operate. In these communities, particularly, bankers realize that they can best serve a certain class of customer and that there is a segment of the market which consumer finance companies can more effectively serve—a segment determined largely by the character of the borrower and his needs.

Bankers who have considered the matter carefully do not wish to handle all of the consumer credit business, and realize that a bank

---

[9] This is developed in the paper by Ernst A. Dauer, "The Nature of Competition in Consumer Credit," in *Proceedings of the Tenth Annual National Consumer Credit Conference* (Columbus, Ohio: The Ohio State University, Bureau of Business Research, 1958), p. 18.

cannot serve all consumers adequately. First, they recognize that sound operating policies require diversification of assets. This principle places a limitation upon the proportion of its assets which a bank can invest in any one field. Second, when bank reserves are under pressure, the responsibility to serve all areas of loan demand in their community limits their ability to expand consumer loans. Third, banks, due to the fact that they generally make much larger consumer loans, must be more selective than consumer finance companies. Ninety percent or more of the funds of a commercial bank are in the form of demand deposits which bear no interest. Its primary responsibility is to its depositors. A bank is examined rigorously to insure that its loans and other assets do not jeopardize the depositors' position. The consumer finance company can take a considerably greater degree of risk, because its creditors are different and its ownership equity is higher. When banks recognize the area in which they can more effectively serve, they usually make the loans involving the least risk and the minimum of service. These are usually loans of larger size.

It is undesirable and uneconomic for either banks or consumer finance companies to attempt to serve the area which the other can serve more effectively. There is an area of overlap, in which the two types of institutions do in fact appropriately compete.

Opinions differ widely as to size of the area of overlap. It is clear that it differs from place to place and from time to time. The outstanding dissertation by Dr. W. David Robbins is one of the few studies in this area.[10] For 1950 and 1951, it sets forth the characteristics of loans made by, and of borrowers from, commercial banks, consumer finance companies, and credit unions, respectively. In his summary, he concludes: "Each of the principal types of lending institutions is important and all make a definite contribution to society. Each type competes with the other types *for a certain segment* of the consumer loan market, but the area of competition is not nearly as important as the fact that all of the principal types are essential." [11]

Legal Impediments to Effective Competition

From the point of view of consumer finance companies, there are various statutory and administrative impediments to effective competition. As indicated in preceding pages, their business is subjected to a much higher degree of regulation than are other credit institutions. This difference in the degree of regulation increases the operating costs of consumer finance companies, and, thereby, their loan charges, and other-

---

[10] W. David Robbins, *Consumer Instalment Loans* (Columbus: The Ohio State University, Bureau of Business Research, 1955).

[11] *Ibid.*, p. 124. Emphasis has been added.

wise makes it more difficult for them to compete with other types of credit institutions. Unjustifiable legal impediments operating to the competitive disadvantage of consumer finance companies fall into three categories.

The largest group consists of outmoded provisions of small loan laws which have survived the original era of modern consumer finance with its different social and economic conditions. Under current conditions, many of these provisions are unnecessary or unduly severe. They are: (1) licensing and bonding, often on an annual basis; (2) payment of substantial annual license, bonding, and examination fees; (3) periodic official examinations; (4) subjection to official rules, regulations, and directives; (5) restraints on advertising; (6) restrictions against making loans outside of the licensed office; (7) restrictions against doing another business in the licensed office; (8) prohibitions against certain types of security; (9) requirements for the keeping of complicated records in a prescribed manner; (10) requirements as to receipts, loan statements, and pass books; and (11) denial of enforcement powers permitted other types of creditors.

Another legal impediment to effective competition has resulted from the failure of certain states to increase the maximum loan permitted under their small loan laws to a size required by present-day economic conditions. Several states still retain the $300 size limit contained in the original (1916) draft of the Uniform Small Loan Law. This is now grossly inadequate. Even the $500 maximum size limit to which the $300 size was increased in a number of states, is now too low.[12] With the consumer price index in 1960 at a level over 2.7 times that of 1916, a loan of $800 in 1960 would have less purchasing power than $300 in 1916. In some states having inadequate size limits, consumer finance companies make larger loans under other regulatory laws. But this expedient is awkward and relatively inefficient, as it entails compliance with different regulatory requirements, and use of different contract forms, loan records, and in some states, a separate corporation. These outmoded restrictions force the customer of the consumer finance company either (1) to secure two or more loans from competing companies or (2) to borrow from lenders of other types. The borrower is thus forced to pay more for his loan than he otherwise would, in view of the common procedure of providing lower rates on larger loans, or he is driven to other types of consumer credit institutions where his needs cannot be met so well—if at all.

A third type of legal impediment to effective competition results from inequality in basic regulatory provisions. Thus, the ability of consumer

---

[12] See F. B. Hubachek, "Progress and Problems in Regulation of Consumer Credit," *Law and Contemporary Problems* (Winter 1954), p. 14.

finance companies to compete is curtailed by inequality in legal provisions as to (1) method of stating and calculating charges and (2) maximum loan maturities.

The Uniform Small Loan Law and laws patterned thereon have historically provided for a single all-inclusive charge in the form of a monthly percentage rate computed on principal balances. Other kinds of regulatory laws often sanction a complex rate structure, such as interest plus fees, and/or permit charges to be deducted from the loan, thus reducing the amount actually advanced. Almost all permit the interest charge to be stated and computed as a percentage of the original or face amount of the loan. This inequality in the form of loan charges operates to the serious disadvantage of consumer finance companies because their rates of charge are thereby made to appear grossly in excess of those of competing institutions operating under such other laws.[13] This inequality could be reduced by permitting consumer finance companies to state and compute their charges as a dollar amount per year per $100 of loan granted. Some states have already done so.

Consumer finance companies are more often restricted as to the duration of loan contracts than other credit institutions, and to the extent that the latter are so restricted their maximum loan maturities are often longer than those prescribed in or under small loan laws. Such inequality reduces the capacity of consumer finance companies to compete for loans which cannot be conveniently repaid within the applicable maximum maturity.

Effective competition by consumer finance companies is also hampered by other inequalities in the extent to which competing institutions are subjected to basic regulatory safeguards which experience has shown to be necessary and which apply to consumer finance companies. Such inequalities range from total absence in some states of laws regulating consumer credit transactions of commercial banks or sales finance companies, to laws omitting important safeguards or casting them in a milder form. For example, there is a wide variation in the sanctions provided for violations. The penalty of total invalidation of loan contracts, provided by small loan laws for violation of loan charge limitations and certain other violations, imposes a heavy burden on consumer finance companies to comply strictly with the statutory restrictions.[14] On the other hand, the milder sanctions commonly provided by other types of laws permit much greater freedom of action and may not deter evasions by unscrupulous persons.

---

[13] See George A. Bogert, *op. cit.*, note 1.
[14] See the decision in *Fisher* v. *Bethesda Discount Corp.* (Md. Ct. of App., 1960) 157 Atl. 2d 265, which applied the invalidity penalty of the Maryland Industrial Finance Law.

Chapter 3

SOURCES OF FUNDS

Comparisons with Other Types of Financing Institutions

Consumer finance companies over the period of their existence have taken essentially all of the common forms of organization, including the individual proprietorship, the partnership, the "Massachusetts" or common law trust, and the corporate form. Today, the corporate form predominates. Generally, sources of funds have been the same as those of similar privately owned organizations in other fields of endeavor. This has been true also of two other types of specialized consumer financing institutions, namely, sales finance companies and industrial loan companies.

This is in contrast to certain other consumer financing institutions (i.e., commercial banks, industrial banks, and credit unions) which obtain their funds from sources peculiar to those types of institutions.

Commercial banks obtain essentially all of their funds, other than the stockholders' investment in net worth, from demand and time deposits. Industrial banks secure their funds in a similar manner. Historically, industrial banks as an institution developed from industrial banking "companies" which sold investment certificates to the general public.[1] When suitable laws were adopted, these companies obtained bank charters and obtained their funds in a manner similar to commercial banks. Over the years, they have taken on the characteristics of commercial banks to an increasing degree.

Credit unions, being mutual institutions, receive essentially all of their

---

[1] Both the industrial banks which accept deposits and their predecessors, companies which sold investment certificates, have been called "investment-type" industrial banking companies by one authority, to distinguish them from the industrial loan companies (or "non-investment-type") referred to earlier. For a full treatment, see Raymond J. Saulnier, *Industrial Banking Companies and Their Credit Practices* (New York: National Bureau of Economic Research, 1940).

funds from the sale of shares to members,[2] as a rule, only an insignificant portion is borrowed, chiefly from other credit unions.

Historical Trends in Sources of Funds

Equity vs. *Long-Term Debt* vs. *Short-Term Debt*

In considering historical trends with respect to sources of funds, it is helpful to recognize three separate and distinct time periods. First, the period prior to 1928; second, the period from 1928 until 1941; [3] and, third, the period since the end of World War II.

Prior to 1928. There is little evidence available about the sources of funds of consumer finance companies in the early period. Initially, consumer finance operations were almost always individual proprietorships or partnerships and their funds were supplied predominantly, if not entirely, by the owners. Expansion, to a very large degree, was limited by the amount of net profits which they were able to retain in the business.

The adoption of the corporate form, with its wider sources of funds, was retarded because, in many states, corporations (other than banks) were not authorized to lend money. Thus, it was not until after the adoption of state laws giving corporations the legal power to lend money, that consumer finance enterprises began to operate as corporations.

The first time that orthodox public financing was made available to a consumer finance company was probably in October 1928, when Household Finance Corporation sold participating preference stock through Lee Higginson and Company. Thereafter, other investment banking houses followed suit.

1929 to 1941. Characteristic of consumer finance companies was the high proportion, compared with other credit institutions, of funds obtained through use of owners' equity or net worth. However, during the period 1929-41, these companies attained flexibility in the sources of their funds through the increased use of borrowed money, chiefly short-term borrowings. They were able, in general, to adjust the volume of funds

---

[2] The "shares" of credit unions occupy a peculiar legal status. Since our interest lies in whether funds are obtained from ownership or from borrowing, emphasis is to be placed upon the fact that these shares are similar to common stock equity. If our interest lay in the analysis of credit union solvency, we should have to consider the shares as the equivalent of deposits, since it is common practice to permit their withdrawal upon demand; the cushion which protects the shareholders is limited to the amount of surplus, undivided profits, and surplus reserves.

[3] The material covering this period is based largely upon Chapter 2 of the study by Ernst A. Dauer, *Comparative Operating Experience of Consumer Instalment Financing Agencies and Commercial Banks, 1929-41* (New York: National Bureau of Economic Research, 1944).

to the demand for their services, increasing borrowings when demand rose and paying them off when demand declined. In effect, they obtained funds at wholesale, chiefly from banks, and retailed them to consumers.

Over the period 1929-41, their sources of funds give evidence of their progress. The chief change was a gradual lowering of the proportion of equity funds in each type of institution. Also, borrowed funds, both long- and short-term, were obtained at much lower rates in the last few years of the period than were available a decade earlier. This resulted from the much wider acceptance of these companies by banks, and in the money market generally, as their sound credit character became evident.

In 1929, 1933, and 1936, years for which data are available from income tax returns of 179 companies, net worth averaged between two-thirds and four-fifths of total assets. In 1936, in materially more than half the companies, net worth represented at least 80 percent of total funds. In addition, net worth was less than half of total funds in only a relatively small proportion (about one-sixth) of the companies. Throughout the entire period, net worth exceeded borrowings of the half dozen largest and most recognized companies in the field.

Until the very end of this period, consumer finance companies did not obtain funds through long-term borrowings, except in rare instances. Their short-term borrowings were a smaller proportion of their total funds than was true of sales finance companies or industrial banks.

The small proportion of short-term debt among consumer finance companies reflected the difficulty encountered in obtaining access to the short-term money market and to commercial banks. The consumer finance company faced the reluctance of the banker to recognize the soundness or the ethical justification of loans for consumption purposes. The stigma that earlier had been attached to the loan shark also carried over in some degree to the consumer finance company. Since their volume of cash loans has been subject to relatively small seasonal or cyclical fluctuation, consumer finance companies do not find it undesirable to derive their funds from relatively permanent sources. Nevertheless, it was not until the very end of the period 1929-41 that the largest companies began the practice of selling long-term securities through public offerings and through investment bankers. Thus, they initiated the trend which spread to middle-sized companies after World War II.

After World War II.[4]   The steady expansion of the demand for consumer loans after World War II presented consumer finance companies with an almost continuous problem of obtaining new funds. From 1945 to 1959, the loans of these companies increased from $0.5 billion to $4.1

---

[4] See also John M. Chapman and Frederick W. Jones, *Finance Companies: How and Where They Obtain Their Funds* (New York: Columbia University, Graduate School of Business, 1959).

billion. They had emerged from World War II with a capital-debt structure that was very similar to the structure that had prevailed before the war. As the demand for loans increased, all available sources of funds were used. The net worth and long-term debt of consumer finance companies increased in every year from 1945 to 1959 and their short-term borrowing increased in all but four years. (See Tables 3-1 and 3-2.) The pattern and rate of expansion in each source of funds varied with the market situation and with the ability of individual companies to obtain funds in the specific markets.

This discussion is based largely on information for a sample of consumer finance companies originally published by the Board of Governors of the Federal Reserve System in their comprehensive study of consumer instalment credit.[5] Data for years subsequent to those previously published were made available for use in this study. The sample includes the five largest companies for the period 1945 to 1952 and the six largest companies for the years 1952-59, and it covers a varying number of companies in the smaller size groups (those with assets of less than $50 million). It included fifteen of the smaller companies from 1945 to 1952; forty-one companies from 1952 to 1955; and twenty-six companies from 1955 to 1959.

The information from the Federal Reserve System was supplemented by data on the sources of short-term funds and for the nature of subordinated obligations from a sample of twenty-one companies that reported information to the National Consumer Finance Association for use in this study. As of June 30, 1959, these twenty-one companies operated 4,283 offices, out of nearly 12,000 licensed offices then in existence. The twenty-one companies held consumer instalment credit of $1,983 million, or 57.9 percent of the receivables then held by all consumer finance companies. Their personal loans outstanding under small loan laws amounted to $1,433 million, or slightly in excess of 50 percent of the total amount of such loans. Thus, the sample is large in proportion to the total loans outstanding in the industry and has a very high representation from the "large" and "moderately large" companies in the field.

The NCFA sample has been classified into four groups on the basis of size of assets. The two companies classified as "large" are the only consumer finance companies with assets exceeding $350 million. The seven companies classified as "moderately large" include all consumer finance companies with assets between $50 million and $350 million, except one operating solely in the State of Ohio, whose capital structure is unique and would not lend itself to inclusion in this study. Excluded

---

[5] Board of Governors of the Federal Reserve System, *Consumer Instalment Credit* (Washington, 1957), Part 1, Vol. 2, pp. 5-39.

TABLE 3-1
Debt and Net Worth of Selected Consumer Finance Companies, 1945-1959

End of Year	Amount in millions of dollars				Percentage Distribution			
	Notes Pay- able	Long- Term Debt	Net Worth	Total Debt And Net Worth	Notes Pay- able	Long- Term Debt	Net Worth	Total Debt And Net Worth
20 companies								
1945	69	48	139	256	27	19	54	100
1946	159	84	154	397	40	21	39	100
1947	188	112	175	475	39	24	37	100
1948	226	147	203	576	39	26	35	100
1949	243	191	229	663	37	29	34	100
1950	317	233	263	813	39	29	32	100
1951	315	352	284	951	33	37	30	100
1952	367	416	340	1,123	33	37	30	100
47 companies								
1952	436	451	384	1,271	34	36	30	100
1953	430	558	427	1,415	30	40	30	100
1954	430	640	453	1,523	28	42	30	100
1955	573	695	495	1,763	33	39	28	100
32 companies								
1955	536	673	478	1,687	32	40	28	100
1956	571	900	530	2,001	29	45	26	100
1957	537	1,077	574	2,188	25	49	26	100
1958	559	1,106	629	2,294	25	48	27	100
1959	640	1,188	663	2,491	25	48	27	100

Source: Board of Governors of the Federal Reserve System.

TABLE 3-2
Percentage Changes in Selected Consumer Finance Companies' Debt and Net Worth, 1945-1959
(Percentage change during year)

End of Year	Total, debt and net worth	Notes Payable	Long-Term Debt	Net Worth
20 companies				
1946	55	129	75	11
1947	20	19	34	13
1948	21	20	31	16
1949	15	7	30	13
1950	23	31	22	15
1951	17	-1	51	8
1952	18	16	18	20
47 companies				
1953	11	-1	24	11
1954	8	-	15	6
1955	16	33	9	9
32 companies				
1956	19	7	34	11
1957	9	-6	20	8
1958	5	4	3	10
1959	9	14	7	5

Source: Board of Governors of the Federal Reserve System.

also from this size group were five companies which are subsidiaries of sales finance companies and hence are not classified as consumer finance companies in the Federal Reserve statistics. Classified as "medium-size" are four of some forty existing companies with assets of from $10 million to $50 million; classified as "small" are six companies, out of about ninety having assets of $1 million to $10 million, and two out of about 3,000 companies with assets of less than $1 million. In spite of the inadequacy of the sample in the smaller size ranges, it is believed that the information obtained from the replies to the questionnaire fairly represents the influence of monetary policy upon the consumer finance industry. Data from the balance sheets of the twenty-one companies are shown in Appendix Tables A-4–A-8, by size of company, as of June 30, 1959.

Data from these samples should indicate the major changes in sources of funds and give some indication of their importance, although they may not be representative of some companies, particularly in the smaller size groups.

Retained earnings and sales of common stock were not large enough to keep pace with the expansion of the industry and the ratio of net worth to total funds employed declined steadily throughout the postwar period. Net worth declined from 54 percent of total of debt plus net worth at the end of 1945 to 27 percent at the end of 1959.

In the early postwar period, the expansion of short-term debt replaced net worth as the largest source of funds for consumer finance companies. In the late 1940's, short-term debt amounted to 40 percent of the funds employed by these companies.

In the early 1950's, long-term debt became the most important source of funds. Outstanding long-term debt increased sharply in 1951 while short-term debt declined fractionally. Beginning in 1957, long-term debt furnished nearly half the total funds employed by these companies and short-term debt and net worth each provided about one-fourth of the total.

Short-Term Borrowing—Commercial banks had traditionally provided most of the short-term funds for consumer finance companies and continued to do so in the postwar period. Bank loans supplied between 74 and 87 percent of their short-term needs from 1949 to 1958. (See Table 3-3.) In recent years, the percentage dropped from 83 in 1955 to 76 in 1958. It can not yet be determined, however, whether the trend away from bank borrowing will continue.

Bank lines expanded with the growth of consumer credit and with the growth in the banking system. Consumer finance companies in an attempt to reduce their dependency on bank borrowing, however, sought other sources of funds. As these sources of funds became available, they have reduced the proportion of bank lines actually used.

Consumer finance companies make less use of the commercial paper

TABLE 3-3
Short-Term Debt of Selected Consumer Finance Companies, 1949-1958

End of Year	Total	To Commercial Banks	Commercial Paper	Other[a]
		(Amounts in millions of dollars)		
1949	236	198	19	19
1950	326	285	18	23
1951	327	277	23	27
1952	373	299	41	33
1953	369	299	30	40
1954	393	291	58	44
1955	514	427	37	50
1956	551	450	41	60
1957	532	417	50	65
1958	532	403	66	63
		(Percentage distribution)		
1949	100	84	8	8
1950	100	87	6	7
1951	100	85	7	8
1952	100	80	11	9
1953	100	81	8	11
1954	100	74	15	11
1955	100	83	7	10
1956	100	82	7	11
1957	100	78	10	12
1958	100	76	12	12

[a] Other short-term debt consists almost entirely of certificates of deposit of one savings and loan association and of one industrial bank. The reports for these two forms of financial institutions were consolidated with the reports of their respective parent consumer finance companies.

Source: Based on Information from twenty-one companies that reported information to the National Consumer Finance Association.

markets than sales finance companies. From 1949 to 1958 they obtained only about 6 to 15 percent of their funds from these markets. The importance of commercial paper as a source of funds for consumer finance companies has varied considerably from year to year and there does not seem to be any clear trend toward an increase or decrease in its importance.

Long-Term Borrowing—Long-term borrowing has increased in importance since World War II. The large companies with excellent credit standing and large bank lines have developed long-term borrowing as a substitute for short-term bank credit. Long-term debt frees them from the vagaries of money market changes and has been less expensive than short-term financing during several recent periods.

Some of the small and medium-size companies have increased their use of long-term subordinated debentures to provide a larger base for bank

TABLE 3-4
Long-Term Debt of Selected Consumer Finance Companies, 1952-1959

End of Year	Type of Debt (In millions of dollars)			Subordinated Debentures as Percent of Total Long-Term Debt	Asset Size (In millions of Dollars)			
	Total	Unsubordinated	Subordinated	All Companies	350 and over	50-349	10-49	Under 10
Number of Companies	(47)	--	--	(47)	(2)	(4)	(14)	(27)
1952	451	384	67	15	--	31	54	54
1953	558	474	84	15	--	31	54	65
1954	640	532	108	17	--	29	56	64
1955	695	576	119	17	--	29	63	67
Number of Companies	(32)	--	--	(32)	(2)	(4)	(10)	(16)
1955	673	571	102	15	--	31	60	64
1956	900	764	136	15	--	34	41	58
1957	1,077	919	158	15	--	32	45	61
1958	1,106	935	171	15	--	32	45	52
1959	1,188	1,009	179	15	--	30	47	49

Source: Board of Governors of the Federal Reserve System.

41

credit.[6] (See Table 3-4.) Junior subordinated debentures were developed as part of this trend and by the late 1950's accounted for one-fourth to one-third of the outstanding subordinated debentures. (See Table 3-5.)

TABLE 3-5
Type of Subordinated Debt of Selected Consumer
Finance Companies, 1949-1958
(Amounts in millions of dollars)

End of Year	Subordinated Debt			Percentage Distribution	
	Total	Senior	Junior	Senior	Junior
1949	26	26	-	100	-
1950	36	36	-	100	-
1951	34	34	-	100	-
1952	41	40	1	98	2
1953	53	50	3	94	6
1954	71	58	13	82	18
1955	77	62	15	81	19
1956	108	76	32	70	30
1957	124	89	35	72	28
1958	139	104	35	75	25

Source: Based on data for twenty-one companies that reported information to the National Consumer Finance Association.

The small and medium-size companies expanded their unsubordinated debt as well as their subordinated debt, and the proportion of subordinated debt to total long-term debt did not change appreciably from 1952 through 1959. Subordinated debentures provided an average of 15 percent of the long-term funds for consumer finance companies for which data are available throughout the 1950's.

Equity Financing—The net worth of consumer finance companies expanded in every year in the postwar period, both as a result of new capital issues and through the retention of earnings. Retained earnings provided two-thirds or more of the additions to net worth each year from 1955 to 1959. (See Table 3-6.)

Ultimate Source of Funds

Consumer finance companies obtain funds directly from all major credit sources. They sell obligations directly to the public, they use all of the major financial market facilities, and they borrow from all major types of financial intermediaries. Regardless of the direct source, however, the funds used by the industry ultimately come either from new money created by the banking system or from the savings of consumers and businesses.

---

[6] Robert W. Johnson, "Subordinated Debenture: Debt that Serves as Equity," *The Journal of Finance* (March 1955), pp. 1-16.

TABLE 3-6
Sources of Equity Funds of Selected Consumer Finance
Companies, 1955-1959

Year	Total	Retained Earnings	Sales of Capital Stock
(Amounts in millions of dollars)			
1955	41	27	14
1956	49	34	15
1957	49	38	11
1958	51	36	15
1959	55	42	13
(Percentage Distribution)			
1955	100	66	34
1956	100	69	31
1957	100	78	22
1958	100	71	29
1959	100	76	24

Source: Board of Governors of the Federal Reserve System. Data are from a sample of thirty-two companies for all years except 1955 when thirty-six companies were included.

Although commercial banks provide three-fourths of the short-term funds used by consumer finance companies, short-term funds account for only about one-fourth of total debt and net worth. As a result, the banks provide only 15 to 20 percent of the total funds used by all consumer finance companies combined.

The ultimate source of bank funds depends in part upon the condition of the banking system at the time. If lending by the banking system is not expanding, the funds used by the consumer finance companies are obtained from repayments of loans of other types and are therefore savings of other sectors of the economy. If, however, the banking system is expanding, the finance companies in borrowing from banks share in the newly created funds.

The 80 to 85 percent of the funds used by consumer finance companies that are not provided by banks ultimately come from the savings of individuals or businesses. These funds flow through many channels. Some of them are obtained directly from consumers. A much larger share, however, comes from large financial institutions such as insurance companies, pension funds and investment companies. Contractual savings of this type provide the bulk of the funds used by consumer finance companies.

The retained earnings of consumer finance companies themselves provide a steady fraction of the total funds. These funds represent the reinvestment of stockholders' equity and are a form of business savings. Business savings in the form of idle balances also provide short-term funds. Nonfinancial corporations frequently buy commercial paper with funds that are temporarily idle.

Contractual savings of consumers ultimately provide the largest share of the funds used by the consumer finance industry. Savings of other sectors of the economy and newly created bank funds channeled to the industry through commercial banks supply another large part of the total and the remainder is obtained from business savings. Statistics on the ultimate sources of funds are not available but the information on direct sources presented in the preceding section gives some indication of the potential size of the various sources of funds.

Large vs. Small Company Pattern

1929–1941. During the period from 1929 to 1941, the influence of size and differences in degree of credit-worthiness was reflected to an increasing degree in the sources of funds of consumer finance companies. Increased size, particularly when accompanied by the greater stability in operations which results from a wider geographic scope, provided more ready access to money markets and resulted in a larger proportion of borrowed, and a smaller proportion of equity, funds.

At the beginning of the period, the use of borrowed funds was exceptional. During the period, the practice spread from the largest companies, gradually, to those of smaller size. By the end of the period, noticeable differences existed between the larger and smaller companies, both with respect to the proportion of total funds borrowed and with respect to the rates of interest required on those borrowings. (See Chart 3.)

The decline in the rate of interest paid on borrowed funds was felt first by the largest companies, reflecting the fact that open-market rates react more quickly to changing conditions than customers' rates. The larger companies had access to a greater variety of sources of borrowed funds, and were able to take advantage of the decline in open-market rates during this period. Thus, they were probably able to exert some influence upon the rates charged on local bank borrowings.

1945–1959. Sources of funds depend upon the size and reputation of the company and upon the amounts needed. The large companies have access to all the major financial markets. The smaller companies frequently are limited to local or regional sources of funds because of the size of their requirements and because of a lack of national reputation or credit standing. As a result, the debt and net worth structure of different companies may show wide variation although their basic financing needs may be similar.

CHART 3

SOURCES OF FUNDS OF CONSUMER FINANCE COMPANIES, 1929-1941

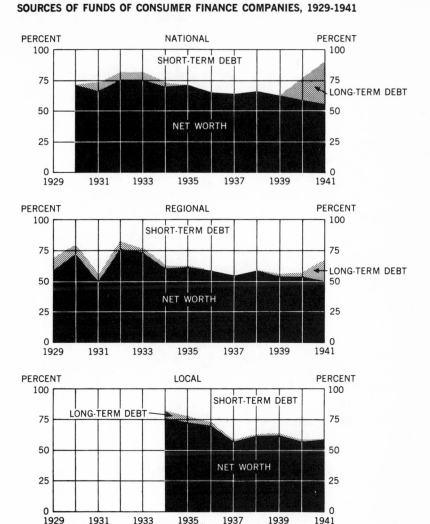

Source: Reproduced from Dauer, *op. cit.*, p. 44.

The proportion of equity funds used by consumer finance companies does not vary greatly by size of company. At the end of 1959, the ratio of net worth to total assets of all companies was about 27 percent. (See Table 3-7.) This is in contrast to the sales finance industry where the ratio of net worth to total assets is generally smaller for the very large companies. The two largest consumer finance companies had a somewhat larger than average ratio—30 percent—and all of the other size groups had smaller ratios. The moderately large group (those with assets between 50 and 350 million dollars) had the lowest ratio of equity to total debt and net worth of 22 percent. These companies reported a consistently lower ratio throughout the entire period for which figures are available.

TABLE 3-7
Net Worth as Percent of Total Debt and Net Worth of Selected Consumer
Finance Companies, 1945-1958
(In percent)

		Asset Size (In millions of dollars)			
End of Year	All Companies	350 and over	50-349	10-49	Under 10
No. of companies	(20)	(2)	(3)	(8)	(7)
1945	54	60	43	43	59
1946	39	44	28	33	45
1947	37	40	30	31	40
1948	35	40	27	29	37
1949	34	38	28	32	36
1950	32	35	28	30	34
1951	30	32	26	30	35
1952	30	33	26	29	32
No. of companies	(47)	(2)	(4)	(14)	(27)
1952	30	33	26	29	32
1953	30	33	27	29	32
1954	30	33	26	29	31
1955	28	31	24	28	31
No. of companies	(32)	(2)	(4)	(10)	(16)
1955	28	31	24	28	30
1956	26	29	22	27	29
1957	26	28	22	29	27
1958	28	30	23	28	27
1959	27	30	22	27	25

Source: Board of Governors of the Federal Reserve System.

Companies of all sizes depend primarily upon retained earnings for the maintenance of their net worth. (See Table 3-8.) The two large companies relied entirely upon retained earnings for new capital in the years 1956-59. Other companies obtained between one-quarter and two-thirds of their equity funds by new security issues during the same period.

The small companies depend more heavily on short-term funds than the larger companies. The small and medium-size companies reported nearly half of total debt and net worth in short-term notes. The moderately large companies obtained only about one-third of their resources from the short-term markets. The two largest companies reported only about 10 percent of their total debt and net worth in short-term funds. (See Table 3-9.)

Commercial banks supplied nearly all the short-term funds for the small companies and the two largest companies. About 90 percent of

TABLE 3-8
Retained Earnings as Percent of Additions to Net Worth of Selected
Consumer Finance Companies, 1955-1958
(In percent)

End of Year	All Companies	Asset Size (In millions of dollars)			
		350 and over	50-349	10-49	Under 10
No. of companies	(32)	(2)	(4)	(10)	(16)
1955	66	67	67	100	25
1956	69	100	39	56	50
1957	78	100	62	55	50
1958	71	100	44	67	50
1959	76	100	52	75	50

Source: Board of Governors of the Federal Reserve System. The sample for 1955 contained a total of thirty-six companies including twelve in the $10-49 million asset size group and sixteen in the under $10 million group.

the short-term debt of both groups was in notes payable to commercial banks during the years 1949-58. (See Table 3-10.) The moderately large companies (assets from 10 to 350 million dollars), however, obtained only about two-thirds of their short-term funds from commercial banks, depending upon other sources for one-third.

The larger companies obtained varying proportions of their short-term funds through the commercial paper market in 1949-58, the highest being 18 percent in 1954 for the moderately large companies. The small companies, however, were largely excluded from these markets.

The use of long-term debt decreases as the size of the company decreases. Long-term debt has accounted for about one-half to two-thirds of the total funds of the two largest companies since 1952, but only between one-third and one-half of those of moderately large companies and only about one-fourth of those of the smaller companies.

The two largest companies used only senior debentures and developed long-term sources of funds as an alternative to bank borrowing. The other companies, however, used subordinated debentures for part of their long-term borrowing. The use of subordinated debentures increases as the size of the company decreases. Moderately large companies used such debentures for about 30 percent of their long-term debt, while the smaller companies depended on subordinated debentures for one-half to two-thirds of their long-term borrowing. In the early 1950's, some of the medium-size companies began to use junior subordinated debentures and by the mid-1950's these securities accounted for half the total subordinated borrowing of this group. (See Table 3-11.)

Secular Influences

The acceptance of consumer credit as a legitimate means of consumer budgeting and the consistent earning record of consumer lenders opened new sources of funds to the industry. Large companies have obtained

TABLE 3-9

Notes Payable and Long-Term Debt as Percent of Total Debt and Net Worth of Consumer Finance Companies, 1945-1959

(In percent)

End of Year	Notes Payable					Long-Term Debt				
	All Companies	Asset Size (In millions of dollars)				All Companies	Asset Size (In millions of dollars)			
		350 and over	50-349	10-49	Under 10		350 and over	50-349	10-49	Under 10
No. of Companies	(20)	(2)	(3)	(8)	(7)	(20)	(2)	(3)	(8)	(7)
1945	27	20	38	40	36	19	20	19	17	5
1946	40	31	55	53	49	21	25	17	14	6
1947	40	32	52	52	51	23	28	18	17	9
1948	39	28	55	56	55	26	32	18	15	8
1949	37	27	48	53	53	29	35	24	15	11
1950	39	32	44	55	56	29	33	28	15	10
1951	33	26	35	53	55	37	42	39	17	10
1952	33	20	43	55	56	37	47	31	16	12
No. of Companies	(47)	(2)	(4)	(14)	(27)	(47)	(2)	(4)	(14)	(27)
1952	34	20	43	52	47	36	47	31	19	21
1953	30	13	42	49	46	40	54	31	22	22
1954	28	15	34	47	42	42	52	40	24	27
1955	33	17	43	47	43	39	52	33	25	26
No. of Companies	(32)	(2)	(4)	(10)	(16)	(32)	(2)	(4)	(10)	(16)
1955	32	17	43	51	43	40	52	33	21	27
1956	29	15	38	47	43	45	56	39	26	29
1957	25	10	34	43	45	49	62	43	29	27
1958	25	9	32	46	44	48	60	45	26	29
1959	25	10	34	48	43	48	60	44	25	32

Source: Board of Governors of the Federal Reserve System.

TABLE 3-10
Commercial Bank Borrowing and Commercial Paper as Percent of Notes Payable of Selected Consumer Finance Companies, 1949-1958
(In percent)

End of Year	All Companies	Commercial Bank Borrowing Asset Size (In millions of dollars)				All Companies	Commercial Paper Asset Size (In millions of dollars)			
		350 and over	50-349	10-49	Under 10		350 and over	50-349	10-49	Under 10
	(21)	(2)	(7)	(4)	(8)	(21)	(2)	(7)	(4)	(8)
No. of Companies										
1949	84	95	75	85	78	8	4	12	10	0
1950	87	96	79	91	79	6	3	8	5	0
1951	85	95	75	87	83	7	5	9	10	0
1952	80	92	73	92	85	11	8	14	4	0
1953	81	93	76	89	86	8	6	9	7	0
1954	74	87	65	88	86	15	12	18	8	0
1955	83	94	76	94	92	7	3	10	4	0
1956	82	89	76	92	93	8	4	9	5	0
1957	78	82	74	93	94	9	10	10	5	0
1958	76	92	69	86	94	12	7	15	11	0

Source: National Consumer Finance Association.

49

acceptance in all the major credit markets and can obtain relatively favorable terms. Many moderately large companies have also obtained acceptance in the major credit markets and, in addition, have been able

TABLE 3-11
Junior Subordinated Debentures as Percent of Subordinated Debt of
Selected Consumer Finance Companies, 1951-1958
(In percent)

End of Year	All Companies	Asset Size (In millions of dollars)		
		50-349	10-49	Under 10
No. of companies	(19)	(7)	(4)	(8)
1951	-	-	-	-
1952	2	-	37	-
1953	6	-	63	-
1954	18	14	49	2
1955	19	15	49	6
1956	30	28	50	6
1957	28	26	57	6
1958	25	23	60	5

Source: National Consumer Finance Association.

to develop regional and local sources. These changes have permitted an increase in the use of debt obligations of all types and have reduced the need for bank funds and equity.

Shifting patterns of savings have also altered the sources of funds. Saving through insurance companies, pension funds, and investment trusts has expanded sources of long-term funds available to consumer finance companies. These sources have permitted greater use of long-term debt and have made this type of financing relatively more attractive and flexible. The long-term needs of finance companies can be tailored to the investment needs of various types of savings institutions to the mutual advantage of both.

The availability of debt funds, the rapidity of the expansion of needs, the profit advantages of debt financing, and the pressures of rising costs, all contributed to a decline in the importance of equity financing. Net worth expanded but not fast enough to keep pace with the growth in loans. The largest companies were able to expand their borrowing. Some of the smaller companies, however, faced difficulties in expanding their borrowing in relation to net worth. Subordinated debt facilitated the expansion of borrowing by providing a larger base for senior debt without the loss of the tax and leverage advantages of debt. The advantages of this type of financing led to the development of junior subordinated debentures and a rapid rise in their importance.

The stability of the consumer finance company loans in the postwar years permitted a shift in borrowing from short-term to long-term debt.

This trend was accelerated by periodic difficulties in obtaining funds in the short-term markets and by the need of assured sources of funds. Some companies reduced their bank borrowings as a result of difficulties in obtaining bank funds during periods of monetary tightness and as a result of higher compensatory balances required on these funds.

A number of secular changes in the relative importance of various sources of funds have appeared since World War II. (1) Long-term borrowing increased in importance. Long-term debt of the two largest companies increased from 20 percent of total debt and net worth in 1945 to 60 percent at the end of 1958. Other companies showed a similar increase in the importance of long-term debt but the ratio of long-term debt to total resources was not as large as that of the two largest companies. (2) Importance of equity funds declined gradually. This trend, which began in the 1930's, continued throughout the postwar period. The ratio of net worth to total debt and net worth for all size groups declined from 54 percent in 1945 to 27 percent at the end of 1958. The decline in importance of equity funds occurred in companies of all sizes and reflected the need for high debt ratios to maintain profit margins and the ability of these companies to obtain funds in debt markets. (3) The use of short-term debt declined in importance. Short-term borrowing supplied a large share of funds needed immediately after the war but was replaced, in part, by longer-term debt as the market for long-term issues developed and as the permanency of the need for additional funds was recognized. The decline in short-term debt was most pronounced at the two largest companies where the growth in long-term debt had been the largest. (4) Since the largest proportion of short-term debt is obtained from commercial banks, the decline in importance of short-term debt was accompanied by a decline in the importance of commercial bank borrowing. The shift from short- to long-term debt resulted, in part, from an attempt of consumer finance companies to transfer their indebtedness from commercial banks to more permanent sources. Increases in compensating balances and difficulties in obtaining accommodations from banks during periods of tight money reduced the attractiveness of bank financing. (5) The use of subordinated debentures by all but the largest companies continued throughout the postwar period. The proportion of long-term debt in subordinated debentures, however, continued at approximately the same ratio throughout the postwar period. (6) Junior subordinated debentures were developed in the early 1950's and by the late 50's, these issues accounted for about one-fourth of the total subordinated debt. (7) Contractual savings as a source of funds increased in importance. Insurance companies, pension funds, and investment companies increased in importance as suppliers of funds and indirectly increased reliance of the consumer finance industry on the savings of consumers themselves.

Cyclical and Seasonal Patterns

The cyclical and seasonal needs of consumer finance companies have traditionally been supplied by bank lines. Equity and long-term funds provide the base for regular operations and for growth; short-term funds provide flexibility for cyclical and seasonal needs. By maintaining bank lines in excess of their normal needs, consumer finance companies can expand their borrowings as the need arises, or reduce their debt when the funds are not needed. The relative stability of the industry in the postwar recessions has reduced the need for short-term provisions. Although bank lines of consumer finance companies have expanded in aggregate, they are a smaller part of total resources and are utilized less completely.

Consumer finance companies adapt their financing to market circumstances and take advantage of the most favorable financing terms. Since conditions in different markets vary with the stages of a business cycle, these adjustments may take cyclical patterns. The stringency in the short-term market during 1959-60, for example, resulted in a shift to long-term funds. The relationship between the long-term and short-term market was only partly of cyclical origin. U.S. Treasury financing in the short-term area distorted the usual relationship between these two markets and added to the advantages of long-term financing. The consumer finance companies accommodate their new financing to varying conditions in the credit markets during various stages of the business cycle.

Seasonal variations in the requirements of consumer finance companies are sizable. The volume of loans in December may run from a third to a half above the average monthly volume. Seasonal demands are also high around Easter and in mid-summer. The requirements for funds in these periods are obtained largely from more complete use of bank lines. Commercial paper also may be used to supply these needs if market conditions are favorable.

Future Prospects

Many of the trends in sources of funds that have been described in the Section on "Secular Influences" can be expected to continue. The social and economic forces that led to the development of these trends are in most cases still operative.

The increased reliance on debt can be expected to continue for a number of reasons. First, the stability and earnings records of the consumer finance industry has justified the use of more debt in relation to equity as a sound financial practice. Second, the increase in debt improves the earning power of these companies. Third, competitive pressures in the market for consumer loans exert a strong force for reduction in rates and increase in services provided with loans. Such competitive pressures can only be met by more efficient operations or by increasing the ratio of borrowed funds to net worth.

The shift toward a larger proportion of long-term debt can be expected to continue. Stability and growth of the industry suggest the ability to use a larger proportion of permanent funds. Short-term funds will remain relatively important, however, to provide a cushion for cyclical and seasonal adjustments.

The widespread use of subordinated debentures will continue. The small and medium-size companies need this type of financing as a source of long-term debt and to improve their borrowing position for senior financing. The use of subordinated instruments will continue as an important source of funds as long as sources of senior debt require the protection they provide.

The decline in importance of bank borrowing can be expected to continue. One reason for this decline is the growing competitive relationship between banks and consumer finance companies in consumer lending. Competition in one market can create difficulties in lending-borrowing relationships in another market. This is reflected by some of the dissatisfaction expressed about bank borrowing by consumer finance companies. The net worth requirements established by banks for smaller companies frequently appear to be unreasonably high. The inability or unwillingness of banks to provide funds during periods of monetary stringency reduces the value of bank lines as a reserve for short-term needs and higher compensatory balances add to the cost of borrowing. Bank lines will undoubtedly continue to be the major source of short-term funds for most consumer finance companies but will decline in importance as increased reliance is placed on long-term debt.

Chapter 4

ANALYSIS OF LENDING PRACTICE

Trends in Assets, 1939-1959

Total Assets

The assets of the consumer finance industry, as defined for this monograph to include the making of loans under effective state small loan laws, are estimated at approximately $3.2 billion for 1958, $3.4 billion for 1959, and $3.7 billion for 1960. These are not exact figures based on a census of the consumer finance industry, but are based on a method of estimating assets used in the business which, though arbitrary, has had industry and governmental acceptance. This method has been widely used for purposes of stating earning rates on a generally comparable basis which eliminates the differences due to varied capital structures.

For over two decades, it has been a general practice to compute the assets "used and useful" in the business as 1.15 times the amount of loans receivable. This formula was derived by Rolf Nugent after extensive studies of the industry led him to the conclusion that a "reasonable" relationship was for assets to equal 1.15 times the average loan balance, i.e., the average of the net receivables outstanding at the beginning and at the end of each year.[1] In addition to the money actually loaned to borrowers, as represented by net loans receivable, other tangible and intangible assets, which are necessary in the operation of a small loan business, are included in assets used and useful. Among the tangible items are cash in the office and in banks, furniture and fixtures, and office machines and equipment. Among the intangible items are prepaid items such as bonds, license fees, insurance, and the cost of organizing and establishing a new office.

---

[1] See Rolf Nugent, "Earnings of Small Loan Licensees, 1929 to 1933," *Harvard Business Review* (January 1935), pp. 249-257.

The data shown in Table 4-1 for total assets used in the consumer finance industry are based on the application of the Nugent formula to the average of small loan balances outstanding at the beginning and end of each year, 1940 to 1960. Thus, they should be taken as orders of magnitude for total assets used and useful in the industry. For com-

TABLE 4-1
Loans and Assets of the Consumer Finance Industry, 1939-1960[a]
(In millions of dollars)

	Amount Outstanding End of Year	Average Outstandings	Estimated Total Assets[b]	Amount Extended During Year	Amount Repaid During Year[c]
1939	431	n.a.*	n.a.	n.a.	n.a.
1940	484	458	527	917	864
1941	525	505	581	969	928
1942	411	468	538	776	790
1943	361	386	444	802	852
1944	381	371	427	867	847
1945	436	409	470	962	907
1946	594	515	592	1,217	1,059
1947	725	660	759	1,478	1,347
1948	854	790	909	1,616	1,487
1949	973	914	1,051	1,782	1,663
1950	1,111	1,042	1,198	1,952	1,814
1951	1,306	1,209	1,390	2,412	2,217
1952	1,514	1,410	1,622	2,769	2,561
1953	1,692	1,603	1,843	2,857	2,679
1954	1,839	1,766	2,031	2,995	2,848
1955	2,088	1,964	2,259	3,460	3,211
1956	2,432	2,260	2,599	3,984	3,640
1957	2,721	2,577	2,964	4,326	4,037
1958	2,816	2,769	3,184	4,117	4,022
1959	3,058	2,937	3,378	4,477	4,235
1960	3,413	3,236	3,721	4,892	4,537

[a] Data are Federal Reserve estimates and cover all consumer loans made under effective state small loan laws as defined by the National Consumer Finance Association. Includes such loans made by consumer finance companies, sales finance companies, and other lending institutions which hold state small loan licenses.
[b] Computed by multiplying 1.15 times the average of outstandings at the beginning and end of each year.
[c] Previous year-end outstandings plus extensions during the year minus current year-end outstandings.
*n.a.-Not available.

Source: Board of Governors of the Federal Reserve System.

parative purposes, Appendix Tables A-9 and A-10 are presented showing summations of end-of-year asset data from state supervisory reports for bench mark years 1950 and 1958, respectively. It will be noted that the 1.15 ratio does not hold exactly for either year, but neither is the margin of error great. The summation of state supervisory reports for 1950 shows total assets at the end of the year to be 1.196 times loans receivable, yielding an asset figure 4 percent greater than that calculated by applying the Nugent formula to Federal Reserve estimates of loans receivable. In 1958, the ratio was 1.121, resulting in assets for that year 2.5 percent less than that calculated by the Nugent formula.

As shown by Table 4-1, the assets of the consumer finance industry decreased during World War II when the financial resources of the United States were diverted to the single purpose of building up an industrial potential capable of winning the war, dropping from $581 million in 1941 to a low of $427 million in 1944. Since that time, there has been an increase in assets each year. Immediately after the war, the assets in the consumer finance industry increased rapidly. Between 1945 and 1949, assets grew by 124 percent. Though the industry has continued to grow, there has been a slackening in the rate of expansion. Between 1949 and 1954, the assets of the industry grew by 93 percent, while the years 1954 to 1959 saw a growth of 66 percent.

It must be remembered that the growth in assets of the consumer finance industry is attributable to two sources: (1) increase in population and the acceptance of consumer credit by an increased percentage of the working population of this country; and (2) more and more states adopting effective state small loan laws. In 1939 only thirty-one states had such laws, while in September 1959, forty-two states had some version of the law in effect.

In addition to the legal definition of the industry, i.e., consisting of the licensees under effective state small loan laws, there are two more definitions which might be used to denote the consumer finance industry.

For statistical purposes, the Federal Reserve defines a consumer finance company as one which holds over 50 percent of its receivables in loans made under effective state small loan laws. In addition to these small loans, many consumer finance companies make cash loans under industrial discount laws which are designed to provide state regulation but are technically different from effective state small loan laws. Consumer finance companies also engage in other consumer credit operations of a somewhat different nature. They purchase automobile paper and other consumer durable goods paper from retailers.[2] The personal cash installment loans of consumer finance companies as defined by the Federal Reserve totaled $3,211 million at the end of 1959, compared to $3,058 million under small loan licenses. Since loans outstanding were the chief asset in each case, the total assets of consumer finance companies (Federal Reserve definition) undoubtedly exceeds the total assets of the consumer finance industry as defined for this monograph.

Though it would be desirable to show the total assets used by con-

---

[2] Some of them acquire paper to finance air travel, and one major company engages on a nation-wide basis in a type of revolving purchase credit under a credit card plan.

sumer finance companies, the diverse nature of their consumer lending operations makes it unrealistic to apply the Nugent formula. Since this formula was derived from a study of lending operations under the traditional small loan law, it is not known if it is applicable to other forms of lending by consumer finance companies. Similarly, it might be misleading to apply it to the personal cash instalment loans made by sales finance companies. Therefore, it is possible to show only the financial resources devoted to the industry (total assets of the industry) which is supervised by authority emanating from effective state small loan laws. Data are not available to show the financial resources devoted to making available all of the credit outstanding of consumer finance companies as reported in Federal Reserve statistics, or the financial resources devoted by consumer finance companies and sales finance companies to making available personal cash instalment loans.

Types of Receivables Outstanding

The receivables outstanding of licensees under effective state small loan laws which are shown in Table 4-1 are all cash loans made to individuals, subject to repayment by instalments. These loans may be secured by tangible goods owned by the borrower or may be unsecured. While there have been many changes since 1939 in the maturities of loans, security for repayment, rates of charge, size of individual loan, and other attributes, the receivables outstanding remain essentially small cash instalment loans.

During the last several years, however, there has been a growing tendency for those finance companies holding small loan licenses to expand the volume of their cash instalment lending more rapidly under related legislation than under effective state small loan laws. As the figures in Table 4-2 indicate, the personal cash loans outstanding, combined for consumer finance companies and sales finance companies, at the end of 1960 ($4,572 million), exceed loans made under effective state small loan laws ($3,413 million) by 34 percent, while at the end of 1955 the excess amounted to only 25 percent. At the same time, the sales finance companies have shown an increasing interest in the cash lending business. As a result, their holdings of personal cash loans increased from $465 million at the end of 1955, or 5.5 percent of their outstanding consumer credit, to $1,001 million or 9.0 percent of their outstandings at the end of 1960. Moreover, the consumer finance companies tended to reduce the proportion of outstandings other than cash loans.

Thus, during the short time interval since 1955 there is a clearly discernible trend toward an increasing volume of lending by finance companies under general legislation permitting a higher loan ceiling (and usually specifying a lower rate of charge), and an increasing entry of sales finance companies into the cash loan business.

TABLE 4-2
Consumer Instalment Credit Outstanding by Consumer Finance Companies
and Sales Finance Companies, Year-End 1955-1960

(In millions of dollars)

	1955	1956	1957	1958	1959	1960
Consumer Credit Outstanding						
Consumer Finance Companies	2,656	3,056	3,333	3,384	3,774	4,212
Personal Loans	2,155	2,500	2,835	2,928	3,211	3,571
Automobile Paper	151	152	139	118	128	127
Other Consumer						
Durable Goods	350	404	359	338	435	514
Sales Finance Companies	8,443	9,100	9,573	8,740	10,145	11,134
Personal Loans	465	567	670	750	899	1,001
Automobile Paper	6,919	7,283	7,470	6,404	7,328	7,695
Other Consumer Goods Paper	1,034	1,227	1,413	1,567	1,883	2,374
Repair and Modernization						
Loans	25	23	20	19	35	64
Total Consumer and Sales						
Finance Companies	11,099	12,156	12,906	12,124	13,919	15,346
Personal Loans of Consumer						
and Sales Finance Companies	2,620	3,067	3,505	3,678	4,110	4,572
Total Loans Under Effective						
State Small Loan Laws	2,088	2,432	2,721	2,816	3,058	3,413

Source: *Federal Reserve Bulletin* (August 1961); Mimeographed releases of the Bureau of
Research and Statistics, Board of Governors of the Federal Reserve System.

Loans, 1939-1959 [3]

Size

Two factors generally control the size of loans made by consumer
finance companies. The maximum loan permitted, i.e., the loan ceiling,
sets an upper limit to the size of loan made. In this case, state legislation
is the determinant. For example, consumer finance companies in Ohio,
where the loan ceiling is $2,000, make larger loans on the average than
in Maryland, where the loan ceiling is $300.

The second controlling factor stems from the interplay between maximum authorized rates and the market for loans of various sizes. Consumer finance companies generally try to offer a "full loan service," i.e.,
try to make available loans of every size permitted by law. However,
the yield on very small loans is below the unit-cost of operation. Therefore, it would be unprofitable for consumer finance companies to have
too large a proportion of their loans outstanding in the form of very small
loans. Since the demand for these very small loans is also limited, few
such loans are made. Moreover, under some state laws, the rate per-

---

[3] Historical data through 1951 on this section may be found in detail in M. R.
Neifeld, *Trends in Consumer Finance* (Easton: Mack Publishing Co., 1954).

mitted on larger loans is too low for such larger loans to be profitable. The average-loan-made, i.e., the total value of loans made during a time period divided by the number of loans made, has increased from $142 in 1939 to $349 in 1957, dropping to $334 in 1958, and increasing to $386 in 1959. (See Table 4-3.) Measured in constant dollars, the size

TABLE 4-3
Average Loans in Consumer Finance Companies, 1939-1959

	In current dollars		Consumer	In constant dollars	
	Average loan made	Average unpaid balance	Price Index 1939 = 100	Average loan made	Average unpaid balance
1939	142	117	100.0	142	117
1940	144	119	100.8	143	118
1941	149	123	105.9	141	116
1942	145	107	117.3	124	91
1943	152	119	124.6	122	96
1944	163	134	126.6	129	106
1945	177	150	129.5	137	116
1946	192	166	140.4	137	118
1947	209	172	160.8	130	107
1948	220	185	173.1	127	107
1949	226	189	171.4	132	110
1950	238	199	173.1	137	115
1951	259	213	186.9	139	114
1952	279	231	191.1	146	121
1953	285	243	192.6	148	126
1954	294	250	193.3	152	129
1955	304	264	192.8	158	137
1956	318	281	195.6	163	144
1957	349	300	202.4	172	148
1958	334	312	207.9	161	150
1959	386	326	209.8	184	155

Source: For years 1939-1951, M. R. Neifeld, *Trends in Consumer Finance* (Easton: Mack Publishing Co., 1954); for years 1952-1958, summation of data in state supervisory reports; constant dollar values were obtained for all years by dividing by the Consumer Price Index of the Bureau of Labor Statistics converted to a base 1939 = 100.

of the average-loan-made fell off through most of the 1940's, due in part at least to the failure of state legislation to permit higher loan ceilings corresponding to the increase in the general price level. As more states passed legislation permitting higher ceilings, and as prices increased less rapidly after 1951, the average loan in constant dollars recovered to the 1939 level. In 1959, the average-loan-made was 30 percent higher in constant dollars terms than in 1939.

The loan ceiling permitted in each state makes for wide variations from the average-loan-made for the United States as a whole. Those states in which high ceilings have prevailed for several years, of course, show a much higher average-loan-made than the United States average. Examples of such states are Ohio and California, where the average-loan-made has generally run roughly one-third higher than the national average. (See Table 4-4.) At the other extreme are states such as Iowa,

TABLE 4-4
Variation in Size of Loan Made, Selected States, 1939-1958

	1939	1948	1950	1954	1958
United States Average	142	220	238	294	334
Relatively High Ceiling States					
Ohio	176	312	327	411	444
California	188	401	351	396	476
Low Ceiling States					
Iowa	133	187	197	222	236
Kentucky	108	180	195	217	231
West Virginia	105	169	181	205	222
States with Raised Ceilings					
Colorado	100	137	137	175	448
Florida	120	195	219	205[a]	352
Oregon	76	172	178	198	411
Virginia	110	177	191	221	365

[a] Data for 1955; data for 1954 not available.

Source: State Supervisory Reports.

Kentucky, and West Virginia, which had not raised their ceilings above $300 during the period. In these low ceiling states, the average size loan has run consistently below the national average. The effect on the average size of loan made resulting from an increase in the ceiling may be illustrated by developments Colorado, Florida, Oregon, and Virginia. The loan ceiling in each of these states was raised considerably between 1954 and 1958. Whereas the nation-wide average-loan-made increased by 8 percent during these years, the average-loan-made in Colorado increased by 156 percent, in Florida by 72 percent, in Oregon by 108 percent, and in Virginia by 65 percent.

The second form of average loan in consumer finance companies is the average-unpaid-balance. As new loans are made and payments are received on loans already on the books, the total of all unpaid balances divided by the number of loans on the books gives the average-unpaid-balance. In current dollars, the average-unpaid-balance at year end was not quite tripled between 1939 and 1959, increasing from $117 to $326.

In addition to the inflationary pressures that raised the average-loan-made in the war and postwar years until 1951, and that, of course, were equally at work on the unpaid balance, there was also the effect of war-time and postwar control of consumer credit. Regulation W, issued by the Board of Governors of the Federal Reserve System, at various times prohibited contracts in excess of eighteen months, fifteen months, and for quite a period during the war, of twelve months. This prescribed faster amortization of new loans resulting in a smaller average-unpaid-balance than would otherwise be encountered.

Subsequently, in 1958, the average-loan-made again decreased in size but this time the volume of loans outstanding from the previous year was sufficiently large that the average-unpaid-balance still showed an increase over 1957.

In constant dollars, the average-unpaid-balance also lost ground in the war years. In 1958, at the end of the 20-year interval, it had reached a level 28 percent above the purchasing power of the unpaid balance at the beginning of the period in 1939.

Purpose

Whether an individual borrows or saves, he considers the numerous factors which bear upon whether his income during the present time period (month, year, or longer) should from his point of view equal his expenditure for the same time period. If he concludes that he may obtain relatively greater satisfaction by increased spending in the future or by a greater accumulation of wealth, he saves, and accordingly spends less than his income during the present time period. If, on the other hand, he concludes that he can obtain greater satisfaction by spending more than his current income in the present time period, he seeks a source of credit. In this case, however, he has committed a part of his future earnings to the repayment of the obligation and must in some future time period restrict his spending to an amount less than his total earning. Thus, in an economic sense, borrowers save after the occurrence of the opportunity or emergency that initiated the expenditure. But the consumer's reasons for borrowing are the same as those for saving.

Consumer finance companies lend to individuals so that they may consolidate overdue bills, refinance existing obligations, and pay for medical, dental, hospital, and other emergencies. Loans are also made to borrowers so they may buy fuel, home furnishings and clothing, and consumer durables. Other loans are made for the purpose of protecting equities in insurance, in homes and in other assets; to make automobile and home repairs; to pay for travel and vacations; to send children to school; and to help friends or relatives in distress.

A survey of consumer finance companies which operated 2,243 offices in June 1959, revealed some changes between 1948 and 1958 in the stated purposes for which loans were made. (See Table 4-5.) The chief reason for borrowing from consumer finance companies was to consolidate overdue bills. In 1958, this was the borrower's stated purpose for nearly 40 percent of the loans extended, compared to 28 percent in 1948.

TABLE 4-5
Distribution of the Number of Loans Extended by Purpose,
Selected Years, 1948-1958[a]

Purpose	(In percent)			
	1948	1950	1954	1958
To consolidate overdue bills	27.8	30.2	33.7	39.5
Travel, vacation, education expense	7.8	7.4	8.4	9.3
Medical, dental, hospital, and funeral	17.6	17.5	11.1	7.9
Automobile purchase or repairs	2.9	4.5	4.7	5.5
Clothing, food, rent, fuel, moving	11.7	10.5	9.7	7.2
Assist relatives	3.9	3.8	3.6	3.5
Home furnishings and appliances	3.3	5.1	5.2	4.7
Taxes, payments on real estate loans, insurance	6.5	6.1	7.7	7.6
Household repairs	8.3	7.3	6.8	5.1
Miscellaneous and not reported	10.2	7.5	9.3	9.7
Total	100.0	100.0	100.0	100.0

[a] Data are for 2,243 offices operated by three consumer finance companies as of June 30, 1959 as reported in answer to a questionnaire sent out by the National Consumer Finance Association.

Rates of Charge

The rate of charge on loans by consumer finance companies is an all-inclusive charge for the use of money and various supplementary services which are rendered to the borrower.[4] The consumer applies for a loan at a consumer finance company without written evidence as to his assets and liabilities. This practice is in sharp contrast to the usual bases upon which business loans are negotiated. The verification of his credit worthiness, therefore, is a highly skilled task and adds considerably to the cost of operations of a consumer finance company. Moreover, the costs of this investigation are just as great for a small loan, which is the traditional specialty of the consumer finance company, as for the larger consumer loans made by other financial institutions. For several years now, consumer finance companies have offered the added service of budgeting and financial counseling to their borrowers. Thus, the rate of charge for small loans, though frequently and erroneously referred to as interest, covers not only the payment for the use of borrowed money (interest) but also the cost of other services.

Each state, in which a law similar to the Uniform Small Loan Law is in effect, sets its maximum rate, which limits the charge consumer finance companies may make. (See the schedule in Appendix Table A-1.) Com-

---

[4] For more detailed information on the rates of charge, see: Clyde William Phelps, "Consumer Finance Company Charges: I," *The Journal of Marketing*, Vol. XVI, No. 4, pp. 397 ff., and M. R. Neifeld, *op. cit.*, pp. 57 ff.

petition may reduce the actual charge and did so in many instances before inflation sharply raised the operating costs of licensed lenders. Faced with higher operating costs and circumscribed by legal requirements which prevented improved efficiency of operation, the maximum rate permitted has become the going rate of charge.

Rates permitted by different states and graduated at varying dollar amounts result in widely varying rates of charge. The States of California, Idaho, and Virginia have been chosen to illustrate these differences. The example shown in Table 4-6 assumes a loan of $600 repayable in twelve monthly instalments. For simplicity, it is assumed that

TABLE 4-6
Comparative Charges on a One-Year $600 Loan in Selected States, 1959[a]

	California	Idaho	Virginia
Monthly Rate of Charge Permitted on $600 Loan Balance			
Up to:	$200 $2\frac{1}{2}\%$	$300 3%	$300 $2\frac{1}{2}\%$
Next bracket:	$200-$500 2%	$300-$500 2%	$300-$600 $1\frac{1}{2}\%$
Next bracket:	$500-$600 $\frac{5}{8}\%$	$500-$600 1%	
Charges Collected Each Month in Dollars[b]			
First Month ($600)	11.83	14.00	12.00
Second Month ($550)	11.42	13.50	11.25
Third Month ($500)	11.00	13.00	10.50
Fourth Month ($450)	10.00	12.00	9.75
Fifth Month ($400)	9.00	11.00	9.00
Sixth Month ($350)	8.00	10.00	8.25
Seventh Month ($300)	7.00	9.00	7.50
Eighth Month ($250	6.00	7.50	6.25
Ninth Month ($200)	5.00	6.00	5.00
Tenth Month ($150)	3.75	4.50	3.75
Eleventh Month ($100)	2.50	3.00	2.50
Twelfth Month ($50)	1.25.	1.50	1.25
Total Charges	86.75	105.00	87.00

[a] It is assumed that repayments of $50 per month were made on the principal starting one month after the loan was made.
[b] Dollar figures in brackets are the amounts owed by the borrower during each time period.

level payments of $50 per month are made on principal. In practice almost all companies schedule payments so that the total principal and charges combined will be constant.[5]

In this example, the total charges vary between $86.75 in California and $105.00 in Idaho. Thus, the average rate per month paid in California by the borrower for the money in his possession was 2.14 percent.

---

[5] For detailed explanations of mathematical methods used in the consumer finance industry, see M. R. Neifeld, *Neifeld's Guide to Instalment Computations* (Easton: Mack Publishing Co., 1951).

During the first month when he had the use of $600, the borrower paid
$11.83 or a rate of 1.97 percent. During the last four months of the loan,
he paid a rate of charge of 2.5 percent. By way of comparison, a borrower of the same size loan, same maturity, and same repayment schedule in Idaho would pay an average rate of 2.57 percent, varying from
a low of 2.33 percent for the first month to 3 percent for each of the
last six months.

In practice, most loans are repaid in equal monthly instalments following an amortization schedule which shows the amount applied to principal, the amount applied to interest, and the balance of the principal
due. Until recent years, consumer finance companies have been required
to provide the borrower with a detailed statement when each payment
was made. For example, the Ohio small loan law requires "For each
payment made on account of any such loan, [the licensee shall] give to
the person making it at the time the payment is made, a plain and complete receipt specifying the date of payment, the amount applied to
charges, and the amount applied to the principal, and stating the unpaid
principal balance, if any, of such loan; provided that an unitemized
receipt may be given temporarily and within five days a receipt as
prescribed above delivered or mailed." [6] This provision in conjunction
with detailed provisions permitting partial repayments at any time and
requiring detailed recalculations of interest on the lapsed time of the
amount of the loan outstanding have imposed onerous record keeping
tasks on consumer finance companies.

Many states have in recent years passed laws which have recognized
that many of the detailed requirements no longer serve a useful purpose.
In 1951, Missouri enacted the first workable provision for precomputing
loan charges at the time a loan was made rather than calculating them
at the time each payment was made.[7] Recognizing the benefits from
increased efficiency, a growing number of the regulated states now permit
consumer finance companies to make "add-on" or "precomputed" loans.[8]

Maturity

The maximum length of the loan contract is limited by the applicable
legislation or regulation in each state. However, company policy may

---

[6] Quoted from Roger S. Barrett, *Compilation of Consumer Finance Laws* (Washington: National Consumer Finance Association, 1952), p. 453.

[7] See Carl A. Dauten, "The Consumer Finance Industry in a Dynamic Economy,"
Consumer Credit Monograph No. 2 (St. Louis, Mo.: American Investment Company
of Illinois).

[8] The technical difference between these two types of loans is that the "add-on"
type specifies a dollar charge which may be added on to the total loan; "precomputed" loans permit a dollar charge calculated from the schedule of rates per month
specified in the law.

result in restricting maturities to a shorter term than that permitted by law.

Loan contracts with consumer finance companies have been increasing in length during the last several years. Responses to a questionnaire sent by the National Consumer Finance Association to consumer finance companies in early 1960 indicate that the average length of loan contract has increased from about seventeen months in 1948 to eighteen months in 1950, twenty months in 1954, and twenty-two months in 1958.

Security

Character of the borrower is the significant consideration in loans made by consumer finance companies. Except in the case of the larger loans, security in the form of tangible personal property frequently has only nominal market value. But to the borrower it may have considerable subjective value and in this respect establishes evidence of his good faith. The record shows that consumer finance companies seldom take possession of security on defaulted loans. Moreover, the proportion of the loans made based on the borrower's signature with no tangible security has increased considerably during the last twenty years. (See Table 4-7.)

TABLE 4-7
Percent Distribution of Loans Extended by Security, Selected Years, 1939-1958[a]

	1939	1950	1954	1958
Household Goods	50.2	44.9	45.7	44.5
Automobiles	15.3	14.1	12.6	12.1
Other Goods	2.6	4.4	4.0	4.4
Unsecured Notes	15.7	25.4	27.3	27.4
Endorsed and/or				
Co-maker Loans	9.6	4.2	3.6	2.7
Wage Assignments	3.7	6.2	6.1	7.7
Real Estate	0.8	0.4	0.3	0.3
Other Considerations	2.2	0.5	0.5	0.8
Total	100.0	100.0	100.0	100.0

[a] Distribution calculated from a summation of available data from state supervisory reports. All states where consumer finance companies made large amounts of loans are included for each year. The total number of states included were: nineteen in 1939, twenty-six in 1950, twenty-seven in 1954 and thirty-three in 1958.

Characteristics of Borrowers

People from all walks of life borrow from consumer finance companies. A survey made by the Michigan Survey Research Center in early 1959 provides data for a rough profile of the "typical" borrower from consumer finance companies. It must be noted that the survey consisted of a small sample covering a very limited geographic area. The results of this survey showed that over half of all borrowers were skilled and semi-skilled workers with incomes of between $4,000 and $7,500 per year, had liquid assets of $100 or more, and had had nine to twelve years of schooling. Two-thirds of the borrowers were between thirty-five and fifty-four years of age, and two-thirds also owned their own homes. These survey results, while subject to a wide margin of error, provide a rough profile of the borrower from consumer finance companies.

Percentage distributions of the income level of borrowers obtained from National Consumer Finance Association data covering two companies operating 1,241 offices in June 1959, are shown in Table 4-8.

TABLE 4-8
Percentage Distribution of the Monthly Income of Borrowers from Consumer Finance Companies, Selected Years, 1939-1958

Monthly Income of Borrowers	(Percent of number of loans extended)				
	1939	1948	1950	1954	1958
$ 0 - 100.00	16.3	1.4	0.9	0.4	0.3
100.01-200.00	62.5	31.5	18.9	7.4	4.6
200.01-300.00	21.1[a]	46.9	46.0	30.7	17.6
300.01-400.00	-	13.0	20.6	32.1	30.6
400.01-500.00	-	4.7	8.7	16.1	22.7
500.01-750.00	-	2.4[b]	4.9[b]	12.0	21.4
750.01-1,000.00	-	-	-	1.3[c]	2.3
Over 1,000.00	-	-	-	-	0.5
Not Reported	[d]	[d]	[d]	[d]	[d]
Totals	100.0	100.0	100.0	100.0	100.0

[a]Over $200.00.
[b]Over $500.00.
[c]Over $750.00.
[d]Less than 0.05%.

Source: From National Consumer Finance Association survey data as reported by two companies which operated 1,241 offices in June 1959.

Just as income levels generally have increased during the last twenty years, so has the income of borrowers from consumer finance companies. Since 1948, the median income of consumer finance company borrowers has increased in about the same proportion as the median income of families generally in the United States. (See the estimates in Table 4-9.)

The percentage of borrowers from consumer finance companies by occupation has changed little during the last several years. (See Table 4-10.) In 1958, somewhat over 30 percent were craftsmen, foremen, and kindred workers; nearly 30 percent were operatives, laborers, and kindred workers; nearly 15 percent were service workers including government civilian and military personnel; nearly 10 percent were clerical and kindred workers; over 5 percent were proprietors, managers, and office workers; and the remaining 10 percent were from various occupational groupings.

TABLE 4-9
Estimated Median Income of Consumer Finance
Company Borrowers and All Families,
Selected Years, 1948-1958

| | (Median annual income in dollars) | |
Year	Consumer finance company borrowers	All families
1948	2,830	3,187
1950	3,190	3,319
1954	4,030	4,173
1958	4,680	5,087

Sources: Survey by the National Consumer Finance Association
for the median income of borrowers from two companies which
operated 1,241 offices in June, 1959. Median family income from
Current Population Reports, Series P-60, No. 33. U. S. Department
of Commerce, Bureau of the Census.

TABLE 4-10
Distribution of the Number of Loans Extended by Occupation of Borrower,
Selected Years, 1948-1958
(In percent)

Occupation of Borrower	1948	1950	1954	1958
Proprietors, managers and office workers, excluding farm	8.8	8.3	6.6	6.5
Craftsmen, foremen and kindred workers	34.4	33.2	32.6	31.6
Operatives, laborers and kindred workers, excluding farm and mine	29.6	31.0	31.6	29.7
Clerical and kindred workers	9.6	9.4	8.3	8.1
Sales persons	3.7	3.8	3.8	4.0
School teachers	1.0	0.9	0.8	0.9
Professional and semi-professional workers, excluding teachers	2.1	2.2	2.1	2.7
Unemployed, pension, or independent income	1.4	1.5	1.6	1.4
Farmers and farm managers	1.0	1.0	0.8	0.5
Farm laborers and foremen	0.1	0.2	0.2	0.2
Service workers, including government, civilian and military personnel	7.9	8.3	11.1	13.9
Occupations not reported and miscellaneous	0.3	0.3	0.3	0.2
Total	100.0	100.0	100.0	100.0

Source: From National Consumer Finance Association survey data reported by three
companies which operated 2,243 offices in June 1959.

Regional Patterns

There is substantial variety in the regional pattern of the consumer
finance business. The variations are due to the concentration in cities,
the degree and type of industrialization, the character of the local community, and many other local conditions.

Consumer finance company loans are most common in family units within the income range of $3,000 to $7,500. This range eliminates the very low income groups, where monthly incomes do not yield a sufficient margin over the requirements for food, clothing, and family necessities to assure repayment of the loan. Hence, we find very little instalment cash loan activity in communities where there is a large concentration of retired couples or in low income small villages and rural communities.

While some consumer finance company loans are made to families with incomes in excess of $7,500, the equities, savings and incomes of such units usually qualify them for credit at commercial banks, and their needs are for larger amounts than consumer finance companies can loan. Therefore, we do not find many consumer finance company offices in high-income suburban communities, nor do we find many borrowers among the executive groups.

The largest concentration of users of consumer instalment loans is in the skilled and unskilled labor groups. Next in order would be the white collar workers, clerks, teachers, and civil employees of federal, state, and local governments. For this reason, the consumer finance business is most highly concentrated in the industrial and population centers. The map (Chart 2) shows that the largest numbers of licensed offices are located in the industrial and population centers in the States of Ohio, Pennsylvania, Illinois, Michigan and California. The least concentration of licenced offices is found in more sparsely settled rural areas. By way of contrast, the State of Illinois in 1960 had 808 licensed offices, while the State of Arizona had only 197; California had 1,095, the State of Idaho, only 72. Ohio, with more than twenty industrial cities, had 1,015 licensed offices, while the State of Maine had only 111 licensees.

Another regional difference is quite apparent in the consumer finance business. There remains a remnant of the old fear and abhorrence of debt which was so long traditional among the farmers and small shopkeepers in Maine, New Hampshire and Vermont, and, to a lesser extent, in Massachusetts and Connecticut. Hence, consumer finance company operations are more limited in that area as compared with more newly developed areas like Florida or the west coast States of California, Oregon, and Washington. As a result, loan volume grows much more rapidly in these newer states to accommodate the rapidly expanding population which accompanies rapidly growing industrial areas. By the same token, loan activity in the agricultural South is considerably slower than in the industrial East and Midwest.

State laws also have much to do with the growth and development of consumer finance companies. Arkansas, for example, has a constitutional provision limiting all interest charges in the state to 10 percent on an annual interest basis. Obviously, no consumer finance company can make small loans at a profit under such a rate limitation; hence, there are no licensed companies in Arkansas.

The State of West Virginia presents an unusual situation with a substantial portion of its area in rough, hilly wasteland in contrast to great industrial centers in locations adjacent to raw materials and transportation facilities. Timber, coal mining, and farming are the principal industries outside of these centers. Furthermore, West Virginia still has a limitation of $300 on the size of loan. With the comparatively low income and low loan ceiling, it follows that the business in West Virginia is quite different in character from the business in Ohio, where industrial areas are more widespread, average income levels are more concentrated in the areas best served by consumer finance companies, and the loan ceiling is more realistic ($2,000).

These illustrations will serve to point up the wide variations in regional patterns for the consumer finance business, and, incidentally, also demonstrate why there is such a variety of provisions in the small loan laws of the several states. Since regional patterns do differ so widely, it is essential that local conditions be recognized and that the legislative authority to regulate and control the business remain vested in the states.

Chapter 5

LOSS EXPERIENCE
IN THE POSTWAR PERIOD

Over-all Trend

A slight trend toward higher loss ratios and lower percent of recovery on loans charged off by consumer finance companies is evident for the years 1948-59. The consumer finance company ratios reported by the First National Bank of Chicago show that the percent of loss to average notes outstanding increased from 1.59 in 1948 to 2.20 in 1960. The percent of recovery on charged off loans decreased from 30.07 in 1948 to 17.52 in 1960. (See Table 5-1.) Though a long-term trend appears evident,

TABLE 5-1
Loss Experience of Consumer Finance Companies, 1948-1960

End of Year	Percent Gross Charge-Offs to Average Notes Outstanding	Percent Recovery on Loans Charged-Off	Percent Net Charge-Offs to Average Notes Outstanding
1948	1.59	30.07	n.a.
1949	1.78	21.71	n.a.
1950	1.64	24.00	n.a.
1951	1.65	26.55	n.a.
1952	1.63	23.84	n.a.
1953	1.90	21.90	n.a.
1954	1.94	18.71	n.a.
1955	1.92	22.03	1.49
1956	1.62	22.69	1.23
1957	1.85	17.71	1.50
1958	2.06	14.56	1.75
1959	1.84	20.28	1.45
1960	2.20	17.52	1.75

n.a.-Not available.

Source: Simi-annual releases of the First National Bank of Chicago, "Small Loan Company Ratios."

the greatest influence is cyclical, following the level of industrial production. In 1954, 1958, and 1960, when industrial production fell off, the loss ratios were comparatively high and the percent of recoveries on loans charged off was low.

Size of Loan

Data on charge offs by size of loan are not available for the industry. Robbins[1] found for 1950-51 that the percentage distribution of charge offs by size of loan for eight consumer finance companies followed fairly closely the percentage distribution of all loans by size made by the industry. (See Table 5-2.) There were proportionally more charge offs

TABLE 5-2
Loss Experience of Consumer Finance Companies by Size of Loan
1950-1951

Loan Size in Dollars	Number of Loans		Percentage Distribution	
	Made by the Industry	Charged Off by Eight Consumer Finance Companies	Loans Made by the Industry	Loans Charged Off by Eight Consumer Finance Companies
50.00 or less	502,674	616	7.61	3.02
50.01 - 100	930,017	2,620	14.09	12.84
100.01 - 150	886,366	3,436	13.42	16.83
150.01 - 200	811,940	2,674	12.30	13.10
200.01 - 300	1,953,981	6,499	29.59	31.84
300.01 - 500	1,256,880	3,170	19.04	15.53
500.01 - 750	153,614	717	2.33	3.51
750.01 - 1,000	89,824	644	1.36	3.16
Over 1,000	17,043	34	0.26	0.17
Total	6,602,339	20,410	100.00	100.00

Source: W. David Robbins, *op. cit.*, pp. 41, 103.

in loans between $100 and $300 and between $500 and $1,000 than in the case of loans of $100 and less, $300 to $500, and of $1,000 and over. However, since the differences are not large, it is very probable that the size of the loan has little bearing on whether it is likely to become a charge off.

Borrower's Occupation and Family Status

Industry data are not available on the relationship between loans charged off and the characteristics of borrowers.

In his study of loans charged off, considering occupation of borrower, Robbins found slight differences for 1950-51 in the percentage distributions of loans charged off by consumer finance companies and of occupa-

---

[1] W. David Robbins, *op. cit.*, pp. 41 and 103.

tions of borrowers. (See Table 5-3.) However, it should be noted that
the ratio of charge offs to total loans made is lower for craftsmen, foremen and kindred workers, and for laborers, except farm and mine. There
were relatively more charge offs for managers, officials and proprietors,
except farm, and for service workers, protective, domestic, and others.
But these differences were small enough so that occupation of borrower
probably bears no real relationship to loan charge off.

TABLE 5-3
Loss Experience of Consumer Finance Companies by Occupation
of Borrower, 1950-1951

Occupation Group	Loans Charged Off as a Percent of	
	Loans Made by the Industry	Loans Charged Off by Eight Consumer Finance Companies
Craftsmen, foremen and kindred workers	23.73	17.94
Operatives and kindred workers	30.46	30.26
Laborers, except farm and mine	11.86	8.95
Clerical and kindred workers	8.20	9.17
Sales workers	3.51	4.88
Professional, technical and kindred workers	2.83	2.66
Manager, officials and proprietors, except farm	9.19	13.37
Farmers, farm managers, and farm laborers	1.14	1.10
Service workers, protective, domestic and others	7.23	9.38
Unemployed, pensions, or independent incomes	1.53	2.24
Occupation not reported	0.32	0.05
Total	100.00	100.00

Source: W. David Robbins, *op. cit.*, p. 108.

It may be that lending to single men is somewhat more risky than
lending to married men, married women, or single women. Robbins
found that while 13.96 percent of all loans were made to single men,
17.18 percent of the charge offs were in that category.

Chapter 6

EARNING POWER

Trends, 1945-1958

The trend of operating earnings ratios has been steadily downward during the period from 1945 through 1958. The effect of this downward trend, on stockholders' earnings, has been offset only partially by expanding the borrowed portion of total funds employed.

As the average size of loan has increased, the monthly rate of charge collected has decreased, reflecting the graduated rate structures in effect in almost all states. As shown in Chart 4, the median rate of charge collected for a group of selected states decreased from 2.46 percent in 1950 to 2.17 percent in 1958. Operating costs have increased despite efforts to offset the factors at work by improving operating techniques and by effecting other economies. The median of the monthly cost per open account for a group of selected states in 1950 was $3.11 and in 1958 it was $4.59. Squeezed between a decreasing rate of charge collected and increasing costs, the industry has experienced declining earnings ratios. In terms of the median for a group of selected states, the earnings before interest on borrowed money decreased from 7.30 percent of assets used and useful in 1950 to 5.51 percent in 1958.

Revenues

The revenues of consumer finance companies, i.e., their gross income, consist largely—usually almost entirely—of the charges collected on loans outstanding. The amount of loans outstanding in consumer finance companies has shown an upward trend due to an increase in average size of loans made, and in the number of borrowers. Concurrently, total dollar charges increased at a slower rate, reflecting the effect of the application of graduated rates of charge on loans outstanding.

Table 6-1 shows, for eighteen states, the average amount of loans outstanding, the dollar charges collected, and the charges collected as

74 *Earning Power*

CHART 4

CHARGES COLLECTED, COST PER OPEN ACCOUNT AND NET EARNINGS,
SELECTED YEARS 1939-1958*

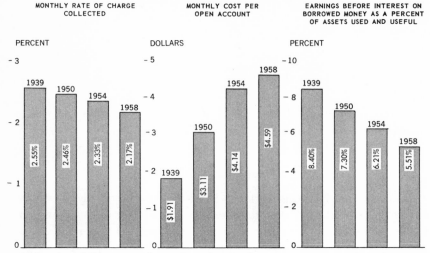

* The plotted figures are the medians for the data shown in Appendix Table A-11
which includes states for which data are available.

a percent of loans outstanding, during the years 1950 and 1958. Since
the data are not complete for the United States, they do not reflect the
total gross income of the consumer finance industry. However, it is
believed that the relationship between charges collected and loans
outstanding of this sample closely approximates the experience for the
country as a whole.

The states shown have rate structures for different size loans and have
loan ceilings comparable to the states not represented. The average
amount of loans outstanding in these states comprised 70 percent of
the United States total in 1950, and 62 percent in 1958.

In these eighteen states, the ratio of charges collected to the amount
of average outstanding loans declined from 26.8 percent in 1950 to 25.3
percent in 1958. This decline reflects chiefly the lower rates of charge
applicable to the larger loans.

Expenses

The proportion of gross income spent for salaries remained reasonably
constant, absorbing about one-quarter of gross income, both in 1950 and
1958. (See Chart 5, which is based on data for twenty-four states in 1950
and twenty-seven states in 1958.) Advertising costs declined from 5.3
percent of gross income in 1950 to 3.8 percent in 1958. The proportion
of gross income absorbed by rent, bad debts, reserves, and all other

TABLE 6-1
Average Amount of Loans Outstanding and Charges Collected by Selected States,
1950 and 1958[a]
(In millions of dollars)

State	Average Amount of Loans Outstanding 1950	1958	Charges Collected 1950	1958	Charges Collected as a Percent of Average Amount of Loans Outstanding 1950	1958
Arizona	3.4	25.5	1.3	7.8	38.2	30.6
California	97.4	279.0	21.7	67.8	22.3	24.3
Florida	33.7	112.3	10.5	33.6	31.2	29.9
Idaho	2.5	12.6	0.9	3.8	36.0	30.2
Illinois	92.8	209.9	27.3	54.2	29.4	25.8
Iowa	19.9	30.5	6.2	9.7	31.2	31.8
Kentucky	22.4	50.5	8.2	18.0	36.6	35.6
Maryland	31.9	64.8	10.4	20.6	32.6	31.8
Michigan	63.1	157.4	17.6	39.1	27.9	24.8
Minnesota	16.1	26.8	5.5	9.1	34.2	34.0
Nevada	0.5	5.5	0.2	1.5	40.0	27.3
New York	123.4	253.6	29.7	54.1	24.1	21.3
Ohio	147.0	316.3	33.5	66.1	22.8	20.9
Rhode Island	7.5	6.2	2.3	1.9	30.7	30.6
Virginia	20.6	82.9	5.8	21.3	28.2	25.7
Washington	10.6	32.8	3.5	10.1	33.0	30.8
West Virginia	17.8	35.5	6.3	12.6	35.4	35.5
Wisconsin	15.7	15.5	4.0	3.8	25.5	24.5
Total	726.3	1,717.6	194.9	435.1	26.8	25.3

[a] Complete data available only for the eighteen states shown.
Source: State Supervisory Reports.

operating expenses increased from 25.9 percent in 1950 to 32.1 percent in 1958. Taxes rose from 13.8 percent to 14.4 percent of gross income. The net effect of these changes was to reduce the proportion of gross income carried over to net income (before interest on borrowed money) from 29.2 percent in 1950, to 24.2 percent in 1958.

The increase in operating expenses as a proportion of gross income has come about despite various efforts to achieve internal economies. Among these efforts has been the support of legislation providing for higher loan ceilings, with the knowledge that the unit cost of making and collecting loans does not increase proportionately with increased size of loan. Other economies have been attained by achieving larger offices, and by expanding multiple office operations. However, the opportunity for increased economy from scale of operation and from specialization of labor is severely limited by the individual nature of each loan transaction.

Another area of effort to achieve economies has been the support of legislation which would reduce some of the detailed operating and reporting requirements of the small loan laws. But the chief reason why

CHART 5

EXPENSES OF CONSUMER FINANCE COMPANIES — THE GROSS
INCOME DOLLAR, AVAILABLE STATES, 1950 AND 1958

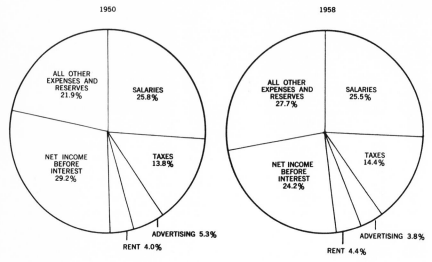

1950   1958

ALL OTHER
EXPENSES AND
RESERVES
21.9%

SALARIES
25.8%

NET INCOME
BEFORE
INTEREST
29.2%

TAXES
13.8%

ADVERTISING 5.3%

RENT 4.0%

ALL OTHER
EXPENSES AND
RESERVES
27.7%

SALARIES
25.5%

NET INCOME
BEFORE
INTEREST
24.2%

TAXES
14.4%

ADVERTISING 3.8%

RENT 4.4%

Sources: R. M. Neifeld, *Trends in Consumer Finance,* p. 70 for 1950; Appendix
Tables A-12 and A-14 for 1958.

operating economies have been unable to offset expense inflation and
declining rates of gross income is the personal service nature of the
business. Automation cannot be applied to a business which requires
personal, individual investigations, follow-ups, counseling, and loan and
collection judgments.

As a result of the various factors at work, several internal changes
have also occurred in the structure of operating expense items. The
proportion of expenses assigned to salaries, not including the cost of
borrowed funds or net income before taxes, dropped from 36.4 percent
in 1950 to 33.6 percent in 1958, and advertising fell from 7.5 percent
to 5.0 percent. (See Chart 6.) Taxes, as a proportion of expenses,
dropped slightly because consumer finance companies were able to
obtain financing from borrowed capital. Since, for income tax purposes,
the interest paid to the holders of notes or debentures is a cost item,
the income tax base did not increase as much as total assets. Other
expenses increased in the same period from 30.0 percent to 36.5 percent
of consumer finance company expenses before interest on borrowed
capital. "Other expenses" include auditing, postage, printing, stationery,
supplies, legal fees, telephone and telegraph costs, travel costs, bad

CHART 6

EXPENSES OF CONSUMER FINANCE COMPANIES — THE
EXPENSE DOLLAR, AVAILABLE STATES, 1950 AND 1958

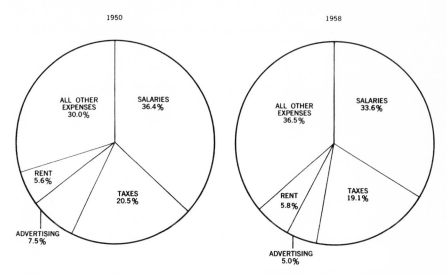

1950   1958

Sources: R. M. Neifeld, *Trends in Consumer Finance,* p. 70 for 1950; Appendix Table A-14 for 1958.

debts and the provision for bad debts, and a miscellany of minor cost items.

Earnings

The earnings of a company or industry may be related to several different bases. The most fundamental relationship for economic analysis, however, is the return on the financial resources committed to the company or industry for a long-term period. In most industrial enterprises, the long-term capital employed represents the fixed assets devoted to production. To a lesser degree, long-term financing has been used by trade enterprises, wholesale and retail, as a means of financing inventories. In the consumer finance business, short-term funds constituted the largest source of outside financing until about 1951. As the short-term rate of interest increased more rapidly than the long-term rate of interest, consumer finance companies relied more and more on long-term financing. In 1958, about two-thirds of the outside financing, excluding net worth, was in the form of debentures. Even before this trend started, however, the short-term borrowings were customarily renewed and therefore were similar in nature to long-term capital.[1] This relationship between earnings and total funds will be used subsequently in this section as one measure of the earnings performance of consumer finance companies. Another measure of earnings performance is the rate of return on assets used and useful.[2] This measure has been used by the regulatory agencies of many states as a device to determine the adequacy of the maximum rates of charge permitted. Net earnings of the consumer finance industry as a percent of assets used and useful has declined steadily almost without exception in states for which data are available. (Appendix Table A-11.) In 1950, the median rate of return on assets used and useful for all states shown was 7.30 percent. The highest rate for any one of the states for which data are available for 1950 was 10.07 percent for West Virginia. The lowest was 4.60 percent for Colorado. In 1954, the median for all states shown was 6.21 percent; 7.52 percent for West Virginia was the highest for any one state, and 2.84 percent for Wisconsin, the lowest. By 1958, the median had dropped to 5.51 percent, with a high of 6.76 percent in West Virginia and a low of 3.19 percent in Wisconsin. These estimates reflect a clear downward trend in the net earnings of the consumer finance industry over the last decade.

For purposes of comparison with other industries, no measure of the earnings performance for the consumer finance industry as a whole is available. The most complete information for such a comparison is contained in *Composite Earnings Performance of the Major Consumer Finance Companies*, prepared by the Stanford Research Institute. The sample in this study comprises the five largest consumer finance companies, all of which are listed on the New York Stock Exchange.[3] These companies constitute a major segment of the industry, as evidenced by the fact that they operate roughly 25 percent of the offices, have perhaps 40 percent of the outstanding loans of the industry, and have total capital comprising somewhat over one-third of the capital employed in the industry. Therefore, this sample is highly useful for comparative purposes with other industries.

To achieve comparability of earnings performance with other industries, the Stanford Research Institute made adjustments of balance sheet

---

[1] For further discussion of this thesis see *Composite Earnings Performance of the Major Consumer Finance Companies*, prepared for Beneficial Management Corporation by Stanford Research Institute, Menlo Park, California, March 1959, pp. 14, 15; S. Cottle and T. Whitman, "Twenty Years of Corporate Earnings," *Harvard Business Review* (May-June 1958), p. 101; J. A. Longstreet, *The Capital Structure of Consumer Finance Companies*, doctoral dissertation, Northwestern University, 1956.

[2] For a further discussion of the background of the use of the concept "assets used and useful" and its use as a base for measuring earnings performance in the consumer finance industry, see Chapter 4, "Trends in Assets, 1939-1958."

[3] These companies are Household Finance Corporation, Beneficial Finance Company, Seaboard Finance Company, American Investment Company of Illinois, and Family Finance Company.

and earnings accounts similar to the method used by S. Cottle and T. Whitman as reported in the *Harvard Business Review*, May-June 1958, and in *Corporate Earning Power and Market Valuation, 1935-1955*, published by the Duke University Press in 1959. These adjustments made it possible to compare the earnings of the consumer finance industry sample with available data on other industries.

In the Stanford study, it was found that the rate of return on total capital, i.e., equity plus long-term borrowing, of the five companies in the consumer finance industry sample declined from 10.3 percent in 1947 to 6.5 percent in 1957. During the same period, the rate of return on total funds, i.e., total capital plus short-term borrowing, declined from 6.7 percent to 5.4 percent.[4] (Table 6-2 and Chart 7.)

TABLE 6-2
Rate of Return on Total Capital and Total Funds for
a Consumer Finance Industry Sample, 1947-1957

	Percent Return	
Year	Total Capital	Total Funds
1947	10.3	6.7
1948	10.2	6.9
1949	9.3	6.5
1950	8.9	6.2
1951	8.3	5.9
1952	7.4	5.6
1953	7.2	5.6
1954	7.0	5.5
1955	6.8	5.3
1956	6.8	5.5
1957	6.5	5.4

Source: *Composite Earnings Performance of the Major Consumer Finance Companies*, (Menlo Park, Calif.: Stanford Research Institute, March 1959), p. 46.

Compared to other industries in the study, it was found that the return on total capital earned by consumer finance companies was comparatively low throughout the period from 1947 to 1957. Though the dollar amount of capital and earnings in the consumer finance industry has expanded more rapidly than most industries, its average earnings performance in 1953-57, as shown by the rate of return earned on capital,

---

[4] *Total capital* is defined in the Stanford study as the sum of the common stock (tangible book value), preferred stock, non-current debt, and minority interests. *Total funds* is defined as the sum of total capital and short-term borrowings. *Earnings available for total capital* is the total of net income after taxes (as adjusted by Stanford) plus tax-adjusted interest on non-current debt. *Earnings available for total funds* is the aggregate of the earnings available for total capital and the tax-adjusted interest on short-term borrowings.

CHART 7

**RATE OF RETURN ON TOTAL CAPITAL AND TOTAL FUNDS
FOR A CONSUMER FINANCE INDUSTRY SAMPLE, 1947-1957**

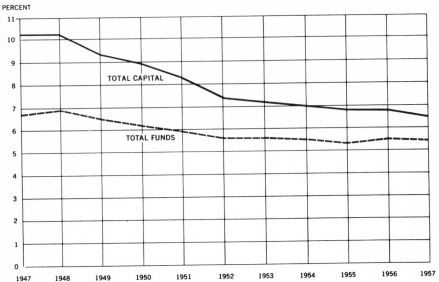

PERCENT

Source: *Composite Earnings Performance of the Major Consumer Finance Companies,* Stanford Research Institute, Menlo Park, California, March, 1959, p. 45.

was exceeded by twenty-nine of thirty-three industries included in the Stanford study.

Regulatory Provisions Affecting Earning Power
and Growth of the Industry and
Recommended Regulatory and Tax Changes

The earning power of consumer finance companies has always been subject to a number of influences which are somewhat beyond the control of the company itself. As a result, these companies are not able to compete with each other and with other types of lenders, in a completely free, competitive situation.

Early small loan legislation, which was designed to eliminate the then existing loan shark operation, contained provisions which restricted the freedom of operation of licensed companies. These included limitations on the rate of charge, amount that could be loaned, number of lenders permissible in a community, and other limitations that will be considered in detail later. In addition to those restrictions which were written into law, there were additional regulations which placed control over advertising practices, accounting procedures, and record-keeping requirements, to which were usually added other restrictive administrative orders issued by some government agency, usually the state banking department.

Once established, these restrictions became difficult to change, even when the consumer income and economy had changed so completely that many of the original provisions, designed to combat loan shark operations, had become unnecessary. Changes could be brought about only through an extensive program to educate the public and legislators as to the need for modernization. Then legislative action had to be secured and executive approval gained.

Since most state laws are based on the Uniform Small Loan Law, an analysis of the three basic tenets on which that law was founded may be in order:

First, it was felt that the potential users of small loan service were people in dire need, economically illiterate, without bargaining power, and, therefore, completely at the mercy of the lender. For that reason, the law consisted of a series of *thou shalt's* and *thou shalt not's,* plus one *may.* Every conceivable restriction designed to protect the borrower was included in the law, and in return for assuming those restrictions, the lender was granted the privilege of charging a rate of 3½ percent per month. Second, it was felt that the only way to prevent manipulation of charges and resultant fleecing of unwary borrowers was to have the total cost of the loan based on the all-inclusive rate, stated as a monthly rate but computed on a daily basis, and applied to unpaid principal balances. Third, it was felt that a ceiling or maximum size of loan of approximately three times the average monthly income of potential borrowers would be ample to take care of all situations. The ceiling was set at $300.

What is the situation today in respect to these tenets on which the small loan law was founded? No longer are customers and the potential users of consumer credit limited to those in dire need, or to those who are entirely unfamiliar with consumer credit and the charges therefor, or who have no bargaining power. Unquestionably, the large majority of consumers are using other forms of consumer credit and are reasonably familiar with various forms of credit. They do have bargaining power, because competition for this business is keen.

The tremendous growth in consumer credit and the various types of charges which have been established and used successfully show that it is possible to prevent manipulation of charges under rate statement and computation, by other means than the monthly rate on unpaid principal balances. When the total charge is expressed in terms of dollars and proper adjustments in charges are clearly spelled out, and the regulatory agency is given adequate powers, manipulation to the detriment of the borrower is not possible.

A $300 ceiling simply does not fit today's economy. The average monthly income of actual and potential customers in 1916 was less than $100. Today it is around $400. A ceiling three times that figure—to maintain the 1916 ratio—would have to be at least $1,200.

The vast improvement in the economic outlook and in the family living pattern during the past forty years is evident to all. Fortunately, many states have been alert to these changing needs, and regulatory laws are being constantly revised. Even so, there is frequently a time lag which places a burden on those in the industry.

Competition and increased volume have helped reduce the rates in many states. In fact, the consumer finance industry is one of the very few in the nation whose charges for goods and services are lower today than they were forty years ago. There are probably two major factors which contributed most to making it possible to maintain reasonable earnings in the industry in the face of increased operating costs pressing against fixed or declining maximum rates of charge. These factors are the increased volume of business and the increased use of borrowed funds by the industry.

Without the leverage of borrowed funds, the industry could not possibly hope to realize a reasonable return on equity capital under present conditions. For example, at the Massachusetts rate hearing in 1957 it was brought out that a lender who had no borrowed funds and was operating entirely on equity capital, would need an average rate of $3\frac{1}{2}$ percent per month on loans up to $1,500 to produce net earnings of 15 percent on capital. And that projection was based on operating expenses of 13.25 percent on average outstandings.

Restrictions on phases other than rate also have a distinct bearing upon the earning power of these companies. One important, as well as restrictive, feature of all small loan laws is that pertaining to the amount of money which may be loaned under these laws. As of September 1, 1959, twenty-seven small loan laws provided for loans in excess of $500: Arizona, Connecticut, Florida, Minnesota, Pennsylvania, Utah, Vermont, and Virginia with $600; Illinois with $800; Alaska, Idaho, Montana, New Mexico, Ohio, Washington, and Wyoming with $1,000; Canada, Colorado, Massachusetts, and Oregon with $1,500; Kansas with $2,100; Maine, Nevada, and South Dakota with $2,500; Nebraska with $3,000; California with $5,000; and Missouri with no limit.

The wide variation reflects to some degree the differing needs of the different state economies, but in some cases the difference is due more to lack of awareness on the part of the state, rather than a contrasting need. For example, if $3,000 is considered necessary in Nebraska, how could $500 be sufficient in the neighboring State of Iowa? Maine, a state with little industry and sparse population, has a law permitting loans up to $2,500, while New York has only recently raised its ceiling from

$500 to $800. In spite of a trend toward higher ceilings, some small loan laws are still inadequate. This causes a low level of outstanding loans, which, in turn, is reflected in the companies' earnings. A more equitable approach to this problem would be to continue rate regulation, but remove the restriction on ceilings and allow competitive forces to work.

The older, national chain lending companies are less seriously affected by present laws containing convenience and advantage clauses. However, the younger companies, with aggressive management desirous of expanding their operations, are stymied in some states because of convenience and advantage clauses which are not always compatible with a free enterprise philosophy. Most companies believe that it should be enough for an applicant for a license to establish financial and moral responsibility. There are too many variables for anyone to administer a convenience and advantage provision in a manner that will at all times be fair to each applicant. This peculiar provision, which does not apply to most businesses, not only affects earnings, but restricts growth of expanding companies. In one state recently, the administrator rejected a small loan license application on the grounds that sufficient other sources of money, including credit unions, already existed in the community. This created a very unfair situation since the competing institutions were not subject to the same restriction.

Most small loan laws prohibit loans on real estate. In many cases, second and third mortgage loans cost the borrower more than the same amount would under small loan laws, particularly those which permit loans up to $1,500 or more. If a person is disposed to borrow money using as security real estate which he owns and which is acceptable as security to the lender, then in a free economy that should be his privilege. Competing credit grantors are not so restricted.

Other provisions which still exist in some states and which restrict the earning power of consumer loan companies include:

1) Requirements making it necessary to complete new papers and cancel existing ones whenever additional funds are loaned to a borrower. Banks and retailers under revolving check and charge arrangements are not required to handle additional advances in this cumbersome manner.

2) Necessity of stating and charging interest on a percent per month basis. Other credit is extended on a dollar cost, discount, or dollar add-on basis. In some cases, such restrictions add to the cost of doing business, because they require time consuming operations and numerous mathematical computations.

3) Some state laws prohibit a consumer loan licensee from engaging in any other business than that of lending money, under the consumer loan or small loan act. In these states it is not permissible to buy retail instalment sales contracts, nor to operate a lending business under

ancillary laws which would permit the accommodation of those borrowers who need more than the amount permitted under the small loan law. Some states, however, permit multiple business in the same office, while others prohibit it.

4) In most states the administrative authority, under small loan laws, is vested in the state banking department. As a result, small loan regulations frequently are authored by a banking commissioner with no background of experience in the consumer finance business.

5) Some laws still require that all advertising copy be submitted to state supervisory officials for approval. This situation can degenerate into a debate in semantics between the copywriter who prepared the advertising and the state official who is acting as a censor. Ridiculous edicts, such as prohibiting the use of the word *can*, but permitting the word *may*, sometimes results. Other regulations on advertising may require lengthy statements in ads explaining rates, loan limits which are permissible, and even license numbers on printed copy. Such requirements increase costs because additional space must be paid for to allow the inclusion of such information. Laws providing that no licensee may use advertising which is false or misleading would seem to be sufficient.

6) Some small loan laws prohibit the offering of life insurance to the borrower, which would liquidate the balance owing at the time of death. The same restriction does not apply to banks, retailers, credit unions, and others engaged in a credit business. This apparent discrimination results in a financial disadvantage, and denies the borrower a desirable service and protection.

7) Another problem arises from the lack of uniformity in the statement of earnings. During the years that the licensed consumer finance companies have filed reports with supervisory departments of the various states, there has been controversy over the proper method of presenting a statement of earnings on a composite basis for the industry. The composite report of the licensed loan business is a public record and is the source of information for both proponents and opponents of the industry within and without the legislatures. The combining of various corporate structures into a single composite report is necessary to reflect the business as a state-wide operation. It is neither practical nor meaningful to show net earnings as percent of net worth in a composite report made up from the figures of many companies, particularly those operating through subsidiaries. Therefore, a form of asset base has been adopted in most states.

Since the asset base is used, the interest cost for borrowed capital must be eliminated from the expense factor and combined with net income after taxes. The point about which there is considerable conflict among the various state regulatory bodies is how to determine the asset base upon which to calculate rate of return.

In addition to state regulations, there are certain federal statutes that have a discriminatory effect on the consumer finance industry.

Many consumer finance companies, especially those of relatively small size, are closely held corporations operating with equity capital supplied by a family or small closely-knit group. Such a form of state-chartered organization not uncommon with small business generally has brought to consumer finance operators a special income tax problem, because interest is the major source of their income. To discourage incorporation as a device to avoid taxation, Section 541 of the Internal Revenue Code imposes a personal holding company tax of 75 percent of the undistributed personal holding company income not in excess of $2,000 plus 85 percent of the undistributed personal holding company income in excess of $2,000. Banks, life insurance companies, surety companies, and consumer finance companies, among others, are excepted from the tax. These exceptions recognize that major sources of income in these operations are typically interest or dividends. The conditions for excepting consumer finance companies are circumscribed.

The Internal Revenue Code follows the traditional language of state small loan laws on permissible rates of charge, i..e, percent per month. Therefore, when the wording of state laws is changed the question arises as to whether the Internal Revenue Service may interpret the intent of the Code as permitting no exception from the personal holding company tax. This question has arisen with respect to laws permitting the dollar add-on computation method of stating charges.

Consumer finance companies organized as closely held corporations which prefer to substitute this method in place of a percent per month statement of charge are restrained by the possibility of having their income taxed at a confiscatory rate. In the past, desirable state legislation has been delayed because of the opposition of those who would be adversely affected under the Personal Holding Company section if the new lending law were passed. Subsequently, appropriate amendments (or administrative rulings) to the Personal Holding Company section only partially alleviated the situation. This failure of federal legislation to keep abreast of changes in state legislation imposes the threat of unintended discrimination against the consumer finance company which happens to be a closely held corporation.

Tax exclusions designed to meet a situation which no longer exists today force consumer finance companies to help subsidize their own competition. Laws giving credit unions or any other competitive business an unfair tax advantage should be adjusted.

Consumer finance companies, sales finance companies, industrial loan companies and commercial banks are all subject to essentially the same state, federal, and local income taxes. These different types of financial institutions are all engaged in competition with one another and, in turn, are also in competition with credit unions, a major component of the financial group making consumer loans. Both federal and state chartered credit unions, however, are exempt from the payment of state, federal, and local income taxes which other competing lenders must pay.

In the early stages of the income tax, rates were low and tax exemption granted credit unions, savings and loan associations, and mutual savings banks represented tangible evidence of support on the part of the government, rather than the creation of an important economic advantage. Today, however, taxes are much higher and tax exemption has become an extremely important economic advantage which credit unions enjoy over other lenders.

Besides total exemption from income taxes, credit unions are also exempt from payment of certain excise taxes, as well as taxes on transportation and communication.

In making a case for tax equality, financial institutions can never hope to have their tax rates reduced. Nor does anyone advocate such a policy, unless all tax-paying corporations' tax rates are so reduced.

If, however, lending institutions are not to seek a reduction in taxes to put them in an equal competitive position, it follows that to preserve a free enterprise economy, credit unions must be required to accept their fair share of the cost of government by paying the same federal, state, and local income taxes on profits as are required of other lenders.

Chapter 7

THE INFLUENCE OF
GENERAL MONETARY POLICY

Cost and Availability of Funds

Portions of this monograph, which trace the history and development of consumer finance companies from the time of their origin, cover a period of almost a half century. Other sections focus attention on the period since the end of World War II. This section, which is devoted to an examination of the influence of monetary policy upon consumer finance companies, and through them on their customers, must be restricted to a much shorter period. The limitations upon the use of general monetary controls were so great in the 1930's, and the character and structure of the consumer finance business was so different from its present structure, that little benefit would be derived from an examination of that period. Throughout World War II and for a considerable period thereafter, monetary policy was subservient to fiscal and debt management considerations; also throughout essentially the same period, consumer credit was restrained by direct regulation. In other words, it is only since the Treasury-Federal Reserve Accord of 1951 and the abandonment of direct regulation of consumer credit in May 1952, that there is any possibility of assessing the influence of monetary policy upon the entire consumer credit area or upon any segment thereof.

At the request of the Chairman of the President's Council of Economic Advisers early in 1956, the Board of Governors of the Federal Reserve System undertook a comprehensive survey of the entire consumer credit field, culminating in the publication of its six-volume study, *Consumer Instalment Credit*, in May 1957. It devoted a considerable measure of its resources of manpower and money to the subject matter of this section, covering in detail the period of credit stringency 1952-53; the period of credit ease 1953-54; and that portion of the subsequent period of credit stringency prior to early 1956. It has not appeared prudent for the National Consumer Finance Association to retrace the same ground,

87

nor would it have had the financial or manpower resources to do so with equal comprehensiveness. Consequently, the National Consumer Finance Association has concentrated on the more recent periods, that of credit stringency 1955-57; and that of credit ease, 1957-58. It has done so by utilizing the replies of a group of twenty-one consumer finance companies to a questionnaire directed to this question, and data showing the sources of funds of these companies at year-end dates, 1949-1958.[1]

Summary data from the balance sheets of the twenty-one companies as of June 30, 1959, appear in Table 7-1.

It is desirable to recognize at the outset that consumer finance companies hold less than 10 percent of the consumer instalment credit outstanding.[2] Sales finance companies throughout the last decade have accounted for from 25-30 percent of consumer instalment credit outstanding and commercial banks have directly supplied about 40 percent of such credit to consumers. The remaining 15 to 20 percent is accounted for by other financial institutions including credit unions. Commercial banks also supply another 15 or 20 percent of total consumer instalment credit indirectly; namely, through loans made to, and commercial paper purchased from, sales finance companies and consumer finance companies. In October 1955, total credit supplied by commercial banks to the consumer sector, directly and indirectly, represented 20 percent of their loans and 8 percent of bank assets.[3] Thus, the impact of monetary policy upon commercial banks is crucial in determining its impact upon the largest segment of the consumer credit market, directly, and upon a large share of the market, indirectly.

Monetary policy impinges most immediately and most directly upon commercial banks, by increasing or decreasing their reserves with the Federal Reserve Banks. The size of these reserves determines the volume of the banks' loanable funds.

In a period of active demand for credit which usually coincides with a period of credit stringency, banks find it increasingly necessary to allocate their loanable funds. Some reach the limit which they consider it prudent to have committed to the total consumer sector. Some restrict their increase in funds to the consumer sector because of insistent demand for funds from other sectors. Within the consumer sector, some banks favor their consumer customers at the expense of their loans to consumer credit institutions. Before examining the manner in which each of these developments has influenced the relationship of commercial

---

[1] A description of the coverage of this survey may be found in Chapter 3. In the questionnaire, a check list was provided for answering all of the questions asked and spaces were provided for comments. For simplicity, negative replies and the failure to reply have not been indicated in some cases in the tables presented.

[2] See Table 2-3 in this monograph.

[3] See "Consumer Credit and the Credit Market," *Consumer Instalment Credit,* Board of Governors of the Federal Reserve System, 1957, Part I, Vol. 2, p. 53.

TABLE 7-1
Summary Data From the Balance Sheets of Twenty-One Consumer Finance Companies, June 30, 1959

Companies Designated as	Range of Assets (In millions)	Number of Companies	Number of Offices Operated	Total Assets	Consumer Instalment Credit (Amounts in thousands)	Personal Loans	Capital and Surplus
Large	$350 and over	2	1,742	$1,103,444	$ 869,511	$ 848,475	$340,885
Moderately large	$50 and under $350	7	2,215	1,070,616	971,880	850,048	224,707
Medium-size	$10 and under $50	4	234	129,815	113,916	78,278	33,332
Small	Under $10	8	92	30,756	27,552	20,961	7,531
Total in Sample		21	4,283	$2,334,631	$1,982,859	$1,797,762	$606,455
Total Consumer Finance Companies		n.a.	n.a.	n.a.	$3,424,000[a]	$2,927,000[a]	n.a.
Licensees Under Effective Small Loan Laws		3,533[b]	11,779[b]	n.a.	$2,811,000[a]	n.a.	n.a.

[a] Estimates prepared and released by Board of Governors of the Federal Reserve System.
[b] Based on small loan licensees as of September 1959, as published in *Roster of Consumer Finance Companies*, National Consumer Finance Association. Includes offices operated by cash lending subsidiaries of companies which Federal Reserve Board classifies as sales finance companies, or otherwise.
n.a.-Not available.

Source: Appendix Table A-10.

89

banks to the consumer finance companies, it is desirable to look briefly at the nature of the demand for personal instalment loans, in general; and for loans from consumer finance companies, specifically, in the last decade.

The nature of this demand has had a profound influence upon the sources from which consumer finance companies have sought their funds in the last decade. Consumer finance companies, since the end of World War II, have been faced with an almost constant growth in demand for their services. The persistence in this rate of growth and the regularity of the rate, which have characterized the entire area of personal instalment cash loans, have been in strong contrast to the much greater degree of fluctuation in rate of growth which has occurred in the other segments of the consumer instalment credit field—automobile paper, particularly, but other consumer goods paper to a lesser degree.[4] The contrast can be readily seen on Chart 8, setting forth consumer instalment credit outstanding, by major parts, reproduced from the Federal Reserve *Chart Book.*

The fairly constant rate of growth in personal instalment loans can be explained by the persistent rate of growth of spending units in the country and the quite regular rate of growth of consumer income, as reflected in the growth in average monthly incomes of spending units. The latter has been significant to the growth of personal instalment loans since the typical personal loan is closely related to the borrower's average monthly income.

The growth of loan receivables of consumer finance companies has been influenced by these factors, namely, the persistent growth in average monthly incomes of most American families, and the growth in number of such spending units. In addition, variations in the rate of growth from year to year have reflected several other factors: variation in intensity of competition with other types of consumer lending agencies; variation in the level of unemployment of various segments of the population—the borrowers from consumer finance companies have suffered from unemployment in recession periods to a greater degree than the borrowers from commercial banks; the adoption of small loan laws in states not previously having such laws—permitting the opening of offices by chain companies in those states; and the upward revision of loan

---

[4] Automobile paper started from a much lower level at the end of the War and has moved up to a greater degree in the period as a whole, but it has been characterized by periods of very rapid growth, alternating with periods of sidewise movement and, in one instance, a marked decline. The periods of sidewise movement and the more recent period of decline have coincided with periods of monetary ease whereas the rapid increases have occurred during periods of monetary tightness. This is the result of the fact that rapid increases in demand for automobiles have occurred during prosperity periods whereas the periods of monetary ease have coincided with those periods in which a reduced sale of automobiles occurred.

CHART 8

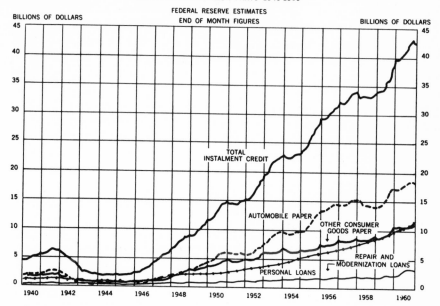

CONSUMER INSTALMENT CREDIT
OUTSTANDING BY MAJOR PARTS 1940-1960
FEDERAL RESERVE ESTIMATES
END OF MONTH FIGURES

Source: Board of Governors of the Federal Reserve System.

limits in the small loan laws in established states. The amount of change in millions of dollars and the percentage change within each year, 1947 to 1960, of loans of consumer finance companies and of loans made under effective state small loan laws, is shown in Table 7-2.

Shift to Long-Term Debt

The persistence in the rate of growth of personal instalment cash loans, which constitute about 85 percent of the assets of consumer finance companies, has made it possible and desirable for management in such companies to make long-range financial plans. In the words of one large company, "generally speaking, it has been less costly for us to obtain funds in the long-term market than in the short-term market throughout the period covered (1949-58). As a result, it has been prudent to acquire additional long-term debt whenever it was our judgment that such funds could be utilized more or less permanently." The manner in which such a policy was accomplished and the reason for it was described by the second large company.

The Company's policy has been to finance its requirements initially through bank borrowings, refinancing from time to time by selling long-

TABLE 7-2
Changes in Outstanding Consumer Finance Company
Loans During Years, 1947-1960

	Increase During Year			
	Loans of Consumer Finance Companies[a]		Loans Under Effective State Small Loan Laws[b]	
	Millions		Millions	
Years	of Dollars	Percent	of Dollars	Percent
1947	c	c	130.7	22.0
1948	c	c	129.2	17.8
1949	c	c	118.8	13.9
1950	c	c	138.2	14.2
1951	269	20.9	194.8	17.5
1952	311	20.0	208.0	15.9
1953	271	14.5	178.5	11.8
1954	120	5.6	147.0	8.7
1955	399	17.7	249.0	13.5
1956	400	15.1	344.0	16.5
1957	277	9.1	289.0	11.9
1958	51	1.5	95.0	3.5
1959	380	11.2	242.0	8.6
1960	360	12.1	355.0	16.1

[a] Consumer finance companies as defined by the Federal Reserve, i.e., have over 50 percent of their outstandings in personal cash instalment loans.
[b] Loans made by all small loan licensees in states with small loan laws classified as "effective" by the National Consumer Finance Association.
[c] Estimates are not available prior to September 1950.

Source: Board of Governors of the Federal Reserve System.

term notes or debentures at prevailing rates. . . . In the earlier years of this period, long-term interest rates were low by historical standards and thus were considered attractive even though higher than short-term rates. In the later years, although long-term interest rates at times were no longer historically low, the above-stated policy was continued for the reason, in part, that funds available to commercial banks for loans were less plentiful.

During the period from December 1949 to December 1958, there was virtually no change in the dollar amount of bank borrowings of the two large companies. Since their total assets increased by $750 million, the percentage of such bank borrowings trended irregularly downward as the amount of long-term debt increased.

Management decision to shift from a dependence upon short-term funds was not limited to the two large companies although it came earlier in their case, apparently prior to World War II. Sources of funds of consumer finance companies over the period 1949-58 is shown in Chart 9.[5] The same deliberate policy decision apparently occurred in

[5] Represents distribution of net worth and liabilities in percent of their total. Miscellaneous liabilities have been omitted from total liabilities in computing the percentages for this chart.

CHART 9

SOURCES OF FUNDS OF CONSUMER FINANCE COMPANIES, 1949-1958

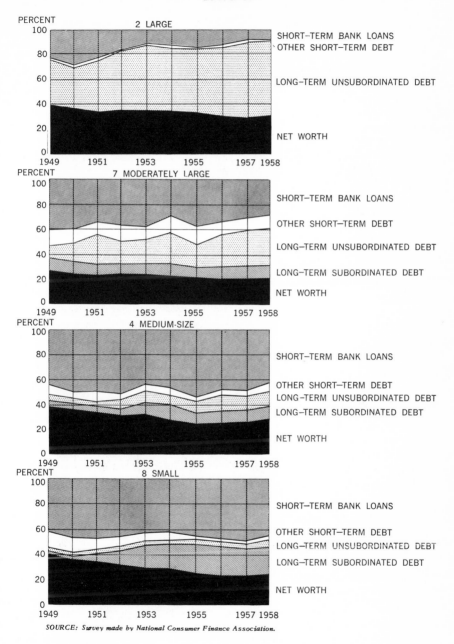

SOURCE: Survey made by National Consumer Finance Association.

Source: Survey made by National Consumer Finance Association.

almost all of the companies in the sample regardless of size. It was not made as early historically as was the case with the two large companies and did not proceed to the same degree. In fact, there was a direct relationship between degree of use of long-term debt and size of company. The greater difficulty encountered by the smaller companies resulted in a relatively greater use of subordinated debt. This also improved the base for bank borrowing. Differences in degree of emphasis of the various factors are evident in a sample of replies.

> The changes in funds represented a change in philosophy, namely, that long-term debt as a non-fluctuating cost was a more desirable arrangement. In addition, some long-term debt certainly strengthened the borrowing base. [Small company.]

> In our opinion, we should have between 40 percent and 50 percent of total debt in long-term funds, . . . (the change in our capital structure was the result of) purposely obtaining more long-term funds. [Moderately large company.]

> [Our lesser use of bank borrowing] has come about as the result of available long-term funds from institutional investors. Long-term debt requires less servicing, no compensating balance and guarantees availability of funds over an extended period. [Moderately large company.]

> We went into a medium-size subordinated debenture bond promotion so as to obtain long-term money, thus enhancing our financial stature with our banking friends. This permitted us to retain a larger unused compensating balance to depend on in future requirements. [Small company.]

> Our bank borrowings have been from 85 percent to 90 percent of total debt because we have relied on bank borrowings and senior subordinated debentures. We have not been in a position to go into the open market for notes. However, we recently have started selling junior subordinated notes throughout our branch offices. [Small company.]

> Continued high retention of earnings—because of conservative policy—financed portion of growth. Remainder of growth principally financed through bank borrowings because long-term market not favorable—from rate standpoint—when securing additional long-term money considered. [Medium-size company.]

> [It is . . .] our policy to use the long-term market and not be at the mercy of banks with their changing position of available funds. [Moderately large company.]

> The company, as a matter of policy, has used substantial amounts of long-term credit. Bank credit requirements are generally kept within the limits which might reasonably be expected in fluctuating business demands. [Moderately large company.]

Seventeen of the twenty-one companies in the sample stated that they had changed the relative portion of short-term debt to total debt during the period. Only one-third of these said the shift was due to changing interest rates, or was made in anticipation of changing interest rates. (See Table 7-3.)

TABLE 7-3
Interest Rates as a Factor in the Changed Debt Structure of Consumer
Finance Companies

	Large	Moderately Large	Medium	Small	Total
Companies reporting change in short-long-term debt structure	2	6	3	6	17
Due to changing interest rates	2ª	2	1	-	5
In anticipation of changing interest rates	2ª	3	-	1	6

ª In part.

Source: Survey made by the National Consumer Finance Association.

Inability to Expand Bank Borrowings

A significant proportion of the companies, ranging from moderately large to small, encountered difficulty in expanding bank borrowings in the tight money period 1956-57. Replies indicate that these companies attempted to, and were unable to, expand bank borrowings: (1) by increasing lines of credit with existing banks; (2) by establishing lines with new banks; and (3) by increasing the number of months during which they used their lines. Some reported this difficulty early in the tight money period, namely, in 1955 and 1956, whereas others did not encounter difficulty until 1957 or 1958. Several reported "from 1956 on" and one reported "during tight money periods." The replies are summarized in Table 7-4.

In describing the reason for their inability to increase bank loans, three small companies reported the reason as the "general tight money" situation, and one said "banks we contacted had all the lines with loan and finance companies they wanted." Two moderately large companies reported that their difficulty was "due to fully loaned position of our major banks." Another reported, "Our policy over these years was to use the lines of credit extended for from seven to nine months of each year and nine months is approximately the maximum use permitted by our credit line banks."

Bank Initiative to Reduce Company Borrowing

Consumer finance companies not only encountered difficulty when they sought to increase their lines of credit, but also encountered situations in which line banks took the initiative to reduce the amount of loans made available to the companies. More than one-half of the companies, of all sizes, were requested not to use their lines of credit for

---

TABLE 7-4
Inability of Consumer Finance Companies to Expand Bank Borrowing[a]

Companies Classified by Size	Number in Sample	Number Reporting Inability to Expand Bank Borrowing by:		
		Increasing Lines	Establishing New Lines	Increasing Use of Lines
Large	2	-	-	-
Moderately Large	7	2	-	2
Medium-size	4	2	2	-
Small	8	3	4	1
Total	21	7	6	3

[a] The question was asked, "Were there any times from 1949 through 1958 when credit was being tightened, under the interest rates in effect at the time, when your company was unable to expand its bank borrowing [by the means shown in the Table] ?"

Source: Survey made by the National Consumer Finance Association.

a period of time. About one-fifth of them, again involving companies of all sizes, were asked by one or more line banks not to utilize their full line of credit; one-third of them were requested to reduce lines of credit. Three-fifths of the companies, again involving all sizes, encountered occasions when banks requested cancellation of lines of credit; and one-quarter reported that they were requested to adhere more closely to compensating balance requirements. Table 7-5 summarizes the replies of companies reporting line bank initiative to reduce company borrowing.

TABLE 7-5
Bank Action to Reduce Borrowing by Consumer Finance Companies

Companies Classified by Size	Number in Sample	Number of Companies Reporting Line Bank Requests of:				
		Temporary Non-Use	Restricted Use	Line Reduction	Line Cancellation	More Strict Adherence To "Rules"
Large	2	1	1	-	2	1
Moderately Large	7	4	1	2	4	2
Medium-size	4	2	1	1	3	1
Small	8	5	1	2	3	1
Total	21	12	4	5	12	5

Source: Survey made by the National Consumer Finance Association.

The reasons given for these actions show that consumer finance companies, which maintain lines of credit with a substantial number of banks, are thus particularly vulnerable to restrictive action when banks are under pressure. In addition, companies of all sizes were requested not to utilize lines when line banks were at their seasonal peaks. A selection of company replies illustrate typical situations:

> The period from November 1957 to January 1958. The reasons given: (1) Tight money market, (2) Bank had over-extended itself, (3) Bank was only extending loans to those finance companies in its geographical area. [Small company.]

> One bank wrote that they were increasing interest rate on finance company lines—we refused to pay them more than other banks so we paid off our notes at maturity. (August 1955.) One bank (in another city) asked that our line be cancelled because they were limiting lines of credit to those finance companies having offices in that city. (March 1957.) A bank in still another city reduced our line in June 1957 but restored it in April 1958. In November 1958, a bank in still another city asked for payment in full within six months because of local demand. [Small company.]

> Several rural banks generally make such requests during last four months of the year due to their local demand for tobacco crop loans. [Medium-size company.]

> We are off-line with each bank at least sixty or ninety days each year. Several banks have asked us if we would arrange our off-line period to coincide with their seasonal peak in loan demand or seasonal low point in deposit balances. In 1957 several banks asked if they could "take their turn" at a specified later date knowing that our lines were ample—the reason given being that their loans were then particularly high, or that they had been borrowing too constantly at the Federal Reserve window and had been asked to cut back, or that they were endeavoring to postpone sales of Government bonds at a loss until their next tax year. [Large company.]

> There was one instance where a bank established a prime rate to finance companies which was higher than its prime rate to other commercial borrowers, and another case where a bank requested an increase in compensating balances higher than that required by other banks. Rather than accede and give preferential treatment to these banks, we took the initiative in discontinuing the line. [Large company.]

> In February 1956 one bank cancelled the line of credit advising that such action resulted from a policy decision to withdraw direct lines of credit in the finance and loan field because it was so heavily in the field on a direct lending basis that its board felt it should contract its total commitments. [Large company.]

Utilization of Bank Lines

Changes in bank loans and in available bank lines of credit suggest that monetary policy has a direct influence upon the operation of consumer finance companies. Chart 10 shows the amount of bank loans as a percentage of bank lines for year-end dates, 1949-58, and the percentage change in bank lines during each year, 1950-58.

CHART 10

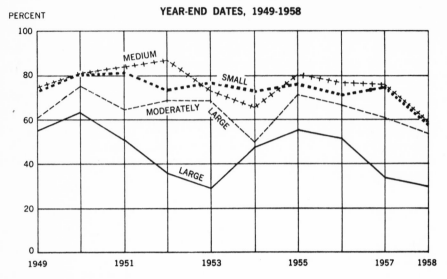

PERCENTAGE OF BANK LINES USED

PERCENT   YEAR-END DATES, 1949-1958

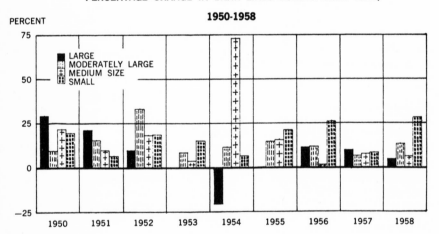

PERCENTAGE CHANGE IN BANK LINES DURING EACH YEAR,

PERCENT   1950-1958

Source: Survey made by National Consumer Finance Association.

During the period under consideration, bank loans made to the small and medium-size companies exceeded 70 percent of their available lines of credit at the end of each year, except in years of credit ease (1958, in the case of small companies and 1954, 1958, in the case of medium-size companies). At the end of 1952, bank loans of the medium-size companies reached a peak of 87 percent of lines, a condition approaching a full utilization of the lines.[6] Apparently the companies involved did not wish to, or were unable to, increase their lines of credit during 1953, a year of credit stringency. Instead, they increased unsubordinated long-term debt by $1,300,000, junior subordinated debt by $2,000,000, sold about $500,000 additional commercial paper, and increased other short-term debt by about $275,000. These additional funds acquired during 1953 enabled the medium-size companies to reduce bank loans by almost $4,000,000, to a figure which was less than 73 percent of available lines of credit. Nevertheless, in this year, when consumer finance companies in the aggregate increased their loan receivables by 14.5 percent, these medium-size companies expanded their total assets (i.e., financial structure) by a smaller percentage than in any other year of the period. This suggests that monetary tightness clearly limited the expansion of consumer loans of this group of companies.

Bank loans of the small companies reached their highest year-end percentage (81.5 percent) of bank lines in 1951. In 1952, they were able to expand lines of credit by more than 18 percent, with the result that utilization of bank lines declined markedly (to 73.4 percent). In 1953, these companies were again able to increase their lines of credit by 15 percent. Despite that fact, loans again increased to a figure in excess of 76 percent of lines. In each of these years, the small companies sold significant amounts of senior subordinated debt (about $750,000 in 1952 and $1,500,000 in 1953) and were able also to increase their loans at line banks by $400,000 and $800,000, respectively. Thus, in 1953, their 16 percent rate of growth exceeded that of the industry as a whole. During 1955-57, years of credit stringency, the small companies had bank loans in excess of 70 percent of their available lines of credit despite increases in lines of 22 percent in 1955 and 27 percent in 1956. Thus, in each of these years of credit stringency, the small companies expanded the dollar amount of their bank loans at a rate which exceeded the rate in growth of their total assets. In 1958, they again obtained a 29 percent increase in bank lines of credit even though their bank loans outstanding declined slightly and their total assets increased at a slower rate than in the preceding years. By obtaining these additional lines of credit, their ratio of loans to bank lines declined to 58 percent, the lowest ratio of the entire decade.

The ability of the small and medium-size companies to increase their lines of credit fourfold (a more rapid rate than the larger companies)

---

[6] December is the seasonal peak of demand for consumer finance companies and would constitute the maximum point of utilization of bank lines from a seasonal point of view. Since all consumer finance companies have short-term bank debt throughout the year, they meet the two-month clean-up requirement by rotation in borrowing among line banks. A two-month clean-up requirement results in a maximum average ratio of bank debt to lines of 83 percent.

at the same time that they were using a high proportion of their existing lines, suggests a close relationship to their line banks and a willingness of those banks to accommodate such companies during a period of credit stringency.

Bank lines of the moderately large companies were typically between 60 percent and 70 percent of available lines at year-end dates, exceeding that range in only two years, 1950 and 1955, and dropping below that range in 1954 and 1958. This suggests a more conservative use of lines of credit by these companies than by the medium-size and small companies. The fact that moderately large companies obtained increases in their lines earlier in the 1952-53 period of credit stringency, and continued to expand their lines of credit at a more regular rate year by year than the other size groups, also suggests conservative management.

The large companies expanded their lines of credit at a rapid rate in the early years of the decade. Thereafter, they went to the long-term market so regularly—in relation to their expanding need for funds —that they considered it prudent to decrease their lines of credit by 0.2 percent in 1953 and by 21 percent in 1954. This decrease in lines enabled them to avoid the expense involved in carrying unnecessarily large lines in view of the low rate of utilization of lines throughout the early period of credit tightness. In 1955, large companies were utilizing 55 percent of their lines of credit. To increase their borrowing leverage, however, the large companies increased their lines of credit by 11 percent in 1956, and by 9.5 percent in 1957. During these years, the large companies further reduced their rate of utilization of lines to a level far below that of companies in any other size group.

Cost of Bank Loans

The cost of loans obtained by consumer finance companies from banks was directly and materially affected by general monetary policy.

The two large consumer finance companies and some of the seven moderately large companies pay the prime rate on their bank loans. This rate is set by the large New York City banks and is also charged by other leading banks on loans to their large and best-rated business borrowers. It is granted only on loans bearing a very low risk and those of considerable size, thus resulting in a very low administrative cost per dollar per loan. It is considered a sharply competitive rate influenced directly and to a substantial degree by conditions in the money market. This prime rate, during the period under consideration, showed considerable variation. (See Table 7-6.)

Companies borrowing smaller amounts or companies whose rating is not "prime" find it necessary to pay higher rates on bank loans. The median rate of interest required on loans of moderately large companies,

TABLE 7-6
Prime Bank Rates, December 1947 to September 1961
(In percent)

December 1947 to August 1948	1.75
August 1948 to September 1950	2.00
September 1950 to January 5, 1951	2.25
January 5, 1951 to October 16, 1951	2.50
October 16, 1951 to December 18, 1951	2.75
December 18, 1951 to April 27, 1953	3.00
April 27, 1953 to March 17, 1954	3.25
March 17, 1954 to August 1955	3.00
August 1955 to October 1955	3.25
October 1955 to April 1956	3.50
April 1956 to August 1956	3.75
August 1956 to August 1957	4.00
August 1957 to January 1958	4.50
January 1958 to April 1958	4.00
April 1958 to September 1958	3.50
September 1958 to May 18, 1959	4.00
May 18, 1959 to September 1, 1959	4.50
September 1, 1959 to August 23, 1960	5.00
August 23, 1960 to September 1961	4.50

Source: *Federal Reserve Bulletin.*

medium-size companies, and small companies, in the sample, reflected just such a differential from group to group, at the end of practically all years during the period. However, after 1953, the median for the moderately large companies was also the prime rate. The differential between the prime rate and the stated rate for the medium-size (0.75 percent) and small companies (1 percent) remained essentially unchanged during the period. Table 7-7 summarizes for the companies in the sample, for year-end dates, 1949-58, the median stated rates on short-term bank loans, the range of stated bank rates, and the range of required compensating balances, by size of company.

There was a significant range of stated bank interest rates within each size group except the largest. This range increased in amplitude, the smaller the size of company, presumably indicating either a greater difference with respect to credit rating within each of the size groups, a greater difference in size of loan amounts, or difference in relationship to line banks.

Stated bank interest rates do not reflect the true cost of bank loans. Companies in the consumer finance business are customarily required to maintain compensating balances with banks with which they have lines of credit. The requirement of maintaining compensating balances increases the effective rate on bank borrowings substantially as does the requirement that the borrower be completely out of debt to the bank for a certain period of time, generally, two or three months in the year. Table 7-8 sets forth effective rates of interest on bank borrowings, assuming either a 10 percent, a 15 percent, or a 20 percent compensating balance requirement and a two-month payout.

TABLE 7-7
Stated Bank Interest Rates and Range of Required Compensating
Balances, 1949-1958
(In percent)

Year End	Large	Size of Companies Moderately Large	Medium Size	Small
No. of companies	(2)	(7)	(4)	(2)
Median Stated Bank Rates				
1949	2	$2\frac{1}{2}$	$2\frac{3}{4}$	3
1950	$2\frac{1}{4}$	$2\frac{1}{2}$	$2\frac{3}{4}$	3
1951	3	3	$3\frac{1}{4}$	$3\frac{1}{2}$
1952	3	$3\frac{1}{4}$	$3\frac{1}{2}$	4
1953	$3\frac{1}{4}$	$3\frac{1}{4}$	$3\frac{1}{2}$	$4\frac{1}{4}$
1954	3	3	$3\frac{1}{4}$	4
1955	$3\frac{1}{2}$	$3\frac{1}{2}$	$3\frac{3}{4}$	$4\frac{1}{2}$
1956	4	4	$4\frac{1}{4}$	$4\frac{3}{4}$
1957	$4\frac{1}{2}$	$4\frac{1}{2}$	$4\frac{1}{4}$	5
1958	4	4	$4\frac{1}{4}$	5
Range of States Bank Rates				
1949	2	2-3	$2\text{-}3\frac{1}{4}$	$2\frac{1}{2}\text{-}5$
1950	$2\frac{1}{4}$	$2\frac{1}{4}\text{-}2\frac{3}{4}$	$2\frac{1}{4}\text{-}3\frac{1}{4}$	$2\frac{3}{4}\text{-}5$
1951	3	$2\frac{3}{4}\text{-}3\frac{1}{4}$	$3\text{-}3\frac{1}{2}$	3-5
1952	3	$3\text{-}3\frac{1}{2}$	$3\text{-}3\frac{3}{4}$	$3\frac{1}{2}\text{-}5$
1953	$3\frac{1}{4}$	$3\frac{1}{4}\text{-}3\frac{1}{2}$	$3\frac{1}{4}\text{-}4$	$3\frac{3}{4}\text{-}5$
1954	3	$3\text{-}3\frac{1}{4}$	$3\text{-}3\frac{3}{4}$	$3\frac{1}{2}\text{-}5$
1955	$3\frac{1}{2}$	$3\text{-}3\frac{3}{4}$	$3\frac{1}{2}\text{-}4$	$3\frac{3}{4}\text{-}5\frac{1}{4}$
1956	4	$3\frac{1}{2}\text{-}4\frac{1}{4}$	$4\text{-}4\frac{3}{4}$	$4\frac{1}{4}\text{-}5\frac{1}{4}$
1957	$4\frac{1}{2}$	$4\text{-}4\frac{3}{4}$	$3\frac{3}{4}\text{-}5$	$4\frac{1}{2}\text{-}5\frac{1}{2}$
1958	4	$3\frac{1}{2}\text{-}4\frac{1}{4}$	$3\frac{3}{4}\text{-}4\frac{1}{2}$	$4\frac{1}{4}\text{-}5\frac{1}{2}$
Range of Required Compensating Balances				
1949	10 - 15	15 - 20	10 - 15	10 - 15
1950	10 - 15	15 - 20	10 - 15	10 - 15
1951	10 - 15	15 - 20	10 - 15	10 - 15
1952	10 - 15	15 - 20	10 - 15	5 - 15
1953	10 - 15	15 - 20	10 - 15	5 - 15
1954	10 - 15	15 - 20	15 - 20	5 - 15
1955	10 - 15	15 - 20	15 - 20	10 - 15
1956	10 - 15	15 - 20	15 - 20	10 - 15
1957	10 - 15	15 - 20	15 - 20	10 - 15
1958	10 - 15	15 - 20	15 - 20	10 - 15

Source: Survey made by the National Consumer Finance Association. For rates of interest paid on commercial paper sold to the public, see Appendix Tables A-15 -A-17.

Obtaining Additional Long-Term Funds

In response to a question as to whether or not the companies could have borrowed a reasonable amount of long-term funds from any source, over and above what they did borrow, a significant minority of the companies indicated that they could not have done so from insurance companies nor from other nonbank sources. The highest proportion

TABLE 7-8
Comparison of Nominal and Effective Interest Rates on Bank Loans[a]
(In percent)

Nominal Rate	Effective rate with 2-month annual payout and compensating balance of:		
	10 percent	15 percent	20 percent
3.0	3.409	3.659	3.947
3.5	3.977	4.268	4.605
4.0	4.545	4.878	5.263
4.5	5.114	5.488	5.921
5.0	5.682	6.098	6.579

[a] It is assumed that the line is drawn down in its entirety whenever utilized, that the requirement as to compensating balance is based upon the amount of the line and that no balances would have been maintained in the absence of a requirement to maintain a balance.

replying in this manner were small and medium-size companies. An additional number replied that they could not have done so at interest rates that compared favorably with the cost of short-term bank borrowings. The large companies replied that they probably could have sold unsubordinated securities on a favorable cost basis, but said their lack of experience with subordinated or junior subordinated securities made them unqualified to comment in that area. It is probable that the nonresponse of other companies can be attributed to a similar reason. Table 7-9 summarizes the replies from the companies with respect, first, to the availability of additional long-term funds and, second, with respect to whether such funds were believed to be available at interest rates that compared favorably with the cost of short-term bank borrowings, during the period, 1949-58.

Consumer finance companies and sales finance companies have apparently issued subordinated and junior subordinated debentures to a greater degree than any other industry.[7] Small and medium-size companies have followed this practice as well as the moderately large companies.

The higher proportion of negative replies from the smaller companies, many of whom issued some subordinated securities, indicates that the sale of such securities by smaller companies is inherently difficult. This is indicated by the following selection of explanatory comments:

Due to size of company and tight money conditions. [Small company.]

We are not large enough to be attractive. [Small company.]

---

[7] Robert W. Johnson, "Subordinated Debentures: Debt That Serves As Equity," *Journal of Finance* (March 1955).

TABLE 7-9
Availability of Additional Long-Term Funds, at Interest Rates Comparing
Favorably with Cost of Short-Term Bank Loans[a]

	Large		Moderately Large		Medium-size		Small	
	No	Yes	No	Yes	No	Yes	No	Yes
No. of companies	(2)		(7)		(4)		(8)	
Additional Funds Available								
From Insurance Companies								
On Unsecured Basis	-	2	-	7	-	4	3	2
On Subordinated Basis	-	2	-	7	1	3	5	1
On Jr. Subordinated Basis	-	2	1	6	1	2	6	1
From Other Nonbank Sources								
On Unsecured Basis	-	2	-	6	-	3	4	2
On Subordinated Basis	-	2	-	5	1	2	4	3
On Jr. Subordinated Basis	-	2	-	6	1	3	4	3
At "Comparable" Rates								
From Insurance Companies								
On Unsecured Basis	-	2	1	6	1	3	3	2
On Subordinated Basis	-	-	1	6	1	3	3	2
On Jr. Subordinated Basis	-	-	2	5	1	2	3	2
From Other								
On Unsecured Basis	-	2	1	6	1	2	5	1
On Subordinated Basis	-	-	-	5	1	2	4	2
On Jr. Subordinated Basis	-	-	-	6	1	3	4	2

[a] The questions to which replies were received were:

(1) Do you believe that you would have been able to borrow a reasonable amount of long-term funds, over and above what you did borrow, from 1949 through 1958 from the following sources and with the following types of securities?

(2) Do you believe that these additional funds would have been available to your company at interest rates that compared favorably with the cost of short-term bank borrowings? Please take into account the difference in the types of securities when comparing the interest cost.

Source: Survey made by the National Consumer Finance Association.

Extent of our market with the public for long-term notes had previously been absorbed. [Small company.]

Because of the somewhat arbitrary balance sheet ratios used as standards. [Small company.]

The small size of our company does not carry the leverage necessary to negotiate for funds at the proper cost. [Small company.]

Had about as much subordinated money as we could expect from sources available to us. [Small company.]

Junior subordinated debt sold direct to the public by the company is unsecured with no trustee. Institutional investors are not interested in participation under such conditions. [Moderately large company.]

Long-Term Senior Borrowings, Issuance, and Cost

The constant increase in demand for the services of consumer finance companies placed pressure upon them to acquire additional funds throughout the period studied. Satisfying this growth in demand, however, was to some degree hindered by monetary tightness which made it more costly and more difficult for consumer finance companies to acquire both long- and short-term funds. The somewhat reduced percentage growth in loan account in 1957, as compared with the other years, can be attributed, in part, to the unwillingness of the companies to pay the rates required to obtain long-term funds in larger amounts than they did acquire.

These companies issued significant amounts of unsubordinated and subordinated debt in each of the years under consideration. There was little variation from year to year in the number of long-term unsubordinated issues, except for a substantial increase in number in 1956—when the companies were feeling the impact of the steps taken by line banks to reduce the amount of bank borrowing. Chart 11 sets forth the

CHART 11

RATES ON NEW LONG-TERM SENIOR DEBT ISSUES, 1949-1958,

BY SIZE OF COMPANY

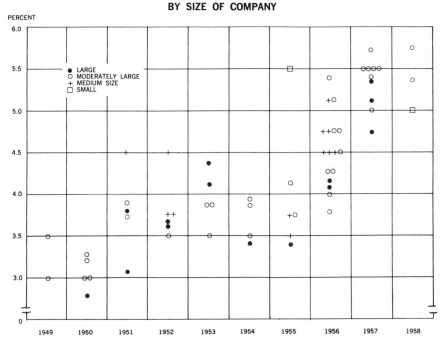

Source: Survey made by National Consumer Finance Association.

number of issues of long-term senior debt, by years, over the period 1949-58, and the effective rate of interest cost on those obligations, as reported by the individual companies.

The large companies and the moderately large companies issued new long-term senior obligations with greatest regularity year after year.

Medium-size companies issued new long-term senior obligations in 1951, 1952, 1955, and, to the greatest degree, in 1956. One small company did so in 1955 and 1958. In addition, one small company continuously offered senior debt obligations—presumably locally—at an unchanged rate of 6.5 percent, and sold varying amounts in each year.

The level of effective interest rates on new long-term senior obligations moved up sharply, beginning in 1955, through 1957, and remained at a high level in 1958. Since no information was provided with respect to the maturity of the individual issues, it is not possible to determine the extent to which the variation in rates shown from year to year reflects differences in length of individual issues, and other terms. Also, since the information provided related only to the year of issuance rather than the actual date, the effect of changes in degree of tightness in the long-term money market during any year cannot be portrayed. It is known, however, that the effective rates on the obligations issued by the large companies, higher in certain years than those of moderately large companies, reflected different degrees of tightness of the long-term market during the course of the individual years. The substantial increase in level of effective interest rates on long-term unsubordinated debt during the period 1955-57 undoubtedly deterred these companies from issuing larger amounts of such obligations than they might otherwise have done, in view of the strength of the underlying demand for their services. The managements of these companies were reluctant to issue substantial amounts of long-term obligations at these rates because they did not wish to increase unduly, for the long-term, the average level of interest burden on their total long-term debt.

It is of interest to note that medium-size companies issued the largest number of long-term obligations in 1956 despite the materially higher rates which those companies were required to pay on such issues as compared with those issued in earlier years.

Subordinated Debt

The growth of long-term subordinated issues of the companies in the sample contains differences from the situation shown for unsubordinated debt. (1) Small companies are represented to a much greater degree, accounting proportionately for as many issues as the medium-size and moderately large companies.[8] (2) There was an increase in number of issues in each year from 1952 to 1957 with very little decline in the number in 1958. Both conditions appear to be a product of the rapid

---

[8] In addition, two companies reported continuing sales of new issues, presumably in the local community, as follows: One small company reported new issues of three to five year maturity subordinated each year, 1951-1958 at 5 percent, and new issues of ten year maturity subordinated during 1954, 1957, and 1958 at 6 percent. One small company reported new issues each year, 1949-1957 at 5 percent and 1958 at 5.5 percent.

rate of growth of these companies over the period studied. This rapid rate of growth made it impossible to augment the common stock equity at a sufficiently rapid rate, through retained earnings, to support the necessary growth in bank credit and other unsubordinated debt. The management of some of the small and medium-size companies, where ownership is closely held, is reluctant to sell additional common stock to a wider group. Under these circumstances, subordinated debt has significant advantages. As contrasted with preferred stock, payment for its use is a tax-deductible expense. From the point of view of bank loans and other unsubordinated creditors, it augments the capital base. This explains the substantial use of subordinated debt on the part of these companies. However, subordinated debt was issued in these years of credit stringency at rates which made it cost as much as short-term bank loans (when the effect of compensating balances are taken into account). Thus, its issuance required the acceptance of the burden of historically high interest rates throughout the life of the long-term obligation in order to accomplish the desired increase in the quasi-equity base. Chart 12 shows the number of issues of long-term subordinated debt,

CHART 12

RATES ON NEW LONG-TERM SUBORDINATED DEBT ISSUES, 1949-1958, BY SIZE OF COMPANY

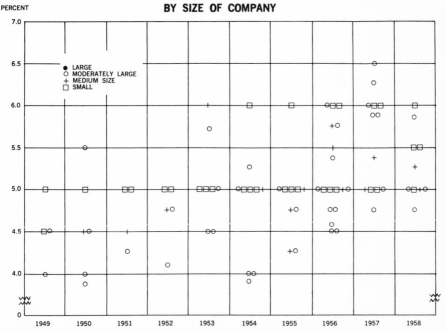

Source: Survey made by National Consumer Finance Association.

by years, over the period 1949-58, and the effective rate of interest cost on those obligations, as reported by the individual companies.

Conclusion

In this chapter, the reactions of consumer finance companies to the varying monetary situation have been set forth. It is clear that the cost of both short-term and long-term funds was directly responsive in periods of monetary restraint, as in 1952-53 and 1955-57. This was true of the consumer finance industry to a degree comparable to business in general. The evidence indicates that the availability of short-term bank funds to consumer finance companies, since all companies except very small ones borrow from several different banks, was affected to a greater degree than was true of companies borrowing only from their local banks.

Concurrently, as a matter of policy, consumer finance companies, in direct relationship to their size, have increased their use of long-term funds throughout the last decade, both those supplied by savers directly, and through institutional sources. By doing so to an increasing degree during recent periods of credit restraint, they have had to pay the higher rates required, and by increasing demand for such funds have also contributed to the increasing of rates. Thus, they have been an influence in transmitting to the long-term market the restraint placed by monetary policy initially upon the short-term market.

The precise degree of effectiveness of monetary policy cannot be determined. To do so, one would have to be able to measure its effect upon what did not happen or against what might have happened in the absence of the policy. It is clear, however, that some of the companies found or believed the long-term market to be closed to them. Others were deterred from greater use of the long-term market by their unwillingness or inability to pay the rates required.

All these conditions occurred during a period of active demand for the services of consumer finance companies. The least that can be said is that the restrictive monetary policy of 1955-57 moderated the rate of growth in the consumer finance industry. It did not prevent growth, and it is submitted that it was not intended to do so.

Funds Made Available to Consumers

The volume of credit made available to consumers by consumer finance companies has been influenced by the supply and cost of funds available to those companies, on the one hand, and by the demand for their services, on the other. In appraising the effectiveness of general credit controls, the expert will inquire into the extent to which the higher cost of funds, during a period of monetary stringency, is passed on to the ultimate user, and, thus, may affect his demand for such funds. It is appropriate to examine this question with respect to consumer finance companies.

Dr. Dawson pointed out in his study that only one of twenty-three consumer finance companies was in a position to raise its rates in the period from 1950 to 1953.[9] The majority of the remaining companies indicated that "they could not raise rates as they were already at the legal maximum." Since 1953, consumer finance companies have generally charged rates which were at the legal maximum. Thus, they were not in a position to attempt to influence the demand for their services by raising the rate of charge.

In the period under study, a minority of the companies reported taking deliberate steps to restrict their extension of loans. These steps included decisions: (1) to appraise the risk of prospective borrowers more strictly; (2) to limit the total loans outstanding by branch or office; (3) to limit certain types of loan activity, generally types involving lower rates of income; (4) to limit the volume of larger size loans and/or those of longer maturity.

Five companies stated that they appraised the risk of prospective borrowers more carefully. Three companies reported this policy as applying "since 1957"; others following this policy stated, "1955-1956, principally in depressed coal areas"; and "1955 and 1957, in our opinion, lack of equity and extended terms resulted in purchasers overbuying to the danger point."

Three companies reported that they had limited the total outstanding by branch or office. One moderately large company indicated that it did so "due to shortage of bank lines and high cost of long-term debt" in late 1956; another reported that "at various times, funds for purchase of retail contracts were restricted." One large company stated the circumstances more fully:

> In the spring and summer of 1956, the company borrowed significant amounts of money at long-term. At that time, it was assumed that the amounts borrowed, together with the amounts available at short-term through bank lines, would be adequate to take care of anticipated growth of the company through the end of 1956. In the summer of that year, demand for loans from customers proved to be much stronger than anticipated. The company had no desire to expand its lines of credit or to acquire additional long-term funds under the conditions and at the rates required at that time. In order to have adequate funds left for the normal seasonal peak demand in December, the company assigned quotas to divisions and offices for each of the last three months in the year of 1956.

---

[9] Ray E. Dawson, "Monetary Policy and Sales Finance and Small Loan Companies' Funds, 1949-1954," unpublished doctoral dissertation, Northwestern University, August 1957. His sample covers almost the same group of companies as the current National Consumer Finance Association sample.

Six companies reported adoption of a policy of increasing the ratio of shorter-term to longer-term loans, thus reducing the average maturity. Three small companies replied that they had done so "in 1955," "since August 1957," and "in 1958," respectively. A medium-size company stated that it had done so in 1955 and 1957 and a moderately large company reported that it had adopted a "gradual program of balancing long- and short-term loans on a 50-50 basis." One small company reported holding its "top loan to $750 and shortening its maturities"; another reported, "Our rate is 8 percent per annum over $300. We cannot have too large a portion of our funds out at this rate. Average loan must be held down."

The responses to a question as to "the major factors, in order of greatest importance, which determine the volume of loans which your company is willing to make," are shown in Table 7-10.

Specific comments indicated that the availability of money and its cost during tight money periods were of influence in deciding the volume of loans which three small companies made, including one which said, "I know I could raise $1,000,000 additional long-term debt right now, but I refuse to pay the going cost (rate) at this time." The availability of customers of "acceptable" credit-worthiness and with appropriate collateral was stressed by a medium-size company. One large company replied more fully:

> At all times, it is the ability and willingness of prospective borrowers to repay their obligations which is crucial in determining total volume.
> There are certain states in which the size of the maximum loan limits to the greatest degree the volume of loans which can be made. There are other states in which the rate of charge permitted under the small loan law or other laws limit the desire to make loans of certain sizes.
> In answering the question, it is also necessary to decide whether long-run or short-run influences are to be emphasized. At certain points in the business cycle, it is the amount of anticipated unemployment and the resultant anticipated collectibility of loans which is the most important factor in determining the amount and the character of loans which we are willing to make in any particular area. From a short-run point of view, there are times and conditions under which the cost of money is an important limiting factor.

Although the first paragraph in the quotation above does not specify a direct connection with monetary stringency, it is nevertheless recognized that a condition of monetary stringency is commonly believed to precede a downturn in general business. Whenever a downturn is expected, the ability of applicants to repay their obligations is evaluated in the light of this prospect.

Effects of Selective Controls on Consumer Credit

Historical Perspective

Before World War II, there was no serious discussion about a limita-

TABLE 7-10
Rank Order of Factors Which Determine the Volume of Loans
Made by Consumer Finance Companies

	Number of companies showing rank order of:				
	1	2	3	4	5
a. Cost of money to you					
Large companies	0	0	0	1	0
Moderately large companies	1	0	0	2	2
Medium-size companies	0	0	2	2	0
Small companies	2	2	3	0	1
Total	3	2	5	5	3
b. Labor cost and availability of personnel					
Large companies	0	0	0	0	1
Moderately large companies	1	3	1	0	0
Medium-size companies	2	1	0	0	1
Small companies	0	1	2	3	0
Total	3	5	3	3	2
c. Size of loan made by you					
Large companies	0	1	0	0	0
Moderately large companies	1	1	1	2	0
Medium-size companies	0	1	0	2	1
Small companies	1	2	2	1	0
Total	2	5	3	5	1
d. Rates you are permitted by law to charge					
Large companies	0	0	1	0	0
Moderately large companies	1	1	3	1	0
Medium-size companies	0	2	2	0	0
Small companies	3	3	0	2	0
Total	4	6	6	3	0
e. All other factors					
Large companies	1	0	0	0	0
Moderately large companies	3	0	0	0	0
Medium-size companies	2	0	0	0	0
Small companies	2	0	0	0	0
Total	8	0	0	0	0

Source: Survey made by the National Consumer Finance Association.

tion on the amount of use of consumer credit nor of a limitation as to the down payment or length of terms involved in financing the sale of consumer durable goods.

When the United States entered the war in 1941, several drastic steps were taken by the federal government under the War Production Act. Among other purposes of the act, two primary objectives became important in a time of great national crisis: (1) to divert the productive capacity of the country into the production of armament and war goods;

and (2) to direct the maximum portion of consumer assets and incomes into the financing of the war effort.

To achieve these objectives, executive orders were issued to curtail or prohibit the production of automobiles and other consumer durables, to direct the flow of steel and other strategic materials into war production. Price controls, wage controls, and rationing of food and other consumption items were instituted.

To give full effect to these executive orders and to the war effort, Regulation W was promulgated by executive order, prescribing minimum down payments and maximum length of terms for consumer credit transactions. The obvious purpose of Regulation W was to make it more difficult for consumers to use their credit and thus curtail demand in the market place in support of the other objectives in war time. People were encouraged to invest all available savings in government bonds to aid in the war effort and the use of consumer credit was discouraged.

After the end of World War II in 1945, Regulation W was retained as an anti-inflationary control while consumer durables were still in short supply and the nation's productive facilities were being converted back from war production to the production of consumer goods. It was not until November 1, 1947 that Regulation W was suspended temporarily. Thereafter, it was reimposed for approximately nine months late in 1948, suspended again in the middle of 1949 and reimposed in late 1950. In May 1952, Regulation W was again suspended, and on June 30, 1952, an Act of Congress terminated the authority of the Federal Reserve Board to impose Regulation W type of controls.

The consumer finance companies have had experience with the Regulation W type of control in war time and in peace time. While the control was designed primarily to limit market demand on durable goods, it did seriously affect the operation of the consumer finance companies and resulted in additional expense in operations, a substantial quantum of ill will on the part of customers, and complete disillusionment as to any good or effective purpose which the regulation was designed to accomplish.

Selective Controls in Operation

Selective controls were designed to reduce the flow of funds into consumer expenditures by tightening contract terms and making it more difficult for consumers to use credit. These controls, if effectively applied, can, to some extent, reduce expenditures on automobiles and other expensive items purchased on credit. A more important question, however, is whether selective credit controls can reduce total effective demand or whether they merely suppress one sector at the expense of others.

The proponents of selective controls assume that the funds that would have moved into consumer credit are held idle so that any reduction in expenditures that results from selective controls will result in a reduction in total expenditures. This assumption, however, has not proved to be valid during periods of strong inflationary pressures. The size of a balloon is not reduced by squeezing one side. Similarly, total expenditures are not reduced, when expansionary forces are strong, by diverting credit from one sector to another.

The opponents of selective credit controls on consumer credit point out that such controls interfere with the allocation of resources and are discriminatory against some sections of industry and of the public. This interference with the market mechanism might be justified if selective controls were effective against inflation, but it has been argued that they do not check inflation, but merely change its shape. By altering the shape of economic activity, selective controls can have far-reaching and unpredictable consequences. Both the growth and efficiency of our free market economy depend upon adjustments in the market place. Selective controls cannot be applied without adversely affecting these important economic adjustments.

Instalment credit has expanded more rapidly than any other type of credit during most of the postwar period, and this expansion has assisted in some important structural changes in the economy. (See discussion in Chapter 8.) When the economy is expanding and operating at a level close to full employment, however, any sector that shows unusual growth or change, attracts attention as an "inflationary force." Hastily designed control programs may destroy natural patterns of growth and adjustment.

Industrial Impact. The impact of selective consumer credit controls on industry is highly selective and concentrated. For a number of reasons, the effects of such controls are limited largely to loans for the purchase of automobiles and major household durables. First, such controls are most effective in limiting demand for credit purchases that can be postponed. Second, credit is more important in the merchandising of automobiles and other expensive durable items than in most other types of consumer goods. Third, contract terms are part of the "price" of a major purchase. Changes in terms can be an important deterrent to the purchase of an expensive item; they are much less of a deterrent for smaller items.

In the two periods of postwar regulation of consumer credit, the impact of controls was much more pronounced on extension of credit for automobiles and other consumer goods than on personal loans. When controls were imposed in 1948, seasonally adjusted extensions of automobile credit declined 17 percent in the first month while extensions of personal loans declined only 8 percent. (See Chart 13.) In 1950, when controls

CHART 13

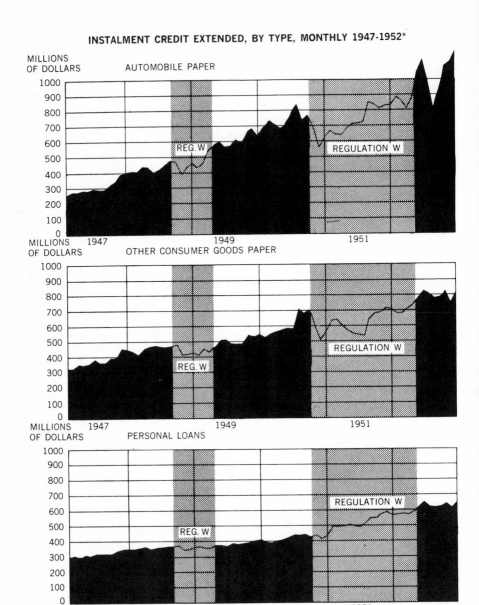

INSTALMENT CREDIT EXTENDED, BY TYPE, MONTHLY 1947-1952*

* Adjusted for seasonal variations and differences in trading days. Regulation W was in effect between September 20, 1948, and June 30, 1949, and between September 18, 1950, and May 7, 1952.

Source: Board of Governors of the Federal Reserve System.

were reimposed, extensions of other consumer goods paper declined 15 percent and extension of personal loans declined only 2 percent. Although part of the differential impact in these two periods can be explained by differences in maturity and down payment requirements, and by the exemption of certain types of loans, part also reflects differences in the nature of the demand for loans to purchase automobiles or other consumer goods and the susceptibility of the demand for these items to changes in contract terms.

Since the effects of selective controls are largely confined to certain types of credit, only a small part of the total national product is adversely affected. Consumer expenditures on automobiles and household durables, including small durables that are not greatly affected, accounted for only 13 percent of total consumption expenditures and about 9 percent of total gross national product in 1958. The remaining sectors may be stimulated by selective controls as funds are diverted from purchases of durables into other expenditures.

The impact of selective controls at the manufacturing level is, of course, also concentrated primarily in the automobile and household durable goods industries. Although, in an inflationary period, it may be desirable to reduce activity in any sector, these industries do not pose unique inflationary problems. The capacity in the automobile industry has never been tested. Even in 1955, when 7.5 million cars were sold, the industry was not at full capacity. Both the automobile and household durable goods industries are able to reduce unit costs as output increases within the limits of existing capacity. Such industries do not add as much to inflationary pressures as industries with increasing costs or those that typically operate close to capacity.

Impact on Lenders. As was pointed out in the preceding section, the impact of selective controls was concentrated in loans for purchases of automobiles or other durables. Lenders specializing in these loans are most directly affected but all lenders are affected to some extent. Nearly all lenders make some loans that are covered by selective controls and all lenders must comply with the administrative provisions of the law. Since the differences in the impact of the law among lenders of different types is largely a matter of degree, this discussion is limited primarily to the effects on consumer finance companies.

A substantial proportion of the loans made by consumer finance companies are for urgent personal needs or emergencies and are not sensitive to changes in terms that accompany selective controls. If hardship cases are provided for in the regulation, many of the loans made by consumer finance companies would be exempt from regulation. More than half of the loans made by consumer finance companies were for the consolidation of overdue bills, medical, dental, hospital and funeral expenses, or for taxes. (See Table 4-5.) In addition, many of the other items, such as home repairs, automobile expenses, and fuel, may include loans for urgent needs.

A statement of purpose from the borrower is probably an essential feature of any selective control that attempts to avoid injustices in hardship cases. Yet, obtaining an accurate statement of purpose involves a number of problems to the lender. Borrowers, under ordinary conditions, are usually willing to provide information essential to the establishment of their credit rating, but under selective controls they tend to state a purpose they think will be favorably regarded.

It must also be recognized that the average personal loan is used for more than one purpose. The purposes may include the payment of past due obligations ranging all the way from doctor bills to auto payments, plus several kinds of personal living items from rent to clothes for the children. When selective controls are applied with different down payments and different payment requirements for different types of goods or services, a personal loan may be made up of several different terms and maturities so that the borrower has to pay various amounts at various times during the period of the loan. It is quite expensive to figure and very confusing to the borrower. The complicated procedure adds to his desire to cheat in stating the purpose of the loan. In the early days of Regulation W, there was one set of down payments for soft goods and another for hard goods, and no down payment was required for medical and dental bills. As a result, during periods of regulation, lenders found a sharp increase in loans for medical expenses or other exempt purposes. Since people, who are otherwise honest, frequently make dishonest statements when they feel a regulation is discriminatory or unfair, such regulations create an atmosphere that encourages petty immorality.

During previous experience with selective credit controls, the expansion of personal loan volume at consumer finance companies may have been slowed but it is not clear that the volume was reduced by the regulation. (See Chart 14.) New volume declined immediately after the imposition of the regulation, but the decline was no larger than the month-to-month fluctuations at several other times. After the imposition of controls in 1950, the volume of personal loans at consumer finance companies rose.

In addition to the possible effects on volume, selective controls introduce additional costs and interfere with efficiency and flexibility of company operations. Larger monthly payments required by selective credit controls do not discourage essential borrowing, but they make it more difficult for the borrower to carry the loan. Numerous studies have indicated that the size of the payment relative to the borrower's income is one measure of the quality of the loan. When the size of the payment becomes excessive, the likelihood of default increases sharply, although the borrower may be able to carry the same size loan with smaller

CHART 14

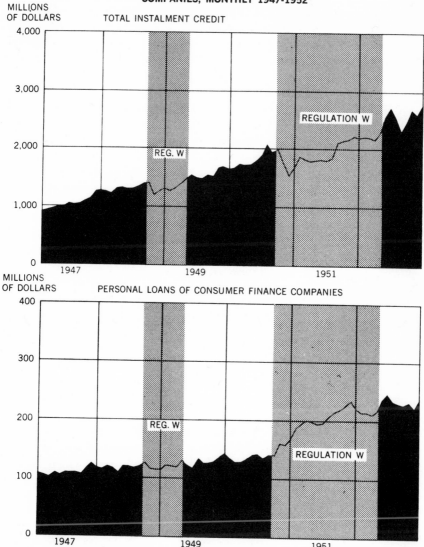

TOTAL INSTALMENT CREDIT EXTENDED AND
PERSONAL LOANS OF CONSUMER FINANCE
COMPANIES, MONTHLY 1947-1952*

* Adjusted for seasonal variations and differences in trading days. Regulation W was in effect between September 20, 1948, and June 30, 1949, and between September 18, 1950, and May 7, 1952.

Source: Board of Governors of the Federal Reserve System.

monthly payments. The inability to tailor the monthly payments to the borrower's capacity to pay results in difficulties for the borrower and higher losses for the lender.

Effective collection techniques frequently require the reduction of the individual's monthly payment or the postponement of the payment until financial difficulties have passed. This type of adjustment is difficult or impossible under selective controls. Thus, effectiveness of collections are reduced and losses are increased.

Selective credit controls also add materially to administrative cost. Since consumer finance companies handle a large number of loans of fairly small size, any addition to the unit cost adds significantly to the total cost of doing business. Selective controls increase the time required in processing loan applications and in the compliance with provisions of the controls.

Company Policies and Objectives of Selective Controls. Although it is not strictly on the subject of the effects of selective controls, it seems appropriate to discuss briefly alternative policies and actions that can accomplish the objectives of selective controls. When lenders are faced with difficulties in obtaining funds or with high cost or unfavorable terms of borrowing, they pursue objectives similar to those of selective controls. They try to limit their volume and speed repayment rates to reduce their need for funds. When the company is free to design its own policies, it can accomplish these objectives with less inconvenience and cost than under the restrictive provisions of selective controls.

A company can reduce its volume by reducing promotional expenses and efforts, by cutting back high cost business, by tightening credit standards, by encouraging borrowers to reduce the size of their requests, or by discouraging renewals. It is important to note the variety and flexibility that can be introduced into the problem of restricting the volume of loans when lenders are free to adopt their own policies. Lenders can and do respond to tight credit market conditions and the results are similar to those desired by the proponents of selective controls but without the inflexibility and attendant problems which accompany selective regulations.

Conclusion

The Regulation W type of consumer credit control in peace time is discriminatory as between cash buyers and credit users, creates distortions in the free flow of market forces, and interferes with the free right of choice and planning.

As developed in other sections of this monograph, general monetary controls already in existence are as effective in consumer credit areas as in other segments of the economy. If it becomes desirable to limit demand in boom times, any federal regulation should be applied without discrimination and across the whole economic structure. Tight money policies have general application and are as effective in the limitation of consumer credit as in the limitation of construction, manufacturing, or other segments of the economy. Thus, the limiting objective can be accomplished without the undesirable side effects of selective controls applied to a limited segment of the economy. In short, selective controls of the Regulation W type are neither necessary nor advisable and should not be reimposed.

Suggestions have been made from time to time for other types of control over consumer credit; for example, complete uniformity in the statement of the amount and rate of charge for consumer credit and mortgage credit extensions, or an outright prohibition of the use of credit for certain instalment purchases. Consumer credit grantors and consumer credit users have established a record of sound judgment in the granting and use of credit. Consumer credit, which supports mass buying, is as important an element in the growth of the American economy as commercial credit, which supports mass production. It should be recognized as a part of the total economic function and should not be made a "whipping boy" in times of economic difficulty.

Chapter 8

ROLE IN THE ECONOMIC
AND FINANCIAL SYSTEM

Place in and Influence on Family Spending and Savings Patterns

Credit adds a third dimension to consumer budgeting. Some consumers must spend their entire income as soon as they receive it. Others are able to save part of their income to provide for future expenditures. Credit adds a third possibility by permitting consumers to pay for current purchases out of future income.[1]

The combined use of credit and savings gives the consumer flexibility in planning his expenditures through time. The average individual's income is not well matched to his expenditure needs at various times during his life. Expenses of most families are heaviest while the family is being established and while the children are young. Incomes, however, tend to increase with the age of the head of the spending unit. Other shorter run discrepancies between needs and income develop with emergencies or accidents. Credit helps coordinate the flow of income and expenditures.

Credit handles two major budgeting problems. It permits the consumer to make purchases in anticipation of income and it provides funds for more urgent personal needs. These two purposes reflect different budgeting problems and pose different problems for lenders. The first type of need is provided largely by retail stores, banks, sales finance companies, and to a limited extent by the personal loans of banks, consumer finance companies, or credit unions. The second type, which accounts for most of the business of consumer finance companies, is furnished by the personal loans of all types of lenders.

Personal Loans and Family Budgeting

Consumer finance companies held 32.3 percent of all outstanding

---

[1] See Table 8-1 for the percentage distribution of spending units in the United States having debt and liquid assets.

TABLE 8-1
Personal Debt and Liquid Assets,[a] Early 1959
(Percentage distribution of spending units)

	All cases	No Debt		Debt	
		No liquid assets	Some liquid assets	No liquid assets	Some liquid assets
All spending units	100	8	32	17	43
1958 income before taxes:					
Under $1,000	100	27	31	34	7
$ 1,000-$1,999	100	21	36	29	15
$ 2,000-$2,999	100	14	30	30	26
$ 3,000-$3,999	100	5	31	23	41
$ 4,000-$4,999	100	4	28	17	51
$ 5,000-$5,999	100	3	27	11	59
$ 6,000-$7,499	100	1	28	6	65
$ 7,500-$9,999	100	1	30	4	65
$10,000 and over	100	-	49	2	49

[a] Includes all short and intermediate term consumer debt except charge accounts. Liquid assets include savings bonds, checking accounts, savings accounts; currency is excluded.

Source: Board of Governors of the Federal Reserve System.

personal cash instalment loans at the end of 1959, sales finance companies held 9.0 percent, banks held 31.4 percent, and credit unions and other types of financial institutions held the remaining 27.3 percent. The operations of all financial institutions in the personal loan field overlapped to some extent. Credit unions are limited to their field of membership which varies depending upon the type of credit union. Consumer finance companies lend to the general public and make a large proportion of their loans to industrial workers.

Personal loans may be used for any purpose. Some of them are used for the purchase of automobiles, durable goods, vacations, and clothing. A substantial proportion of personal loans, however, are used for urgent personal needs, such as medical expenses, repair bills, funerals, to assist relatives, or to consolidate debts. About 40 percent of the loans of the three largest consumer finance companies that reported information on the purpose of loans for this monograph were for the consolidation of debts. Some of these loans stem from improvident financial management by the borrower. Many of them, however, involve unanticipated expenditures or the unexpected loss of income. Whatever the cause, they often involve difficult financial adjustments.

A large proportion of the other loans made by consumer finance companies are for personal needs. Nearly 8 percent of the loans of the reporting companies were for medical, dental, or funeral expenses. Over 3 percent were to assist relatives. Many of the others, such as those for repairs, taxes, etc., may stem from serious needs, the urgency of which may not be indicated by the stated purpose.

The borrower's need for personal loan credit usually results from temporary and unexpected variations between needs and income. Unforeseen difficulties may arise to face borrowers of all ages and financial status. The problem is most difficult, however, for borrowers in the medium and low income groups, and those with large necessary expenses. Personal loan credit is used most frequently by the same groups that borrow to purchase durable goods. Young families with children are generally less able to cope with unexpected financial problems than older families that have had time to accumulate liquid assets or have smaller demands on their incomes.

Emergency credit needs can be a serious social problem. Few families are able to protect themselves adequately against all eventualities. Liquid assets and insurance of various types provide some protection but the accumulation of assets and the cost of insurance payments reduces the funds available for family consumption. Not many families can afford the luxury of protection against relatively remote possibilities, yet improbable accidents or emergencies do happen to an unfortunate few.

Emergency loans are often difficult for the borrower to obtain. The urgency of the situation frequently indicates financial stress and raises some question about the ability of the borrower to repay the loan. If the need cannot be met by legitimate lending institutions, the borrower must turn to loan sharks or any other source he can find. This is a problem that has been nearly forgotten because it has been largely solved. Historical actions against usury were symptomatic of the problem but they did not provide a solution. The solution came with the legal approval of rates that were adequate to cover the risks and costs of this type of lending. The state small loan laws and the federal and state credit union laws have permitted the establishment of institutions designed to handle emergency lending.

Consumer finance companies provide an important share of emergency loan funds. They serve a somewhat lower income group than the average of all instalment credit borrowers. Three-fourths of the loans of the two large companies that provided information on the characteristics of their borrowers were made to families with incomes of $6,000 or less. Only about 60 percent of the spending units that used consumer credit in 1958 had incomes of less than $6,000 in that year. A substantial proportion of the loans of consumer finance companies are made to industrial workers. About 70 percent of all loans of the reporting companies were made to foremen, skilled, semi-skilled, or unskilled workers in service and manufacturing industries where variations in income are the highest.[2]

When emergency facilities are available, the consumer is free to plan his expenditures through time and to match his expenditure pattern with his expected income as well as he can. He can be fairly sure of obtaining credit in the case of a serious emergency. This enables the medium and lower income groups to obtain a higher standard of living than would be possible if they had to maintain the liquid assets or carry insurance to protect them from all contingencies.

Credit for Consumer Goods

In dollar terms the most important type of consumer credit is that for the purchase of automobiles or goods of a similar substantial nature.

Seventy-five percent of total instalment credit at the end of 1959 was either in automobile goods paper or in other types of credit for purchases. Most of this credit is used for purchases of durable items. Some of it is for soft goods but not a substantial proportion. In addition, some small part of personal cash loans is used for the purchase of consumer durable goods.

The use of credit for the purchase of durable goods has made possible important changes in the pattern of consumption. Consumers now own automobiles and other assets that supply shelter, transportation, household services, and recreation. Before the availability of instalment credit these services were provided to a large extent by business establishments.

The shift to consumer ownership of durables has also led to the substitution of credit payments for payments formerly made to suppliers of various services. The instalment payments for the washing machine may be regarded as an alternative to payments to the laundry establishment or for wages of domestic servants. Ownership of a television set replaces, to some extent, admissions to theaters and sports events. Some of the shifts are indicated by the changes in expenditures shown in Table 8-2.

Consumer ownership of durable equipment is similar to business ownership of capital equipment. Automobiles and other durables give rise to a stream of services just as business capital gives rise to a stream of income. Consumer ownership of durables introduces new budgeting and financial problems that are also similar to those of business financing. The consumer must make a large initial outlay for the equipment but he receives the services over a period of years, just as a business receives income from equipment over a period of years. Instalment credit makes it possible for the consumer to spread the cost of equipment over a period of time while the services are being received.

---

[2] From information obtained by a survey made by the National Consumer Finance Association.

TABLE 8-2
Comparative Growth of Selected Consumer
Expenditures, 1929 to 1957

	Growth of Type of Expenditure as a Percent of Growth In Total Consumer Expenditure
Total consumer expenditures	100
Laundering in establishments	33
Domestic service	35
Admissions to motion pictures	21
Purchased local transportation	31
User-operated transportation	177

Source: United States Department of Commerce.

The use of consumer durable goods for services has become so widespread that adequate substitutes frequently are no longer available through commercial channels or are prohibitively expensive. Commercial laundry facilities cannot compete on a cost basis with home laundry equipment, and they may not be as convenient. Public transportation cannot compete with the automobile for flexibility in route and timing. In many areas commercial transportation facilities are not available to serve as a substitute.

The living standards and habits of today imply the use of consumer durables. They are a necessary part of ordinary living and consumers are faced with the problems of buying durables to provide these services. Such purchases are a major budgeting problem for most families, particularly for new families where the needs are heaviest and incomes are the smallest. It is not surprising that 80 percent of the spending units where the unit heads were between twenty-five and thirty-four years of age were using instalment credit in early 1959. (See Table 8-3.) The proportion is even higher when the spending units include young children. The need for durable goods varies with changing family status and the use of instalment credit diminishes as the family grows older and as its financial situation improves.

Consumers use credit for durable goods purchases as part of their regular budgeting plan. Although some consumers may be too optimistic or may have unanticipated difficulties in executing their plans, most budgeting plans are successful. This type of credit differs from emergency credit because it is usually part of the planned activities of a solvent spending unit. As a result, the credit on durable goods generally involves a low degree of risk.

TABLE 8-3
Personal Debt Within Income and Age Groups, Early 1959[a]
(Percentage distribution of spending units)

Income or age group	All cases	No debt	Some debt
All spending units	100	40	60
1958 money income before taxes:			
Under $1,000	100	58	42
$ 1,000-$1,999	100	57	43
$ 2,000-$2,999	100	44	56
$ 3,000-$3,999	100	36	64
$ 4,000-$4,999	100	32	68
$ 5,000-$5,999	100	30	70
$ 6,000-$7,499	100	29	71
$ 7,500-$9,999	100	31	69
$10,000 and over	100	49	51
Age of head of spending unit:			
18-24	100	30	70
25-34	100	20	80
35-44	100	29	71
45-54	100	36	64
55-64	100	59	41
65 and over	100	74	26

[a] Includes all short and intermediate term consumer debt except charge accounts.

Source: Board of Governors of Federal Reserve System.

Financial Position of Consumers

New borrowing increases the consumer's liability and is, therefore, a form of dis-savings only if it is not used to acquire new assets or to replace existing debt. The over-all impact of the use of credit is quite complicated. The use of credit makes possible additions to assets that may exceed the amount of the debt either originally or after some time, and may thus result in an increase in savings in the form of durable assets. As the debt is repaid the consumer's net worth is increased by his increased equity in the remaining value of the item purchased. The Federal Reserve Board has estimated that consumers in 1960 owned durable goods worth about $125 billion after allowances for depreciation. (See Table 8-4.) Much of the savings in this form has been made possible by the use of instalment credit. Credit can in this way add to consumer savings.

A substantial part of the loans made by consumer finance companies do not affect the consumer's net worth. Loans for the consolidation of debt do not increase the total amount of debt but only reorganize the form of the debt. These loans frequently make it possible for the individual to work out financial difficulties without default or repossession. Default on debt may improve the borrower's financial position in a strict

TABLE 8-4
Total Value of Consumer Held Durable Goods[a]
(In billions of dollars)

End of year	Total	Automobiles	Other durables
1946	29.2	3.7	25.5
1950	65.7	19.3	46.4
1954	90.4	31.9	58.5
1958	113.5	41.3	72.2
1959	119.8	43.8	76.0
1960	125.0	46.3	78.7

[a] Estimates on original cost basis minus depreciation.

Source: Board of Governors of the Federal Reserve System.

accounting sense by reducing his liabilities but the repossession of durable goods results in financial loss both to the borrower and the lender.

Some consumer loans, however, are not used for the consolidation of debt or for the purchase of durable goods that are considered assets. These loans reduce the consumer's net worth although some may add intangible assets such as the potential earning value of education loans. Consumer debt of this type involves a choice on the part of the borrower to exchange future income for the advantages of current spending.

The existence of debt of any type reduces the individual's financial maneuverability. It increases the problems he must face in event of an unexpected financial reverse or the loss of income, and reduces his ability to borrow in the event of unexpected need. It also limits the use of credit as an instrument for future budgeting. The larger the debt the greater the risk and the greater the loss of flexibility.

Consumer credit is a financial tool for consumer planning. If it is used properly, it adds a great deal to the individual's freedom in handling his finances. It permits him to adjust his income and expenditures through time. It adds to the range of activities that he can undertake and to the assets that he may own. It also provides for emergencies and its availability serves as a partial substitute for insurance or liquid assets. The use of credit, however, involves costs, not only in interest payments and charges but in added risks. Most consumers make sure the advantages to be gained through the use of credit are sufficient to justify the costs involved.

Implications for Economic Stability

Implications of the activities of consumer finance companies for economic stability must be discussed in the broad framework of total instalment credit. Many aspects of their operations are similar to those of other lenders and have much the same impact on economic activity. Since consumer finance companies specialize in personal loans, however, their loan volume is much more stable than that of companies engaged in lending for purchases of durable goods. Mild cycles in extensions of personal loans are observable but the range of fluctuations is much smaller than that of durable goods credit.

A substantial share of the loans made by consumer finance companies are used to consolidate debts, or for emergency personal needs of various types. Their experience with loans of this type has led to the development of practices designed to avoid forced debt liquidation in times of personal financial stress. These practices contribute to the stability of this type of credit during periods of general business difficulty.

The use of instalment credit is closely related to fluctuations in business activity. It responds to the enthusiasm of good times and to the apprehension of bad times. Credit is a means to an end and is under the influence of the strong forces of demand for automobiles and other consumer items purchased on credit. An examination of the fluctuations of instalment credit shows that variations in credit are closely related to variations in the demand for automobiles and other durable goods.

Credit is not entirely passive, however. It can accentuate or soften pressures for expansion and contraction. During the expansionary phase of the business cycle the conditions that lead to rising activity are also favorable to the use of credit. Consumers are sensitive to changes in business conditions and adjust their use of credit accordingly. Rising incomes and high levels of employment make the consumers more willing and able to use credit. During a down-turn in business activity, a decline in incomes and employment creates apprehension about the future and consumers are less willing to assume new debts. Lenders are also affected by the climate of business opinion and tend to relax standards and terms during good times and to tighten standards and screen loans more carefully during bad times. Conditions in the credit market can, in this way, accelerate the expansion of business activity during boom periods and accentuate the contraction during recessions.

During the later stages of expansion and contraction, however, credit can reduce and soften cyclical pressures and contribute to the stability of the economy. The role of the interest rates in checking or stimulating business activity has been widely discussed but some of the stabilizing possibilities of instalment credit have not been widely recognized.

The growth of instalment credit has been so rapid that the cyclical pattern has been partly obscured and the interpretation has been complicated. The changes in instalment credit reflect the influence of growth and the influence of changing business conditions. Thus the analysis of past fluctuations gives a one-sided picture of the cyclical aspects of instalment credit. Some of the reactions that develop to the rapid expansion during boom periods are hidden by the forces for growth. Although instalment credit can be expected to continue to grow, it seems unlikely that the rate of growth relative to the rest of the economy will be as rapid as it has been in the recent past and some of the internal restraints to expansion in this sector are likely to be more important.

Errors in credit judgments show up very quickly in the form of slow payments and delinquencies. A downturn in business activity is not necessary to show up such problems. A rise in delinquencies usually signals the problem to lenders and leads to remedial action. Problems of this type can develop during boom conditions and tend to check forces for expansion of consumer credit. The early detection of errors in credit judgment is possible largely because of the instalment nature of the consumer credit industry. It is not as easy in non-instalment or non-amortized types of lending.

Instalment credit lenders respond to money market conditions and tend to screen loans more carefully and to ration credit when money conditions are tight. Conditions in the money market depend upon the monetary authorities as well as upon business conditions. As the credit market tightens in the later stage of a business expansion or as the result of restrictive monetary policies the impact is felt on instalment credit.

Market reactions to rising repayments and errors in credit judgment tend to temper the cyclical swings in instalment credit and to reduce extremes in expansion or contraction. These reactions arise from the contractual nature of instalment repayments and do not appear to the same degree in non-amortized lending. In addition, money market conditions may reduce the amplitude of fluctuations in credit extensions. The strength of these forces for stability has never really been tested. Scare buying, strong growth trends, or heavy spending in other sectors of the economy can sometimes overcome these forces for restraint. As the growth trend in consumer credit slows, these forces will be more effective in limiting credit fluctuations.

Pattern of Instalment Credit Fluctuations

Seven cycles in extensions of instalment credit have occurred from 1929 to date, excluding the World War II period from 1940 to 1946. Five of these cycles corresponded approximately to fluctuations in general business activity. The other two occurred during periods of strong general business activity; the first in 1950-51 and the second in 1955-56.

During the 1930's, extensions of instalment credit followed the same general pattern as business activity. (See Chart 15.) Extensions of credit reached a peak in 1929 at about the same time as the peak in business activity, as indicated by the reference cycles prepared by the National Bureau of Economic Research. Personal income and industrial production dropped about 50 percent in the depression that followed, while extensions of instalment credit declined by 70 percent from the peak to the trough in 1933. The trough in extensions of credit coincided with the low point in general business activity in March 1933. Extensions of instalment credit expanded two and a half times during the recovery that followed, while personal income increased only about 80 percent and industrial production returned to a level of only slightly above that of 1929.

Extensions of credit reached a second peak in 1937, somewhat before the peak in business activity, but remained at a high level for several months. In contrast to the experience in the depression in the early 1930's, the decline in credit in 1937 was not as deep as the decline in industrial production. The trough was reached in 1938 at about the same time as the trough in general business activity and the expansion in credit that followed contributed vigorously to the recovery.

The pattern of fluctuations in instalment credit after World War II did not conform as closely to general business activity as in the 1930's. The first peak in extensions of instalment credit occurred in 1948 just before a peak in general business activity. Two months after the downturn, extensions of credit turned up so that the trough in credit preceded the trough in general business activity by almost a year.

The next downturn in extensions of instalment credit began with the reimposition of Regulation W after the outbreak of the Korean War. The reduction in extensions of credit was not accompanied by a drop in general business activity. Other types of expenditures continued strong and personal income expanded steadily. The decline in extensions of credit was sharp—25 percent from peak to trough—but it lasted only four months. Though Regulation W remained in effect, the recovery was rapid and extensions of credit moved to a new high in nine months.

The peak in extensions of instalment credit in 1953 occurred several months before the peak in general business activity that preceded the recession of 1953-54. Although the recession affected most sectors of the economy, the decline in extensions of instalment credit was smaller than in 1950. The recovery that followed was strong and rapid. The expansion of extension of credit particularly on automobiles led to the record growth in outstanding credit in 1955.

A short cycle of extensions in instalment credit began with a peak in the third quarter of 1955. A small drop of about 5 percent occurred from the third quarter of 1955 to the first quarter of 1956. Most other segments in the economy continued upward. After this short decline, extensions of credit continued to rise and exceeded the previous highs by the end of 1956.

The recession of 1957-58 was the most severe of the postwar recessions according to measures developed by Geoffrey Moore of the National

CHART 15

TOTAL INSTALMENT CREDIT EXTENDED, MONTHLY 1929-1940 AND 1947-1960 *

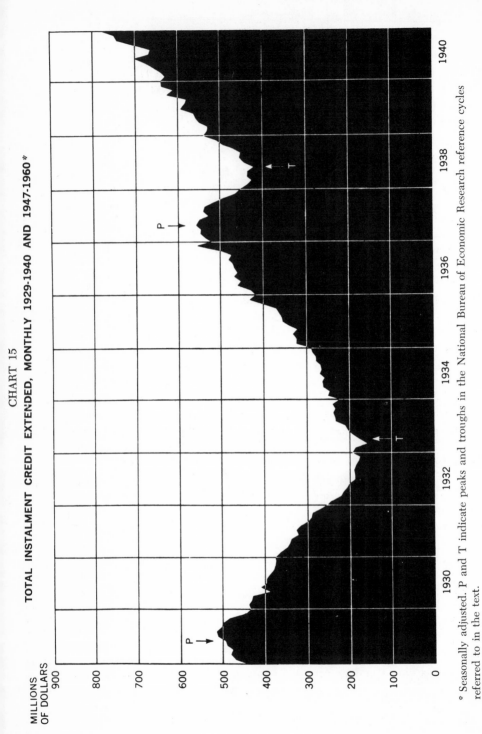

* Seasonally adjusted. P and T indicate peaks and troughs in the National Bureau of Economic Research reference cycles referred to in the text.

Source: Board of Governors of the Federal Reserve System.

CHART 15 (Continued)

MILLIONS
OF DOLLARS

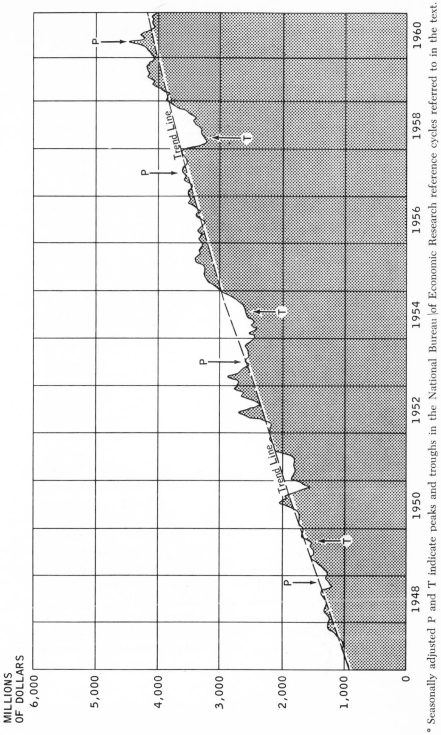

° Seasonally adjusted P and T indicate peaks and troughs in the National Bureau of Economic Research reference cycles referred to in the text.

Source: Board of Governors of the Federal Reserve System.

DATA FOR CHART 15

(In millions of dollars)

	1958	1959	1960
Jan.	3,466	3,793	4,160
Feb.	3,243	3,921	4,197
Mar.	3,261	3,926	4,259
Apr.	3,283	4,011	4,499
May	3,276	4,122	4,255
June	3,316	4,119	4,313
July	3,349	4,171	4,214
Aug.	3,406	4,172	4,072
Sep.	3,339	4,244	4,125
Oct.	3,484	4,262	4,108
Nov.	3,618	4,185	4,134
Dec.	3,748	4,119	4,007

The above data for Chart 15 are revised figures for 1958 and 1959 and latest estimates for 1960.

Bureau of Economic Research.[3] The downturn in general business activity began in the third quarter of 1957 but the decline in extensions of instalment credit did not begin until the first part of 1958. Extensions of credit declined 13 percent in three months and reached a trough at about the same time as the trough in general business activity.

Although the fluctuations in instalment credit have followed in a broad way the fluctuations of general business activity, the relationship is not close or consistent. Extensions of credit have on some occasions reached a peak before the general business peak and on some occasions after. The troughs in extensions of credit, however, have nearly always preceded or coincided with lows in business activity. On two occasions fluctuations in instalment credit have been largely independent of fluctuations in business activity. The first, in 1950, probably reflected the impact of consumer credit controls. The second, in 1955-56, probably reflected unusual market conditions for durable goods. These exceptions and the lack of any close relationship in the timing of cycles of instalment credit

---

[3] Geoffrey H. Moore, "The 1957-58 Business Contraction: New Model or Old?" *American Economic Review* (May 1959), pp. 292-308.

and general business activity, however, suggest that the forces affecting instalment credit are related to but not entirely dependent on the forces that shape the cycles in general business activity.

Demand for Commodities and Fluctuations of Credit

Most consumers borrow to buy things. Some borrowing is used to consolidate earlier debts, but for the most part these debts have in turn been incurred in making purchases. Demand for automobiles and other items bought on credit plays a dominant role in the determination of the amount of credit that is used.

Cash purchases of automobiles and other items reflect the conditions of demand and supply in the markets for these commodities. Credit purchasers of the same items are subject to the same market forces of supply and demand and, in addition, are influenced by conditions in the credit markets. Although it cannot be assumed that changes in demand will affect both cash and credit buyers in precisely the same way, differences between cash and credit expenditures give some indication of the special role of credit forces.

Cash and credit purchases of automobiles moved together during the 1930's. The amplitude of the fluctuations in credit purchases was somewhat larger than those in cash purchases.[4] In the 1929 depression and in the 1937-38 recession the timing of changes in both series was similar.

Cash and credit expenditures on durable consumer goods other than automobiles also moved in the same general pattern in the 1930's. Cash expenditures declined somewhat more than credit expenditures in the depression of the early 1930's and increased somewhat less during the recovery. Both types of expenditure reflected the 1937-38 recession with cash expenditures showing a somewhat sharper decline.

The correlation between cash and credit sales of automobiles and other durable goods in the period after World War II is not as close.[5] Scare buying of automobiles was much more pronounced in the cash sector than in the credit sector during the Korean War. On the other hand, the boom in automobile sales in 1955 was more pronounced in the credit sector than in the cash sector. The difference between cash and credit sales in 1955 can be explained in large part by the lengthening of terms that occurred during that year. The smaller monthly payments that accompanied the longer maturities stimulated credit sales. Comparison of credit and cash sales of household durable goods in the postwar period shows minor variations in movement but general agreement in the broad pattern of fluctuations.

---

[4] For comparison see Board of Governors of Federal Reserve System, *Consumer Instalment Credit,* Part I, Vol. I, Chart 26, p. 219.

[5] *Ibid.,* pp. 219, 221.

The similarity in the pattern of fluctuations of cash and credit sales suggests that cyclical changes in the demand for goods purchased on credit play a prominent role in the use of instalment credit. Purely credit factors can affect the level of expenditures and can explain some of the differences between cash and credit expenditures. These factors, however, have not been responsible for any of the major fluctuations in credit expenditures. Demand factors must be introduced to explain the major cyclical changes.

Credit Market Conditions

Although the demand for goods and services is probably the dominant force in changes in extensions of credit, changes in demand do not explain all the fluctuations. Conditions in the credit market also affect the level of credit extensions. The availability and cost of funds affect the willingness and ability of lenders to make new loans. The attitudes and financial prospects of consumers affect their willingness and ability to assume new obligations. These forces may supplement the forces of demand for goods and services or they may restrain these forces.

A number of forces operating on both the consumer and the lender tend to reinforce or accentuate fluctuations in general business activity. The wider amplitude of fluctuations in credit expenditures than in cash expenditures during the depression in the early 1930's can probably be explained by these factors. The severity of the depression and the resulting psychological and financial impact on both consumers and lenders was a strong force for a reduction in the use of credit. Credit factors added to the already strong forces reducing demand.

The easing of credit terms has historically occurred during periods of rising business activity when lenders are optimistic and confident. This stimulates the use of credit and the rise in business activity. The move from twenty-four to thirty-six months in maturities on loans for the purchase of new cars in 1954-55 is a recent example that demonstrates the potential of easier credit terms.

Although there have probably been cases where credit terms have been tightened, no evidence exists of any significant tightening in terms on a nation-wide basis. When business conditions deteriorate, terms are checked but by varying degrees and methods. The reaction to the easing of terms in 1955 may have contributed to the drop in the extensions of credit early in 1956. The restrictive possibilities of tightening credit terms were demonstrated by consumer credit regulations in 1948 and 1950.

Some of the forces that affect the use of instalment credit are not related to changes in general business activity. Such forces account for the deviations in the pattern of extensions of credit from that of general business activity and are particularly important in understanding the role of consumer credit in cyclical behavior. These forces do not necessarily reinforce swings in general business activity, but may at times help stabilize the economy.

Existing obligations in the form of old debts limit the consumer's use of new credit. The ratio of payments to income is a rough measure of the burden of the existing debt on consumers. As the ratio increases the resistance to the use of new credit also increases. As credit expands, the ratio of repayments to income increases and at the advanced stages of the business cycle the high level of repayments creates resistance to a further rise in credit. After a business downturn, the decline in income relative to repayments results in a further increase in the burden of repayments. In the early stages of a business downturn the burden of repayments restricts the use of credit and adds to the downward movement. In the later stages of the contraction, however, the ratio of repayment to income again declines and the use of credit is encouraged. The drop in repayment can act as a stimulant late in a recessionary period and the increase in repayments as a restraint late in a boom period.

The full cyclical potential of the burden of repayment as a restraining factor will not be felt until the ratio of repayment to income approaches some maximum level. At the end of 1957, this ratio rose to a high of 13.6. In the 1958 recession it dropped for the first time since World War II, except during the period of credit regulation. This suggests that this ratio may be a more important restraining force in the future than it has been in the past.

The tight money market conditions that usually develop in the advanced stages of a boom make it difficult and expensive for lenders to expand their loans to consumers. Lenders respond in various ways to high rates and the scarcity of funds and most of these adjustments limit the expansion of loans. There was some evidence that tight money market conditions had a restrictive effect on lenders in 1953, when extension of credit declined before the general business downturn. Recent evidence of the restrictive effects of a tight credit market is presented in Chapter 7 of this monograph.

In the face of strong demand pressure, tight credit market conditions may merely slow the expansion of consumer credit. As a result, it is difficult to detect the effects of credit market conditions. Considerable evidence is available from the study of individual company adjustments to indicate that lenders do respond to tight credit market conditions.[6]

Since credit market conditions depend in part upon monetary authorities, the restrictive effects of the credit market on instalment lending

---

[6] *Consumer Instalment Credit*, Part I, Vol. I, chap. 13, pp. 257-286 and Part I, Vol. II, chap. III, pp. 143-172. Also see Paul F. Smith "Response of Consumer Loans to General Credit Conditions" *The American Economic Review* (September 1958), pp. 649-655.

CHART 16

MONTHLY CHANGES IN OUTSTANDING INSTALMENT CREDIT, 1929-1938 AND 1949-1960*

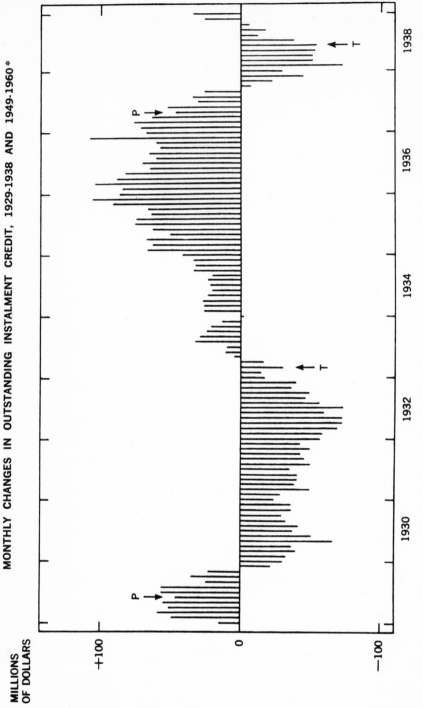

* Seasonally adjusted P and T indicate peaks and troughs in the National Bureau of Economic Research reference cycles.

Source: Board of Governors of the Federal Reserve System.

136

CHART 16 (Continued)

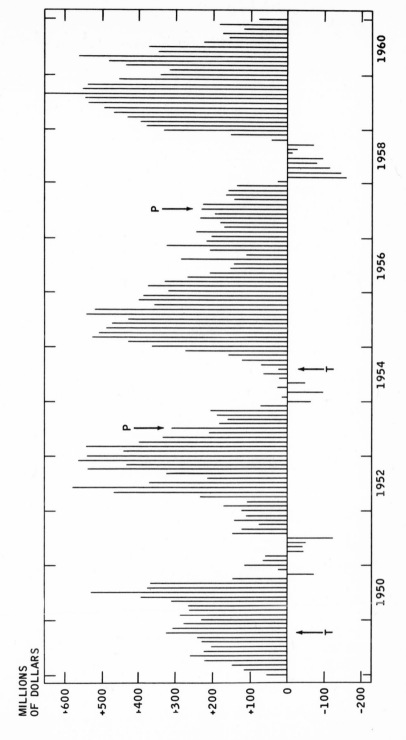

MILLIONS
OF DOLLARS

° Seasonally adjusted. P and T indicate peaks and troughs in the National Bureau of Economic Research reference cycles.

Source: Board of Governors of the Federal Reserve System.

137

DATA FOR CHART 16

(In millions of dollars)

	1958	1959	1960
Jan.	27	376	312
Feb.	-161	398	432
Mar.	-153	439	482
Apr.	-117	466	564
May	-77	499	344
June	-97	531	379
July	-8	539	217
Aug.	-18	645	154
Sep.	-63	558	167
Oct.	41	540	114
Nov.	169	458	188
Dec.	331	346	76

The above data for Chart 16 are revised figures for 1958 and the latest figures for 1959 and 1960.

can be itensified by the use of general monetary controls to reduce funds available in credit markets. The response of the instalment credit industry to varying conditions in the credit market tends to slow the expansion in the later stages of a business boom and to encourage expansion in the last stages of a recession. General monetary policies can be used to make the natural response of the industry to conditions in the credit markets more effective.

Instalment Credit and Consumption Expenditures

Extensions of credit provide some consumers with extra funds for consumption. Repayments withdraw funds from income that would otherwise be available for consumption. The combined effects of extensions and repayments as a source of funds to consumers is indicated by the difference between extensions and repayments or the net change in outstanding credit.

Change in outstanding credit shows all seven of the cycles that were observed in extensions of credit. The pattern of fluctuations is similar except that the timing is somewhat different. The peaks and troughs in changes in outstanding credit occurred before those in extension of credit and usually before the turning points in general business activities as shown in Chart 16. The maximum increase in outstanding credit occurs early in the expansionary period when extensions of credit are expanding at a constant or increasing rate. When the growth in extension of credit slows repayments rise faster than extensions and the change in outstanding credit slows. This relationship is reversed during periods of contraction.

Instalment credit provides the largest sources of funds early in the expansion period of business. As the boom progresses the funds provided by credit decline. As the downturn develops, instalment credit withdraws funds from consumption, if the downturn is severe enough to result in a decline in outstanding credit. Since World War II only the decline in 1958 was large enough to result in any extended decline in outstanding credit, although both the cycles in the 1930's resulted in sizable decreases in outstanding credit. The maximum withdrawals of funds from consumption usually occur in the early stages of the downturn and diminish as the recession proceeds.

Special Factors in Consumer Finance Company Lending

Personal loans comprised about 86 percent of the total consumer finance company receivables at the end of 1959. The remainder consisted of 3 percent in automobile loans, both direct and indirect, and 11 percent in other consumer goods paper. The loans for automobiles and other durable goods reflect primarily the diversified activity of some consumer finance companies. This business is usually conducted by separate subsidiaries and often from separate offices. It is not part of the normal personal lending business of the consumer finance companies in their operations under the state small loan laws.

Fluctuations of personal loans since World War II appear only as variations in the rate of growth. Outstanding credit has increased steadily throughout all of the postwar recessions. Variations in the rate of growth do appear in extensions of loans, however, as shown in Chart 17. These variations correspond approximately to the major cycles in business activity as indicated by the National Bureau reference cycles. The two cycles (in 1950 and 1956) that appeared in total instalment credit but not in general business activity do not show up in the data for personal loans.

Comparable figures for the 1930's are not available for personal loans, but data for the loans of consumer finance companies indicate that personal loans declined during the depression in the early 30's and again in the 1937-38 recession.[7] The drop in personal loan volume at con-

---

[7] Duncan McC. Holthausen, *The Volume of Consumer Instalment Credit, 1929-1938*, National Bureau of Economic Research, 1940, pp. 88-90.

CHART 17

TOTAL INSTALMENT CREDIT AND PERSONAL LOANS EXTENDED, MONTHLY 1947-1960°

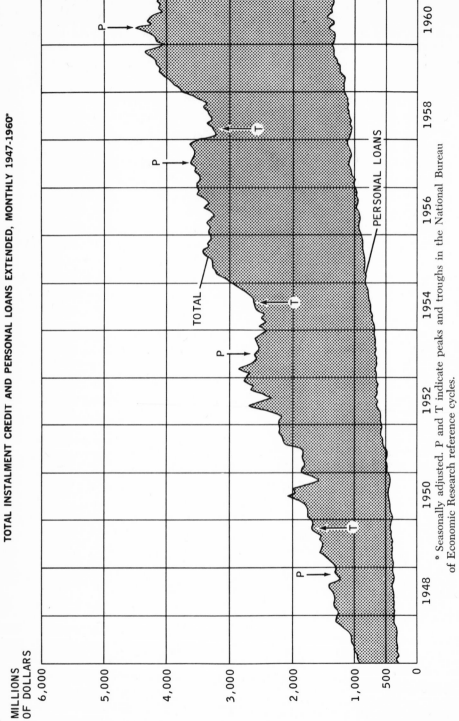

° Seasonally adjusted. P and T indicate peaks and troughs in the National Bureau of Economic Research reference cycles.

Source: Board of Governors of the Federal Reserve System.

DATA FOR CHART 17

(In millions of dollars)

	Total Instalment Credit			Personal Loans		
	1958	1959	1960	1958	1959	1960
Jan.	3,466	3,793	4,160	1,079	1,168	1,321
Feb.	3,243	3,921	4,197	1,041	1,187	1,314
Mar.	3,261	3,926	4,259	1,031	1,169	1,313
Apr.	3,283	4,011	4,499	1,073	1,175	1,415
May	3,276	4,122	4,255	1,025	1,249	1,337
June	3,316	4,119	4,313	1,065	1,233	1,341
July	3,349	4,171	4,214	1,073	1,266	1,453
Aug.	3,406	4,172	4,072	1,104	1,277	1,358
Sep.	3,339	4,244	4,125	1,092	1,339	1,377
Oct.	3,484	4,262	4,108	1,107	1,327	1,323
Nov.	3,618	4,185	4,134	1,130	1,329	1,333
Dec.	3,748	4,119	4,007	1,154	1,347	1,335

The above data for Chart 17 are revised figures for 1958 and 1959 and the latest figures for 1960.

sumer finance companies in the depression was only about half as large as the decline in total extensions of instalment credit.

The demand for loans from consumer finance companies arises primarily from personal needs not necessarily related to changes in business conditions. As a result, the lending of consumer finance companies is a relatively stable component of credit and is not subject to severe changes in business conditions, as are most other types of credit. Consumer finance companies are also experienced in handling financial problems, adapting their policies to the needs of their consumers. By postponing, deferring, or reducing the payment requirements during difficult periods, they avoid some of the destabilizing effects of credit during a downturn in business activity.

Implications for Economic Growth

One important impact of consumer credit on economic growth lies outside the usual measures of growth. The services provided by automobiles and household durable goods are not included in measures of output. If these services were performed by business capital, they would be included in statistical measures of output and would add to the national product and to the growth rate. Implications of this omission can be illustrated by assuming that small power plants were developed that could replace the gas and electricity now used by consumers. Payments for utilities, in 1958, amounting to more than $10 billion were included in gross national product. If these utilities were provided by consumer-owned power plants, these expenditures would be reduced markedly or eliminated from the national product and would be only partly offset by purchases of equipment.

The automobile provides the most striking example of the expansion of services through consumer capital. It introduced a personalized transportation that was not confined to a fixed time schedule or to a fixed route. The services of the fifty-nine million cars now in existence, at commercial rentals, would amount to a fantastic figure of over $100 billion a year, an amount one-third as large as total consumption expenditures under the conventional system of national accounts.

The Board of Governors of the Federal Reserve System estimated that consumers owned major durable goods worth about $114 billion (on an original cost basis and after allowance for depreciation) in 1958. It is impossible to estimate the value of the service that is performed by these assets. Comparisons with commercial facilities are not adequate because privately owned durables provide convenience and flexibility that cannot be achieved by commercial facilities. Consumers spent $200 billion on durable goods of all types in the five years, 1955-59. During the same period, business spent only about $130 billion for durable equipment; clearly, the value of services produced by consumer capital is sizable and adds appreciably to final output of the United States economy.

Consumer credit is essential for the purchase of a large proportion of consumer durables and provides a substantial part of the funds for such expenditures. More than half of major household durables and about 60 percent of new automobiles are purchased with instalment credit. Consumer ownership of durable goods could not have reached its present size without instalment credit. There is no reason to think that the full potential of the growth in services provided by consumers' capital goods has been realized.

Consumer ownership of capital goods shifts the problem of financing from business to consumer lending. Credit will be needed for further expansion of consumer owned capital, just as it will be needed for expansion in business capital. As in the past, any further expansion of services derived from consumer owned capital goods will not be reflected in national output, but such services add materially to our standard of living. Even though the value of the services of consumer capital cannot be measured, the increase in the value of these services should be recognized as one of the important economic developments of recent decades and, as such, be taken into consideration in an analysis of economic growth.

Consumer Demand and Growth

In a free economy the assurance of a profitable market is a strong stimulus to productive activity, efficiency, and growth. Consumer credit, by assisting in the distributive process, can strengthen the market for expensive consumer items and under some conditions can stimulate overall demand.

Market Size. Much of the growth in the United States economy has resulted from the specialization and mechanization that has been made possible by mass markets for the products. The high levels of efficiency and output in the automobile and appliance industries depend in large part on the mass markets that have been developed through the use of instalment credit.

The growth of expenditures for consumer durable goods is closely related to the rise in instalment credit. (See Chart 18.) Currently, about 60 per cent of all new cars and between 50 and 75 percent of all major appliances are bought on credit. Credit re-enforces the demand for automobiles by providing more than half the funds for used car purchases. The funds from the used car markets provide much of the cash, in the form of trade-ins, for new car purchases.

The ability of the appliance industry to reduce prices despite increased wages and raw material costs is one of the results of larger scale production. Output of major appliances in 1958 was about 25 percent above the 1947-49 average, and the increase in capacity was much larger. During the same period, the price index for household appliances declined from a 1947-49 average of 100 to 83 in 1958 in contrast to an increase in the index of all items, other than food, to 126. (See Table 8-5.) This comparison understates the full decrease in prices in the appliance industry because improvements in products cannot be adequately reflected in price indexes.

The television industry provides a specific example of the advantages achieved by mass production attuned to an expanding market. Production of television sets has increased several thousand percent since the early postwar years. At the same time, prices have been reduced. The full extent of the reduction cannot be measured, because price indexes are not available for the early years of small output, high cost production. Prices of television sets declined from an index of 115.1 in 1951 (January 1953 = 100) to 86.2 in 1955.

The pleasure boat industry appears to be a more recent example of

CHART 18

ANNUAL EXPENDITURES ON DURABLE CONSUMER GOODS AND
OUTSTANDING INSTALMENT CREDIT, 1929-1940 and 1947-1960

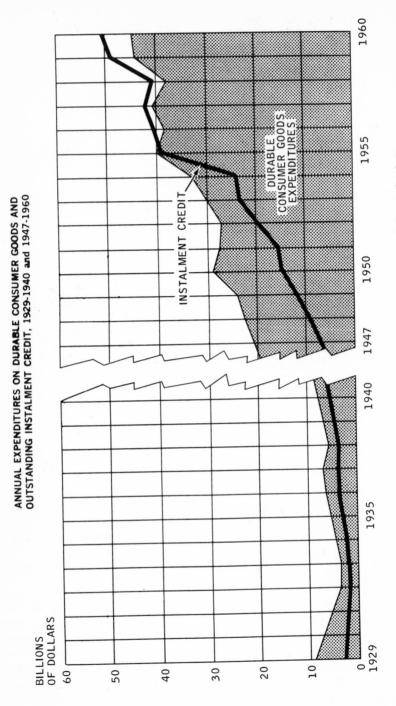

Source: U.S. Department of Commerce and Board of Governors of the Federal Reserve System.

144

DATA FOR CHART 18

(In billions of dollars)

	Annual Expenditures on Durable Consumer Goods	Outstanding Instalment Credit
1955	39.6	39.0
1956	38.5	40.2
1957	40.4	42.5
1958	37.3	40.8
1959	43.5	49.0
1960	44.3	50.3

The above data for Chart 18 are revised figures for 1955-58 and the latest figures for 1960.

the increased efficiency possible in a broadening market. The small boat industry was, until recently, almost entirely a handicraft industry building boats for a relatively small segment of the population. With increased demand, boat building has become a factory process with an accompanying increase in productivity and efficiency. The introduction of instalment credit into boat financing has been an important factor in the expansion and development of this market.

TABLE 8-5
Indexes of the Production of Home Appliances and Prices,
Selected Years, 1935-1958
(1947-1949 average = 100)

Year	Appliances Output	Appliances Prices[a]	Television Sets Output	Television Sets Prices[b]	Prices, all items except food
1935	n.a.	57.4	n.a.	n.a.	65.8
1937	n.a.	61.0	n.a.	n.a.	68.9
1940	n.a.	57.8	n.a.	n.a.	69.4
1947	96	98.4	13	n.a.	95.1
1949	90	98.5	217	n.a.	103.0
1951	136	102.3	396	115.1	110.8
1953	123	97.0	541	97.9	115.7
1955	138	88.3	558	86.2	116.7
1957	127	84.3	453	90.2	122.8
1958	127	82.9	365	92.0	125.5

[a] Includes prices of radios and television sets.
[b] January 1953 = 100.
n.a.-Not available.

Sources: Price indexes, Bureau of Labor Statistics, Production indexes, Board of Governors of the Federal Reserve System.

Full Utilization of Resources. The capacity and efficiency of an economy is irrelevant if resources are not utilized. A serious depression results in a loss of output that takes years of growth to replace. Unemployment and stagnation not only waste resources, but discourage innovations and the adoption of new equipment. The growth in instalment credit in the last three decades has contributed to growth by stimulating demand during periods of stagnation and recession.

Instalment credit was one of the few vigorous economic forces in the period of stagnation that followed the depression in the early 1930's. Expansion in instalment credit began shortly after the banking holiday in 1933 and continued throughout the rest of the 1930's except for a brief decline in the recession of 1937-38. From 1933 to 1940, instalment credit expanded nearly twice as fast as the gross national product. The growth in instalment credit provided funds for a substantial part of the increase of consumption expenditures. During these years, the increase in instalment credit amounted to between 5 percent and nearly 30 percent of the increase in consumption expenditures. (See Table 8-6.)

TABLE 8-6
Changes in Outstanding Instalment Credit, and Consumption
Expenditures, 1934-1940
(Amounts in millions of dollars)

Year	Change in - Instalment Credit	Change in - Consumption Expenditures	Change in Credit as Percent of Change in Expenditures
1934	283	5,502	5.1
1935	823	4,395	18.8
1936	929	6,327	14.6
1937	392	4,643	8.5
1938	-324	-2,618	12.4
1939	812	2,937	27.8
1940	1,011	4,303	23.7

Source: Board of Governors of the Federal Reserve System and
United States Department of Commerce.

The rapid growth of instalment credit after World War II reduced the impact of the postwar recessions. In the 1949 recession, instalment credit continued to expand throughout the recession. Outstanding instalment credit increased at the rate of $250 million a month for several months before the trough in the business cycle which came in October of 1949, and expanded at the rate of nearly $300 million a month during and immediately following the low point in the recession.

Again in the recession of 1954, instalment credit expanded almost without interruption throughout the entire period. The expansion of credit slowed at the low point of the recession in the third quarter of 1954, but accelerated in the fourth quarter, adding impetus to the very rapid and strong recovery that followed.

Instalment credit played a smaller role in the recovery from the 1958 recession than in either of the earlier postwar recessions. Outstanding credit declined for several months before and after the trough in April, 1958. Instalment credit began to expand again by the fourth quarter of the year and was an early force for strength in the recovery that developed in late 1958 and early 1959.

Consumer Credit and the Labor Force

Consumer credit has had an impact on both the size and efficiency of the labor force. The widespread adoption of home labor saving devices has permitted large numbers of domestic workers to move into other occupations and has freed housewives for entry into the labor force. The resulting expansion of the labor force has permitted further growth in industrial output.

The number of domestic workers in relation to the population has declined in the United States from 20 per thousand in 1910 to 16 per thousand in 1940 and an estimated 13 per thousand in 1958.[8] Although other forces have contributed, this decline was caused, in part, by the increased use of labor saving devices. Only 3,000 washing machines were sold in 1909; in recent years over four million a year have been sold. In 1921, 700,000 vacuum cleaners were sold; in recent years over three million a year have been sold. In addition, clothes driers, dishwashers, and numerous small appliances have reduced household work and the unpleasantness associated with some aspects of it.

The proportion of married women in the labor force has increased from about 5 percent of all married women in 1890 to 30 percent in 1958.[9] The shift in population to urban areas, the growth in white collar work, and the long-term decline in the size of families have contributed to this change, but the increased efficiency of household equipment has also been an important factor in this shift.

The significance for the labor force of the decline in domestic servants and increase in working wives can be illustrated by assuming that each of these developments was reversed. If only 5 percent of married women

---

[8] George J. Stigler, *Domestic Servants in the United States, 1900-1940*, Occasional Paper 24, National Bureau of Economic Research, April 1946. Estimate for 1958 based on data for number of domestic servants obtained from Bureau of Labor Statistics.

[9] *American Workers Fact Book*, U. S. Department of Labor, 1956, p. 11. Additional information in this area is available from the Bureau of Labor Statistics.

were in the labor force and domestic servants amounted to 20 percent of the population as was the case at the turn of the century, the labor force available for other types of work would be reduced by eleven million or about 15 percent.

In addition to its effects on the size of the labor force, consumer credit has contributed to mobility by assisting in the purchase of automobiles. Recent estimates of the proportion of the labor force that depends on automobiles to get to work are not available. In World War II, 75 percent of the workers in a group of war plants surveyed used automobiles for transportation.[10] The percentage is probably larger at the present time because of shifts in the location of industry and the increased number of cars. The automobile has a number of advantages for industry that could add to productivity. A broad labor market permits a higher degree of specialization and permits adjustments and changes that are not possible in a smaller market. Workers released from a dying industry can be quickly absorbed into an expanding one and special skills needed for new processes can be located more quickly.

To the extent that consumer credit reduces financial problems of labor, it may also have added to the effectiveness of the labor force. Personal financial problems interfere with productivity. Before the widespread availability of consumer credit, employers frequently had to assist in the solution of employees' financial problems. This need has been reduced by the availability of credit through lending institutions.

Consumer finance companies, which make available to consumers a source of cash instalment loans, provide, to a certain extent, a safety valve for other forms of consumer credit. This safely valve factor comes from the willingness and ability of these companies to refinance and consolidate the obligations of consumers who have over-reached their credit limits or whose incomes have been unexpectedly interrupted. This service makes it possible for these consumers to continue to pay out the balance of the money they owe on past purchases without losing the equity they have built up, or drastically reducing their expenditures in the area of necessities such as food and clothing.

Competition with Capital Outlay

Consumer credit has added a new element into the credit markets and has become an important competitor for funds. Consumer credit has increased its proportion of total private debt from 4.0 percent in 1929 to 9.6 percent in 1960. (See Table 8-7.) It now draws funds from every credit market and has developed new instruments for tapping new markets.

The competition between consumer expenditures financed by con-

---

[10] *Automobiles and National Defense*, Automobile Manufacturers Association, p. 5.

TABLE 8-7
Net Private Debt, Selected Years, 1929-1960

Year	Total Private Debt	Consumer Debt	1- to 4- Family Mortgage Debt	Business and Farm Debt[a]	Consumer Debt as Percentage of Total Debt
1929	161.5	6.4	n.a.	155.1	4.0
1939	125.5	7.2	n.a.	118.3	5.7
1950	250.9	21.4	n.a.	229.5	8.5
1954	348.4	32.5	71.9	243.9	9.3
1955	402.5	38.9	83.8	279.8	9.7
1956	439.4	42.5	94.1	302.8	9.7
1957	468.2	45.3	102.2	320.7	9.7
1958	499.9	45.5	111.8	342.5	9.1
1959	547.5	52.1	124.4	371.0	9.5
1960	581.9	56.0	134.7	391.1	9.6

[a] Includes 1- to 4- family mortgage debt prior to 1954.
n.a.-Not available.

Sources: United States Department of Commerce and Board of Governors of the Federal Reserve System.

sumer credit and business expenditures financed by credit takes place on two levels. First, the potential borrowers must compete for funds in the credit markets. Second, the borrowers must compete for the real factors of production necessary to produce either consumer goods or capital goods. The outcome of the competition and the effects on the economy depend upon conditions in the credit market and conditions in the markets for factors of production. When credit market conditions are easy, both consumers and investors are able to obtain the necessary funds. When credit market conditions are tight, some consumers or some investors will be unable to get funds. Similarly, when the factors of production are not fully employed, both consumers and investors are able to obtain the goods they need. Under conditions of full employment, however, consumers and investors must compete for the available resources. This competition necessarily leads to higher prices and some allocation of the resources between consumers and investors.

Conditions of ease or tightness in the money market and in the markets for the factors of production usually occur at about the same time so that the problems of the competition between consumers and investors in these two markets can be discussed together. The possibilities of different conditions in the two types of markets, however, should be recognized, although such possibilities will not be examined separately.

When the factors of production are not fully employed, any demand, either from consumers or producers, stimulates economic activity and contributes to fuller utilization of resources. Easy credit conditions make it relatively easy for consumers and investors to obtain the funds they need. Growth of credit in either the consumer or business sector contributes to the effectiveness and development of the economy.

When factors of production are fully employed, however, some allocation between consumer demand and business demands must be made. Not all demands can be satisfied. The allocations in both the credit market and the markets for resources are based on price and the numerous non-price elements that affect all markets. There is no reason to assume that these adjustments will be unfavorable to economic growth.

The market selection during periods of full employment should be favorable to growth rather than unfavorable. Business borrowers can find credit if they are willing to pay the market rates and if they can persuade the lenders that prospects for their investment are good. This process should select the best investment prospects and eliminate the worst. If the borrower is confident that his investment will provide a high enough yield to cover interest costs, high rates will not deter him. Lenders try to select borrowers who have the greatest prospects of success. This natural process of market selection encourages business expenditures with the greatest growth possibilities and discourages those of questionable value.

The same selective process applies to lending to consumers except that emphasis probably should be placed on the lenders' appraisal of the credit worthiness of the borrower rather than on the interest rate as a basis for selection. In periods of tight money, business borrowing and consumer borrowing may face the possibility of discouragement or rejection.

The competition between consumers and businesses for funds and resources in boom periods may result in some curtailment of capital outlays, but it is not clear that this reduces the growth potential of the economy. Growth implies some direction to economic activities, and in a free market economy the market determines the direction.

Not all capital outlay contributes to growth. Capital adds to productivity only if it produces something that is needed and can be sold. Business failures testify to the economic waste that is possible through bad business judgment and capital waste can occur without resulting in business failure. During boom periods, business expansion is often misdirected by an overestimation of potential markets. Capital outlays, as well as other expenditures, should be subject to a critical review and scrutiny of the market during boom periods.

Chapter 9

SUMMARY, CONCLUSIONS, AND RECOMMENDATIONS

Summary and Conclusions

The regulated consumer finance business arose in response to an urgent social and economic need for a cash loan service to small borrowers. The Russell Sage Foundation, other welfare organizations, and a few farsighted business leaders worked together to create a new form of credit institution which would fill this need and do away with the black market operator who preyed upon people with little bargaining power in time of financial crisis. Until the advent of the Uniform Small Loan Law, personal debt was actively discouraged by a prohibitory type of legislation based on laws designed for commercial credit operations. Sporadic efforts for remedial legislation through eleemosynary or quasi-charitable organizations had failed to provide an adequate avenue of help for the consumer who needed a small cash loan.

Experimental at first, the Uniform Small Loan Law has proved to be a sound and efficient method of providing the necessary financial services and preventing abuses in the field of family financing. Overcoming great initial resistance in the state legislatures, this new plan met with favorable acceptance after testing in a few states. One state after another accepted the philosophy of a protected loan service under law and joined the group of regulated states until the number of regulated states is now forty-three, with approximately 12,000 licenses issued.

American families have endorsed the beneficial and necessary services of consumer finance companies by increased use, and today the consumer finance industry serves the financial needs of more families than any other cash instalment lending institution.

The companies in this industry have taken on the same forms of organization and have the same characteristics as companies in other dynamic industries in the United States. There are a few large corporations, a sizable number of medium-size corporations, and many small

151

corporations, partnerships, and proprietorships. All offer personal cash loan services and provide without additional charge a valuable financial counseling service to individual consumers.

Consumer finance companies have become adept at searching out sources of capital funds. Depending on the size of company and the condition of the money market, the long-term capital market is tapped through the use of debentures which are sold to both institutional investors and in the open market. In recent years, with the increase in the short-term interest rate, the long-term capital market has played a growing role in financing consumer finance companies. Supplementing this form of financing and that of owners' equity, is the short-term borrowing, usually from commercial banks, which serves to provide for seasonal fluctuations in consumer finance companies' total available funds.

Since World War II, assets in the business have increased rapidly, and total assets of the consumer finance industry were estimated at $3.4 billion in 1959. The combined personal cash instalment loans outstanding of consumer finance companies and sales finance companies at the end of 1959 was $4.1 billion.

The trend in recent state legislation has been toward increased maximum loan limits, lower average interest rates, and some variation as to method of computing and stating rate. There is no attempt (nor should there be) to dictate the purpose for which loans are made, for most loans are actually made for a combination of purposes. Length of the loan contract is to some extent governed by state legislation, but company policy usually is the major determining factor. Average length of contract in 1958 was about twenty-two months. Character of the borrower is still the prime consideration, with most loans made on single signature only or on security which has negligible market value.

The regulated consumer finance loan service and the state laws under which it operates have been tested in two World Wars, in our greatest depression, and in periods of great economic growth and expansion, and have been proved sound and in the public interest. Variations in state laws generally reflect the conditions peculiar to the different sections of the country. Though there is an understandable time lag between the recognition of consumer needs and the enactment of legislation to provide ways to meet these needs, much has been accomplished in the way of modernizing small loan legislation in most states. Maximum loan ceilings have been raised in many states, and though the changes have not entirely kept pace with increases in the wage and price level, the trend continues. These higher loan ceilings have made possible graduated rates of charge which resulted in a reduction in the average rate of charge on loans made by consumer finance companies.

As the consumer finance industry continues to expand its services, a trend toward slightly higher loss ratios has been noted over the last ten years, but the percent of loss to average notes outstanding was 1.84 in 1959 compared with 2.06 in 1958. Neither the size of the loan nor the occupation of the borrower appears to have much bearing on whether or not it is likely to become a charge off. There is some evidence, however, that loans to single men carry the greatest risk.

Increased maximum loan sizes, increased volume of business, and an increased number of borrowers, have enabled consumer finance companies to continue profitable operations at a declining rate of charge' for loans. However, the inherent nature of the industry limits the possibilities for increased efficiency. The results have been a rising volume of loans outstanding, a higher level of gross income generally, but a lower rate of return on assets. A compilation of state supervisory reports revealed that net income before interest on borrowed money as a percent of assets used in the business declined from a median of 7.30 in 1950 to 5.51 in 1958.

The influence of governmental policy measures on the savings flow and the loan investment process is most effective in the area of general monetary policy. Monetary policy impinges most immediately and most directly upon commercial banks by increasing or decreasing their deposit balances maintained with the Federal Reserve Banks. The size of these balances determines the volume of the banks' loanable funds. These factors also limit the operating funds available to consumer finance companies and increase the cost at which they are available. To guarantee a steady flow of funds, these companies have shifted to long-term debt. At the same time, increasing cost of bank funds because of off-line and compensating balance requirements, uncertainty resulting from the heavy invasion of banks into the direct loan field, and occasional reduction or cancellation of bank lines, have led finance companies to secure additional funds through long-term senior and subordinated borrowings.

In the area of selective controls, experience has shown that Regulation W type peace time consumer credit controls are highly discriminatory between cash and credit users, that they distort the free flow of market forces, and that they interfere with the free right of choice and financial planning of the family. Since general monetary controls already in existence are as effective in consumer credit as in other business areas, there is no need for selective peace time controls.

In recent years, as rising incomes and inflationary prices have brought needs for larger consumer loans, a number of states have permitted larger loans. In many cases, however, restrictive provisions of small loan laws have stood in the way of continuing service to this market, and as a result, commercial banks and credit unions have come to play a prominent role in this area. In states which have permitted larger loans by consumer finance companies, they have been able to operate competitively, even though these other financial institutions have sources of funds which are less costly than funds borrowed in the money market. The consumer finance industry has become an essential and increasingly important element in the financial structure of the United States. Responding to the demand of consumers for loans, it searches out sources of capital and makes available cash loans, frequently on an unsecured basis, thus helping the individual consumer to consolidate existing debts, to meet emergency expenses, to purchase needed goods, or to improve the family level of living. In serving this function, the consumer finance industry has contributed to economic stability, making it possible for individuals to level out their expenditures and income over time.

In an expanding economy, with rapid increases in population and family formation, the need for consumer credit will be greater in the coming years. The several consumer credit institutions have arisen in response to recognized needs for specialized financial service. Consumer finance companies will continue to serve an important segment of the over-all field of consumer credit as long as fair treatment is accorded to them under tax laws and regulatory state laws, permitting them to reach their full potential for service in a free enterprise economy. These services have won for the consumer finance industry an important and an honored place in the socio-economic structure of America.

Recommendations

This monograph has presented a profile of the consumer finance industry—its beginning, its growth and development, and its present place as an integral part of a complicated economy. From the industry's vantage point of nearly half a century of experience in cash instalment lending, certain problem areas present themselves. It is believed that the following recommendations, if carried out, would permit consumer finance companies to improve and broaden their service as financial intermediaries performing essential economic functions.

Selective Controls

The consumer finance industry is opposed to peace time selective controls by the federal government on the purpose, term, and use of consumer credits.

Over-all monetary and credit regulation through the Federal Reserve System and fiscal measures applied by the federal government are effective in restraining the expansion of consumer credit as well as other types of credit. The consumer finance industry has responded in periods of monetary restraint by a moderated rate of growth. (See Chapter 7, "Cost and Availability of Funds," and "Funds Made Available to Consumers.")

The Regulation W type of credit control interfered with the freedom of choice of the family, and led to widespread public evasion. Because of its discriminatory nature, it created a disrespect for law and government. The "red tape" involved in administration and enforcement increased costs to grantors and users alike. (See Chapter 7, "Effects of Selective Controls over Consumer Credit.")

Tax Equality

All lending institutions should be subject to the payment of the same taxes. The existing unfair advantage in this area should be corrected and this indirect subsidy eliminated. Consumer finance companies should have equal opportunity for service and should be given incentive equivalent to other lending institutions, so that competition may evolve the best service to the consuming public.

Credit unions, with their tax-favored and subsidized status, have grown rapidly. Many are multimillion dollar organizations whose operations are professionally managed and essentially motivated by the prospects for profit. Through broadening the basis of membership eligibility and expansion of the scope of purpose for which they lend money and the amounts which they lend, they have become serious competition to the private enterprise companies which must pay all expenses of operation, raise their own capital, and pay income taxes on earnings before any return may be made to investors. While it is true that credit union loan service is not available to all of the public, their tax exemptions and other subsidies warrant an objective study to determine their ultimate effect (possibly undesirable), upon our money and credit system, with respect to safety of investors' funds, loss in federal revenue, and effect on taxpaying enterprises. (See Chapter 2, "Competitive Position and Nature of the Competition," and Chapter 6, "Regulatory Provisions Affecting Earning Power and Growth of the Industry and Recommended Regulatory and Tax Changes.")

Personal Holding Companies

Provision should be made to insure that technicalities in the Personal Holding Company section of the Internal Revenue Code not encumber the operation of consumer finance companies.

As its inception, the purpose of the Personal Holding Company Act was to discourage incorporation as a device for avoiding personal taxation of income from interest, dividends, rents, etc., arising out of "inactive" investments. In drafting exemptions for consumer finance companies, the Treasury Department utilized the language of the rate sections of the state regulatory laws. As a result, changes in various state laws exposed small, incorporated, closely held consumer finance companies to the possibility of having to pay an 85 percent tax on undistributed corporate profits. (See Chapter 6, "Regulatory Provisions Affecting Earning Power and Growth of the Industry and Recommended Regulatory and Tax Changes.")

Legislation and Supervision

Legislation and supervision affecting the consumer finance industry properly rests at the state level. The legislation and supervision of lending practices historically have been the responsibility of each state. The states should continue to exercise full authority in this field.

Because of the widely varying economic development of the different states, consumer finance needs of the citizens of each state can best be determined at the state level. Here also, supervision is most effective, and legislatures most sensitive to needs for revisions in existing laws. (See Chapter 2, "Distribution," and Chapter 4, "Loans, 1939-1959.")

Competitive Equality

The state legislatures and supervisory officials in exercising their regulation of lending practices should take all necessary steps to insure a fair competitive climate for all lenders.

Restrictions imposed by artificially low ceilings on loans by consumer finance companies, while other institutions offering similar services are free to loan larger amounts, create a competitive inequality which cannot be justified. Broadening the area of competition would guarantee every lender an equal chance, and would benefit the borrower by providing the best possible service at the lowest possible rates. Sometimes equality in competitive opportunity can best be gained by permitting a reliable lender to operate in more than one lending area, perhaps under two or more separate licenses. It is as logical to expect a consumer credit institution to be able to serve all the different credit needs of its customers as it is to expect an insurance broker to be able to handle all the different insurance needs of its customers. Some institutions are free to offer all varieties of lending services. Others are expressly forbidden to do so. This discrimination is not in the best interest of either the lenders or the borrowers. (See Chapters 2, 6, and 8.)

APPENDIX TABLES

State Small Loan Laws: Year Enacted and Rates of Charge, September 1, 1961

State	Year First Operative Law Was Passed	Maximum Rates[a]
Alabama	1959	3-2% @ $200 to $300; $1 per $5 of loans not exceeding $75
Alaska[b]	1955[b]	4-2½% @ $300, 2% @ $600 to $1000; 5% on loans not exceeding $50; default fee of $3
Arizona	1919	3-2% @ $300 to $600
Arkansas	b	b
California	1939	2½%-2% @ $200 to $500, (2% if security insured) ⅝% @ $500 to $5000; no maximum above $5000
Colorado	1913	3-1½% @ $300, 1% @ $500 to $1500
Connecticut	1919	3-2% @ $100; ¾% @ $300 to $600; 12% a year after 20 months
Delaware[b]	b	6% a year discount; 2% service fee; 5% fine; various limitations; industrial law; loan size based on capital and surplus
District of Columbia	b	
Florida	1925	3-2% @ $300 to $600; 10% a year 12 months after maturity
Georgia	b	8% a year to $2500, fee of 8% of first $600 and 4% of excess; charged on initial balance as discount for 18 months, as add-on for longer maturities; plus other charges
Hawaii	1937	3½%-2½% @ $100 to $300
Idaho	1943	3%-2% @ $300, 1% @ $500 to $1000
Illinois	1917	3%-2% @ $150, 1% @ $300 to $800
Indiana	1917	3%-2% @ $150, 1½% @ $300 to $500
Iowa	1921	3%-2% @ $150, 1½% @ $300 to $500
Kansas	1955	3⅝% @ $300 to $2100; 10% a year 6 months after maturity
Kentucky	1934	3-2% @ $150, 1% @ $600 to $800; or add-on rates, $20-$15 a year per $100 @ $150, $11 @ $600 to $800, charged on initial balance
Louisiana	1928	3½%-2½% @ $150 to $300; 8% a year 1 year after maturity
Maine	1917	3-2½% @ $150, 1½% @ $300 to $2500; 25¢ minimum
Maryland	1918	3% to $300
Massachusetts	1911	2½%-2% @ $200, 1¾% @ $600 to $1000, ¾% @ $1000 to $1500; 6% a year one year after maturity
Michigan	1921	3-2½% @ $50, ¾% @ $300 to $500

(Continued)

Table A-1 (Continued)

State	Year First Operative Law Was Passed	Maximum Rates[a]
Minnesota	1939	$2\frac{3}{4}\%-1\frac{1}{2}\%$ @ $300 to $600
Mississippi	[b]	
Missouri	1927	2.218% to $500; 8% a year on remainder
Montana[b]	[b]	$20-$16 a year per $100 @ $300, $12 @ $500 to $1000; charged on initial balance for full contract period; special rate for loans up to $90
Nebraska	1943	$3-2\frac{1}{2}\%$ @ $150, $\frac{3}{4}\%$ @ $300 to $3000
Nevada[b]	1943[b]	9-8% a year @ $1000 - $2500 plus monthly fee of 1¢ per $1 to $200 and $\frac{1}{2}$¢ per $1 from $200-$400; all charged on initial balance for full contract period
New Hampshire	1917	Add-on rates $16-$12 a year per $100 @ $600 to $1,500
New Jersey	1914	$2\frac{1}{2}\%-\frac{1}{2}\%$ @ $300 to $500
New Mexico	1947	$3-2\frac{1}{2}\%$ @ $150, 1% @ $300 to $1000; 10% a year 1 year after maturity and in certain other cases
New York	1932	$2\frac{1}{2}-2\%$ @ $100; $\frac{3}{4}\%$ @ $300 to $800
North Carolina	1961	Add-on rates, $20-$18 a year per $100 @ $100; $15 @ $200; $6 @ $300 to $600
North Dakota	1960	$2\frac{1}{2}\%-2\%$ @ $250; $1\frac{3}{4}\%$ @ $500 to $750; $1\frac{1}{2}\%$ @ $750 to $1000
Ohio	1915	Add-on rates, $16-$9 a year $100 @ $500; $7 @ $1000 to $2000
Oklahoma[b]	1941[b]	10% a year plus service charges not exceeding an initial 5% and monthly 2% but not more than $2, subject to various limitations to $300
Oregon	1935	3-2% @ $300; 1% @ $500 to $1500
Pennsylvania	1915	3-2% @ $150; 1% @ $300 to $600; 6% a year after 24 months
Rhode Island	1923	3% to $300
South Carolina	[b]	
South Dakota[b]	1953[b]	$3\frac{3}{4}\%$ @ $300 to $2500; $2 minimum, 8% a year 6 months after maturity
Tennessee[b]	[b]	$\frac{1}{2}\%$; monthly fee not exceeding 1%
Texas	[b]	
Utah	1917	3-1% @ $300 to $600
Vermont	1937	$2\frac{1}{2}\%-2\frac{1}{4}\%$ @ $125; 1% @ $300 to $600
Virginia	1918	$2\frac{1}{2}\%-1\frac{1}{2}\%$ @ $300 to $600; 6% a year after 23 months and in certain other cases

(Continued)

160

Table A-1 (Continued)

State	Year First Operative Law Was Passed	Maximum Rates[a]
Washington	1941	3-1½% @ $300; 1% @ $500 to $1000; $1 minimum
West Virginia	1925	3½-2½% @ $150 to $300
Wisconsin	1927	2½-2% @ $100; 1% @ $200 to $300
Wyoming[b]	1945[b]	3½-2½% @ $150; 1% @ $300 to $1000; plus $1 fee on loans of $50 or less; $1 recording fee

[a] Rate per month on unpaid balance, unless otherwise indicated. Where more than one rate is given, each rate applies to that part of the loan balance as indicated. Thus, in Colorado, the maximum charge for a month during which the loan balance is $700 would be: 3% of $300 or $9.00; 1½% of $200 or $3.00; 1% of $200 or $2.00. Total charge $14.00. As of September 1961, twenty states permitted add-on or pre-computation of charges under laws similar to the Uniform Small Loan Law: Alabama, Arizona, California, Colorado, Idaho, Illinois, Kansas, Kentucky, Massachusetts, Minnesota, Missouri, Montana, Nevada, New Hampshire, New Mexico, New York, North Carolina, Ohio, Utah, and Washington. Several other states having laws similar to the Uniform Small Loan Law permitted add-on or pre-computation of charges for loans made under authority of other types of legislation such as the discount-type license in Florida, loans of over $300 in Louisiana, Maryland, and Wisconsin, and of loans of over $600 in Pennsylvania.

[b] The States of Arkansas, Mississippi, South Carolina, Texas, and the District of Columbia, as of September 1, 1961, in most cases had regulatory statutes of one form or another under which consumer finance companies could or did operate. The States of Alaska, Delaware, Georgia, Montana, Nevada, Oklahoma, South Dakota, Tennessee, and Wyoming as of September 1, 1961, had laws dissimilar to the Uniform Small Loan Law with varying degrees of effectiveness.

Source: *Roster of Consumer Finance Companies*, Washington, National Consumer Finance Association, 1960-1961; Wallace P. Mors, *Small Loan Laws*, Educational Pamphlet No. 2, Western Reserve University, Bureau of Business Research.

TABLE A-2
Consumer Finance Industry: Number of Licensees, Loans Made, Loans Outstanding, and Personal Income, 1929-1960

Year	Licensees[a] (Number)	Loans Made (In millions of dollars)	Loans Outstanding at year-end (In millions of dollars)	Personal Income (In billions of dollars)	Index Numbers (1957-1959 = 100)[b] Licensees	Loans Outstanding	Personal Income
1929	n.a.	463	263	85.8	--	--	--
1930	3,520	503	287	76.9	31.4	10.0	21.1
1931	3,687	498	289	65.7	32.9	10.1	18.0
1932	3,596	376	257	50.1	32.1	9.0	13.7
1933	3,363	304	232	47.2	30.0	8.1	12.9
1934	3,305	384	246	53.6	29.5	8.6	14.7
1935	3,271	423	267	60.2	29.2	9.3	16.5
1936	3,325	563	301	68.5	29.7	10.5	18.8
1937	3,553	619	350	73.9	31.7	12.2	20.2
1938	3,619	604	346	68.6	32.3	12.1	18.8
1939	4,036	763	431	72.9	36.0	15.0	20.0
1940	4,658	917	484	78.7	41.6	16.9	21.6
1941	5,021	969	525	96.3	44.8	18.3	26.4
1942	4,747	776	411	123.5	42.4	14.3	33.8
1943	4,210	802	361	151.4	37.6	12.6	41.5
1944	4,192	867	381	165.7	37.4	13.3	45.4
1945	4,434	962	436	171.2	39.6	15.2	46.9
1946	5,002	1,217	594	179.3	44.7	20.7	49.1
1947	5,414	1,478	725	191.6	48.3	25.3	52.5
1948	5,722	1,616	854	210.4	51.1	29.8	57.6
1949	5,974	1,782	973	208.3	53.3	34.0	57.1

Year							
1950	6,358	1,952	1,111	228.5	56.8	38.8	62.6
1951	6,738	2,412	1,306	256.7	60.2	45.6	70.3
1952	7,352	2,679	1,514	273.1	65.6	52.8	74.8
1953	7,862	2,857	1,692	288.3	70.2	59.1	79.0
1954	8,225	2,995	1,839	289.8	73.4	64.2	79.4
1955	9,271	3,460	2,088	310.2	82.8	72.9	85.0
1956	10,160	3,984	2,432	332.9	90.7	84.9	91.2
1957	10,745	4,326	2,721	351.4	95.9	95.0	96.3
1958	11,080	4,117	2,816	360.3	98.9	98.3	98.7
1959	11,779	4,477	3,058	383.3	105.2	106.7	105.0
1960	12,250	4,892	3,413	402.2	109.4	119.1	110.2

a Number of Licensees as of the end of January 1930, July 1931 to 1948, and September 1949 to date.
b Index numbers were computed from the following averages for the years 1957–1959: Licensees–11,201; Loans Outstanding–2,865; Personal Income 365.0.

Sources: *Roster of Consumer Finance Companies*, Washington, National Consumer Finance Association, annually, 1930–1960; *Federal Reserve Bulletin*, January 1947, p. 84, Washington, Board of Governors of the Federal Reserve System; "Consumer Loans Made Under Effective State Small Loan Laws," Board of Governors of the Federal Reserve System, Division of Research and Statistics, November 1956, January 1959, and February 3, 1961, Mimeographed; *U. S. Income and Output*, Washington, U. S. Department of Commerce, 1958; *Survey of Current Business*, July 1961, Washington, U. S. Department of Commerce.

TABLE A-3
Number of Licensees by States, Selected Years, 1931-1960[a]

State	1931	1939	1948	1954	1958	1959	1960
Alabama	n.a.	n.a.	n.a.	n.a.	n.a.	n.a.	n.a.
Alaska	--	--	--	--	10	13	15
Arizona	20	42	50	117	192	201	197
Arkansas	n.a.	n.a.	n.a.	n.a.	n.a.	n.a.	n.a.
California	n.a.	n.a.	446	664	902	997	1,095
Colorado	28	118	146	192	290	329	342
Connecticut	178	81	74	89	100	103	106
Delaware	n.a.	n.a.	n.a.	21	22	20	21
Florida	48	86	275	456	740	790	783
Georgia	65	8	8	2	n.a.	n.a.	n.a.
Hawaii	--	--	--	3	10	11	17
Idaho	n.a.	n.a.	48	48	71	72	72
Illinois	369	379	555	606	731	767	808
Indiana	340	339	372	495	670	710	717
Iowa	176	152	196	236	262	289	298
Kansas	n.a.	n.a.	n.a.	n.a.	301	319	334
Kentucky	n.a.	36	117	185	303	314	330
Louisiana	102	93	177	289	375	405	443
Maine	43	34	42	74	103	104	111
Maryland	95	121	138	272	307	324	332
Massachusetts	218	188	208	236	308	317	321
Michigan	262	219	249	369	487	515	544
Minnesota	n.a.	62	84	113	142	153	157
Mississippi	n.a.	n.a.	n.a.	n.a.	n.a.	n.a.	n.a.
Missouri	101	111	n.a.	255	355	366	413
Montana	n.a.	n.a.	n.a.	n.a.	n.a.	118	111
Nebraska	52	124	138	156	181	186	179
Nevada	n.a.	n.a.	9	12	21	24	30
New Hampshire	19	16	25	42	60	62	64
New Jersey	121	113	164	221	260	265	267
New Mexico	n.a.	33	95	106	130	130	162
New York	23	289	288	371	444	462	469
North Carolina	n.a.	n.a.	n.a.	n.a.	n.a.	n.a.	n.a.
North Dakota	n.a.	n.a.	n.a.	n.a.	n.a.	n.a.	n.a.
Ohio	494	524	576	792	949	996	1,015
Oklahoma	n.a.	n.a.	103	108	138	159	164
Oregon	84	47	60	119	177	184	188
Pennsylvania	580	510	538	737	897	883	888
Rhode Island	73	71	66	74	80	83	103
South Carolina	n.a.	n.a.	n.a.	n.a.	n.a.	n.a.	n.a.
South Dakota	n.a.	n.a.	n.a.	73	82	85	91
Tennessee	31	17	10	7	9	n.a.	5
Texas	n.a.	n.a.	n.a.	n.a.	n.a.	n.a.	n.a.
Utah	4	41	55	72	132	142	149
Vermont	n.a.	12	14	21	25	26	26
Virginia	65	78	77	113	209	220	233
Washington	n.a.	n.a.	79	101	149	162	166
West Virginia	26	47	101	161	188	190	195
Wisconsin	70	45	139	183	216	222	228
Wyoming	n.a.	n.a.	n.a.	34	52	61	61
Total above	3,687	4,036	5,722	8,225	11,080	11,779	12,250

[a] See footnotes to Table A-1 for classification of laws, and footnotes to Table A-2 for month and day applicable to each year.

n.a.-Not available.

Source: *Roster of Consumer Finance Companies*, Washington, National Consumer Finance Association, published annually.

TABLE A-4

Composite Balance Sheet of Twenty-One Consumer
(In thousands of

Item

Assets

1. Cash and bank balance. . . . .
2. Accounts and notes receivable
   a. Retail passenger automobile paper . . . .
   b. Other consumer goods paper . . . .
   c. Residential repair and modernization loans. . . . .
   d. Personal loans. . . . .
   e. Retail paper on commercial vehicles, trucks, taxicabs, and farm equipment . . .
   f. Wholesale paper on automobiles . . . .
   g. Other wholesale paper. . . . .
   h. Business loans. . . . .
   i. Other accounts and notes receivable . . . .
   j. Less: reserves for unearned income . . . .
   k. Less: reserves for losses . . . .
3. Other loans and investments (including investment in subsidiaries excluded
   from this statement) . . . .
4. Other assets . . . .
5. Total assets (sum of items 1 through 4 minus 2j and 2k) . . . .

Liabilities, Capital, and Surplus

6. Short-term notes payable to banks (excluding commercial paper) . . . .
7. Commercial paper and other short-term indebtedness . . . .
8. Long-term notes payable to banks . . . .
9. Other long-term indebtedness (excluding subordinated debentures) . . . .
10. Subordinated debentures . . . .
11. Other liabilities . . . .
12. Capital and surplus. . . . .
13. Total liabilities, capital and surplus (sum of items 6 through 12) . . . .

14. Amount of loans outstanding under State small loan licenses . . . .
    Amount of these loans included above in item 2d, Personal loans . . . .
15. Number of offices covered by above figures . . . .

_____

ᵃ Size of company by asset size: Two large companies with assets of $350 million and over;
seven moderately large companies with assets of $50 million and under $350 million; four medium-
size companies with assets of $10 million and under $50 million; eight small companies with assets
of under $10 million.
ᵇ See footnote to Appendix Table A-12 for an explanation of the unusually large proportion of
"Commercial paper and other short-term indebtedness" for moderately large companies.

Source: Survey made by the National Consumer Finance Association.

166

Finance Companies, June 30, 1959
dollars)

	Size of Company[a]			
Large	Moderately large	Medium size	Small	Total
35,550	93,531	14,497	3,789	147,367
0	13,652	28,760	2,709	45,121
21,036	106,821	6,878	3,460	138,195
0	1,359	0	422	1,781
848,475	850,048	78,278	20,961	1,797,762
0	0	0	40	40
0	3,598	4,419	188	8,205
0	1,706	561	0	2,267
0	8,640	489	0	9,129
0	534	106	81	721
(47,666)	(58,267)	(4,526)	(307)	(110,766)
(18,360)	(27,541)	(3,992)	(1,330)	(51,223)
238,797	37,992	1,004	0	277,793
25,614	38,541	3,342	743	68,240
1,103,444	1,070,616	129,815	30,756	2,334,631
49,086	244,359	56,547	13,368	363,360
18,869	129,452[b]	6,862	1,251	156,434
0	1,000	3,000	0	4,000
663,965	307,888	13,101	1,764	986,718
0	119,562	12,270	6,381	138,213
30,640	43,646	4,703	459	79,448
340,885	224,707	33,332	7,531	606,454
1,103,444	1,070,616	129,815	30,755	2,334,630
683,592	650,575	78,278	20,956	1,433,401
683,592	650,575	78,278	20,956	1,433,401
1,742	2,215	234	92	4,283

TABLE A-5
Liabilities and Ownership Equity of Two Large Companies, 1949-1958[a]
(In thousands of dollars)

Balance Sheet Item	1949	1950	1951	1952	1953
Notes Payable					
Short-Term					
Bank	87,694	135,659	128,244	96,027	77,526
Commercial Paper	3,400	4,625	6,335	8,000	5,075
Other	792	867	887	822	901
Long-Term Debt					
Unsubordinated	133,625	148,585	224,609	280,306	360,936
Subordinated (Senior)					
Subordinated (Junior)					
Other Liabilities	22,045	33,456	41,357	46,265	52,576
Preferred Stock	28,890	29,979	25,654	33,281	30,793
Common Stock Equity	115,920	137,477	155,520	175,666	201,990
Total Liabilities and Ownership Equity	392,366	490,648	582,608	640,366	729,797

Balance Sheet Item	1954	1955	1956	1957	1958
Notes Payable					
Short-Term					
Bank	94,339	120,810	123,775	87,050	91,753
Commercial Paper	12,628	4,280	6,225	10,802	6,755
Other	1,036	3,180	8,611	8,847	1,664
Long-Term Debt					
Unsubordinated	369,171	422,392	539,354	647,023	642,323
Subordinated (Senior)					
Subordinated (Junior)					
Other Liabilities	52,551	56,137	54,492	58,497	58,121
Preferred Stock	28,800	28,400	28,000	56,918	56,220
Common Stock Equity	219,618	241,958	271,173	261,602	285,867
Total Liabilities and Ownership Equity	778,143	877,157	1,031,630	1,130,738	1,142,703

[a] End of calendar year.

Source: Survey made by the National Consumer Finance Association.

TABLE A-6
Liabilities and Ownership Equity of Seven Moderately Large Companies, 1949-1958[a]
(In thousands of dollars)

Balance Sheet Item	1949	1950	1951	1952	1953
Notes Payable					
Short-Term					
Bank	89,637	122,822	118,225	166,958	188,431
Commercial Paper	14,160	12,290	14,205	31,355	23,415
Other[b]	15,844	19,870	24,241	30,345	36,432
Long-Term Debt					
Unsubordinated	22,250	46,100	82,214	83,193	99,300
Subordinated (Senior)	23,730	33,166	31,286	37,597	44,708
Subordinated (Junior)	0	0	0	0	0
Other Liabilities	28,181	36,212	52,337	47,658	51,369
Preferred Stock	25,636	22,434	25,428	42,849	40,480
Common Stock Equity	36,014	52,303	60,545	75,299	89,509
Total Liabilities and Ownership Equity	255,448	345,197	408,481	515,252	573,643

Balance Sheet Item	1954	1955	1956	1957	1958
Notes Payable					
Short-Term					
Bank	149,898	240,445	260,500	258,877	251,222
Commercial Paper	41,695	30,159	32,452	36,159	52,867
Other[b]	40,532	45,313	49,200	54,406	59,437
Long-Term Debt					
Unsubordinated	134,745	129,928	193,629	240,252	260,099
Subordinated (Senior)	49,173	52,326	65,654	79,402	94,001
Subordinated (Junior)	7,944	9,593	26,012	28,356	27,551
Other Liabilities	58,333	51,736	58,689	59,616	63,389
Preferred Stock	30,975	28,991	34,092	39,515	46,024
Common Stock Equity	100,451	112,974	128,541	140,096	152,328
Total Liabilities and Ownership Equity	613,745	701,463	848,767	936,678	1,006,917

[a] End of calendar or fiscal year.

[b] Other short-term notes payable in this table consist almost entirely of certificates of deposit at one savings and loan association and at one industrial bank. The reports for these two forms of financial institutions were consolidated with the reports for the respective parent consumer finance companies.

Source: Survey made by the National Consumer Finance Association.

169

TABLE A-7
Liabilities and Ownership Equity of Four Medium-Size Companies, 1949-1958[a]
(In thousands of dollars)

Balance Sheet Item	1949	1950	1951	1952	1953
Notes Payable					
Short-Term					
Bank	15,915	21,135	23,970	29,330	25,460
Commercial Paper	1,845	1,152	2,725	1,435	1,925
Other	1,026	1,012	938	1,031	1,304
Long-Term Debt					
Unsubordinated	1,644	1,944	2,256	4,646	5,937
Subordinated (Senior)	1,800	2,050	1,994	1,712	1,766
Subordinated (Junior)	0	0	0	1,000	3,000
Other Liabilities	1,809	2,217	3,414	3,822	3,634
Preferred Stock	1,418	1,459	1,486	1,516	1,518
Common Stock Equity	12,527	13,914	15,196	16,610	17,976
Total Liabilities and Ownership Equity	37,983	44,882	51,980	61,102	62,519

Balance Sheet Item	1954	1955	1956	1957	1958
Notes Payable					
Short-Term					
Bank	39,558	56,177	54,469	57,654	47,529
Commercial Paper	3,705	2,414	2,870	3,188	5,900
Other	1,599	1,232	1,562	1,315	1,555
Long-Term Debt					
Unsubordinated	6,424	8,968	15,444	15,906	15,531
Subordinated (Senior)	5,034	5,015	5,470	4,670	4,470
Subordinated (Junior)	4,786	4,750	5,512	6,250	6,650
Other Liabilities	5,219	4,987	5,073	6,276	4,640
Preferred Stock	2,310	1,392	1,994	1,988	1,984
Common Stock Equity	22,823	25,256	27,692	30,032	32,082
Total Liabilities and Ownership Equity	91,459	110,191	120,086	127,279	120,341

[a] Data available for three companies 1949-1953, and for four companies 1954-1958 and refer to end of calendar or fiscal year.

Source: Survey made by the National Consumer Finance Association.

170

TABLE A-8
Liabilities and Ownership Equity of Eight Small Companies, 1949-1958[a]
(In thousands of dollars)

Balance Sheet Item	1949	1950	1951	1952	1953
Notes Payable					
Short-Term					
Bank	4,217	5,431	5,992	6,384	7,201
Commercial	0	0	0	0	0
Other	1,206	1,429	1,206	1,099	1,191
Long-Term Debt					
Unsubordinated	342	302	412	470	502
Subordinated (Senior)	225	312	786	1,545	3,128
Subordinated (Junior)	0	0	0	0	0
Other Liabilities	652	793	895	987	994
Preferred Stock	1,706	1,651	1,597	1,443	1,420
Common Stock Equity	2,369	2,656	2,904	3,208	3,650
Total Liabilities and Ownership Equity	10,718	12,574	13,793	15,136	18,088

Balance Sheet Item	1954	1955	1956	1957	1958
Notes Payable					
Short-Term					
Bank	7,347	9,332	10,989	12,818	12,750
Commercial Paper	0	0	0	0	0
Other	1,172	839	772	755	858
Long-Term Debt					
Unsubordinated	584	798	791	867	1,713
Subordinated (Senior)	3,492	4,627	4,904	5,239	5,879
Subordinated (Junior)	74	320	337	325	321
Other Liabilities	989	1,181	1,158	1,189	1,184
Preferred Stock	1,291	1,019	1,027	1,102	1,567
Common Stock Equity	3,942	4,381	4,764	5,143	5,588
Total Liabilities and Ownership Equity	18,889	22,497	24,742	27,437	29,858

[a] End of calendar or fiscal year.

Source: Survey made by the National Consumer Finance Association.

TABLE A-9
Assets of the Consumer Finance Industry, 1950[a]
(In thousands or millions of dollars as indicated)

State	Cash in Office and Bank (Thousands)	Loans Receivable (Millions)	Real Estate (Thousands)	Furniture, Fixtures, and Equipment (Thousands)	Deferred Charges (Thousands)	Other Assets (Thousands)	Total Assets (Millions)
Arizona	203	3.4	8	60	7	1,027	4.7
California	8,034	105.0	493	934	--	5,139	119.6
Colorado	1,872	6.0	1,100	375	48	31,705	41.1
Connecticut	442	14.3	--	138	14	106	15.0
Idaho	321	2.8	73	95	17	5,392	8.7
Illinois	9,714	102.5	124	1,457	999	3,421	118.2
Indiana	2,903	42.1	64	649	833	2,351	48.9
Iowa	1,690	21.0	--	314	76	820	23.9
Kentucky	1,210	24.5	29	391	160	3,510	29.8
Maryland	1,664	36.6	51	511	107	16,667	55.6
Massachusetts	1,630	25.7	26	343	25	1,476	29.2
Michigan	3,342	69.4	91	723	215	1,729	75.5
Minnesota	1,369	17.6	--	256	74	301	19.6
Nebraska	828	14.6	76	164	20	252	15.9
Nevada	138	0.7	--	29	22	2,090	3.0

New Hampshire	124	3.2	11	43	85	237	3.7
New Jersey	1,463	55.1	47	630	104	3,000	60.3
New York	3,888	135.7	– –	820	165	327	140.9
Ohio	10,850	157.4	350	1,252	217	2,231	172.3
Oklahoma	1,011	10.0	325	264	35	14.565	26.2
Ohio	18,891	313.5	1,366	3,436	1,191	29,746	368.2
Oklahoma	1,532	54.2	524	485	197	7,919	64.8
Oregon	1,456	31.7	88	472	84	887	34.7
Pennsylvania	11,723	239.7	– –	2,838	2,688	24,052	281.0
Vermont	137	6.3	– –	59	2	123	6.6
Virginia	2,906	85.3	21	992	122	2,991	92.3
Washington	1,613	41.4	40	541	40	3,116	46.8
West Virginia	1,488	35.7	63	520	112	2,704	40.6
Wisconsin	1,430	14.4	– –	132	– –	748	16.7
Totals	127,324	2,603.6	5,659	33,452	13,751	134,587	2,918.5

a Covers twenty-nine states for which data are available.

Source: Reports of State Supervisors.

173

TABLE A-10
Assets of the Consumer Finance Industry, 1958[a]
(In thousands or millions of dollars as indicated)

State	Cash in Office and Bank (Thousands)	Loans Receivable (Millions)	Real Estate (Thousands)	Furniture, Fixtures, and Equipment (Thousands)	Deferred Charges (Thousands)	Other Assets (Thousands)	Total Assets (Millions)
Arizona	1,364	27.0	24	496	94	1,220	30.3
California	19,170	320.3	669	3,407	786	7,052	351.4
Connecticut	716	33.3	--	285	43	25	34.3
Florida	4,257	122.4	443	2,110	877	9,341	139.4
Hawaii	32	0.9	--	28	--	50	1.0
Illinois	16,247	214.2	224	2,898	1,297	2,382	237.2
Indiana	8,045	118.1	459	1,855	323	7,470	136.3
Iowa	2,091	31.3	15	567	402	1,314	35.7
Kansas	2,437	62.8	429	860	475	969	68.0
Kentucky	2,935	52.4	26	1,314	171	6,246	63.1
Louisiana	2,647	35.6	708	1,008	369	3,809	44.2
Maryland	3,054	61.4	22	1,057	2,203	8,163	75.9
Michigan	6,995	158.7	352	1,819	517	2,093	170.5
Minnesota	1,995	25.7	--	490	158	586	28.9
Missouri	3,762	97.7	164	1,135	428	1,016	104.2

Nevada	149	6.0	4	109	13	1,269	7.5
New Hampshire	197	3.0	--	196	69	887	4.3
New Jersey	2,662	115.3	18	1,080	391	4,776	124.2
New Mexico	1,254	35.5	--	843	347	2,499	40.5
New York	6,139	259.8	--	2,420	352	1,134	269.9
Oregon	877	8.3	67	258	28	270	9.8
Pennsylvania	4,768	96.9	231	1,807	365	11,529	115.6
Utah	439	4.5	184	105	26	5,177	10.4
Vermont	76	2.0	--	13	1	110	2.2
Virginia	614	21.7	--	266	42	1,214	23.8
Washington	831	11.8	105	131	17	2,916	15.8
West Virginia	979	19.2	49	236	37	1,098	21.6
Wisconsin	1,733	16.0	9	144	--	414	18.3
Totals	63,013	1,028.0	3,513	12,408	3,739	119,074	1,229.6

ª Covers twenty-eight states for which data are available.

Source: M. R. Neifeld, *Trends in Consumer Finance* (Easton: Mack Publishing Co., 1954), page 87.

175

TABLE A-11
Monthly Rate of Charge Collected, Monthly Cost Per Open Account, and Annual Percent Net Earnings on Assets Used and Useful, by States, Selected Years, 1939-1958[a]

	Monthly Rate of Charge Collected (In percent)				Monthly Cost per Open Account[b] (In dollars)				Annual Percent Net Earnings on Assets Used and Useful[c] (In percent)			
	1939	1950	1954	1958	1939	1950	1954	1958	1939	1950	1954	1958
Arizona	n.a.	3.17	n.a.	2.56	n.a.	3.85	n.a.	6.49	n.a.	5.62	n.a.	4.97
California	2.31	1.92	n.a.	1.86	n.a.	4.70	4.91	5.13	n.a.	9.00	n.a.	n.a.
Colorado	n.a.	2.44	2.71	n.a.	n.a.	3.45	4.45	5.73	n.a.	4.60	4.45	3.48
Connecticut	2.39	2.22	2.04	1.81	n.a.	3.53	4.14	4.45	6.33	7.30	5.02	n.a.
Florida	2.92	n.a.	n.a.	2.49	n.a.	n.a.	n.a.	5.37	7.82	n.a.	n.a.	5.44
Idaho	n.a.	2.80	2.85	2.52	n.a.	3.07	4.83	7.93	n.a.	5.93	6.88	5.84
Illinois	2.64	2.45	2.32	2.15	n.a.	3.33	4.38	5.57	8.20	6.70	5.03	4.54
Indiana	2.52	2.47	2.20	n.a.	n.a.	2.93	4.14	n.a.	8.51	6.70	5.53	n.a.
Iowa	2.68	2.59	2.60	2.64	n.a.	3.94	3.87	3.95	8.98	7.18	6.61	6.14
Kentucky	3.12	3.06	3.01	2.97	n.a.	3.60	4.49	4.68	8.40	7.70	6.14	5.49
Maine	2.86	2.68	n.a.	n.a.	n.a.	3.12	n.a.	n.a.	n.a.	6.99	6.32	6.27
Maryland	2.84	2.70	2.70	2.64	1.91	2.55	n.a.	n.a.	n.a.	7.64	6.22	5.51
Michigan	2.51	2.33	2.23	2.07	n.a.	1.91	4.35	4.59	8.13	8.20	6.21	5.89
Minnesota	2.37	2.85	2.87	2.82	n.a.	n.a.	n.a.	4.51	Loss	8.85	6.88	6.56
Nevada	n.a.	2.81	2.32	2.18	n.a.	n.a.	n.a.	n.a.	n.a.	n.a.	5.10	5.47

New Jersey	2.38	2.01	2.07	1.97	n.a.	n.a.	n.a.	n.a.	2.08	7.33	n.a.	n.a.
New Mexico	n.a.	2.37	n.a.	n.a.	n.a.	2.42	n.a.	4.69	n.a.	n.a.	n.a.	n.a.
New York	2.58	2.01	1.87	1.78	n.a.	2.85	n.a.	4.46	9.06	6.50	4.65	4.45
Ohio	2.24	1.91	1.83	1.79	2.13	3.59	4.04	4.15	6.45	n.a.	n.a.	n.a.
Utah	2.74	2.70	n.a.	n.a.	n.a.	n.a.	n.a.	n.a.	9.60	n.a.	n.a.	n.a.
Vermont	2.90	2.34	2.33	2.00	2.12	2.48	3.06	3.99	9.05	n.a.	n.a.	n.a.
Virginia	3.01	2.43	2.41	2.14	1.75	2.56	3.26	4.44	10.40	8.70	6.36	6.49
Washington	n.a.	2.70	2.57	2.57	n.a.	3.16	4.18	5.08	n.a.	7.46	7.14	6.31
West Virginia	n.a.	2.76	2.96	2.95	n.a.	3.09	3.98	4.50	n.a.	10.07	7.52	6.76
Wisconsin	2.28	2.11	2.06	2.03	1.61	2.27	3.02	2.72	8.40	7.10	2.84	3.19
Median	2.55	2.46	2.33	2.17	1.91	3.11	4.14	4.59	8.40	7.30	6.21	5.51
High	3.12	3.17	3.01	2.97	2.13	4.70	4.91	7.93	10.40	10.07	7.52	6.76
Low	2.24	1.91	1.83	1.78	1.61	1.91	3.02	2.72	2.08[d]	4.60	2.84	3.19

[a] Covers states for which data are available.
[b] Not including interest on borrowed money.
[c] Before interest paid on borrowed funds.
[d] Excluding Minnesota where a net loss was reported.
n.a.-Not available.

Source: State Supervisory Reports.

177

TABLE A-12
Gross Income of Consumer Finance Companies and Its Uses, by States, 1958[a]
(In millions of dollars)

State	Gross Income	Expenses Before Interest	Net Income Before Interest	Interest Paid	Net Income After Interest
Arizona	11.1	8.8	2.3	1.6	0.7
California	69.1	51.2	17.8	11.5	6.3
Connecticut	7.3	5.6	1.7	1.0	0.7
Florida	34.2	26.4	7.8	4.8	3.0
Illinois	55.1	44.3	10.8	7.9	2.9
Iowa	9.9	7.7	2.2	1.0	1.2
Kansas	17.5	13.5	4.0	2.0	2.0
Kentucky	18.5	14.8	3.7	1.6	2.1
Louisiana	12.6	9.0	3.6	1.5	2.1
Maryland	21.1	16.8	4.3	n.a.	n.a.
Michigan	39.7	29.7	10.0	6.5	3.5
Minnesota	9.4	7.5	1.9	0.9	1.0
Missouri	20.0	15.4	4.6	2.5	2.1
Nevada	1.5	1.1	0.4	0.2	0.2
New Hampshire	0.7	0.5	0.2	-	0.2
New Jersey	26.3	18.6	7.7	n.a.	n.a.
New Mexico	7.3	4.4	2.9	0.9	2.0
New York	54.2	41.3	12.9	9.3	3.6
Ohio	67.2	50.6	16.6	10.6	6.0
Oklahoma	2.2	1.7	0.5	0.2	0.3
Oregon	8.5	6.3	2.2	1.1	1.1
South Dakota	4.5	3.1	1.4	0.9	0.5
Vermont	1.2	0.8	0.4	0.2	0.2
Virginia	21.7	15.5	6.2	3.3	2.9
Washington	10.3	7.8	2.5	n.a.	n.a.
West Virginia	12.6	9.7	2.9	1.2	1.7
Wisconsin	3.8	3.0	0.8	0.6	0.2
Total	547.5	415.1	132.3[b]	71.3[b]	46.5[b]

[a] Covers twenty-seven states for which data are available.
[b] The total for interest paid and net income after interest does not equal the total for net income before interest because no breakdown of these two items is available for the States of Maryland, New Jersey, or Washington.
n.a.-Not available.

Source: State Supervisory Reports.

TABLE A-13
Liabilities and Net Worth of Consumer Finance Companies
by States, 1958[a]
(In millions of dollars)

State	Liabilities Including Reserves	Net Worth	Total Liabilities and Net Worth
Arizona	34.8	13.5	48.3
California	269.8	81.8	351.6
Connecticut	25.8	9.9	35.7
Florida	105.9	33.5	139.4
Illinois	n.a.	n.a.	237.2
Iowa	21.8	13.9	35.7
Kansas	68.4	19.7	88.1
Kentucky	45.0	18.1	63.1
Louisiana	23.0	21.2	44.2
Maryland	85.3	21.7	107.0
Michigan	160.6	34.5	195.1
Minnesota	17.9	11.0	28.9
Missouri	75.3	28.9	104.2
Nevada	6.4	1.1	7.5
New Hampshire	2.7	3.6	6.3
New Jersey	110.5	13.7	124.2
New Mexico	24.8	15.7	40.5
New York	236.6	33.3	269.9
Ohio	290.4	77.8	368.2
Oklahoma	4.4	3.8	8.2
Oregon	n.a.	n.a.	34.7
South Dakota	19.1	7.1	26.2
Vermont	4.5	2.1	6.6
Virginia	77.0	15.3	92.3
Washington	38.6	8.2	46.8
West Virginia	26.7	13.9	40.6
Wisconsin	12.1	4.6	16.7
Total	1,787.4[b]	507.9[b]	2,567.2[b]

[a] Covers twenty-seven states for which data are available.
[b] The total of the column "Liabilities and Net Worth" exceeds by $271.9 million the sum of the two components because no breakdown is available for the States of Illinois and Oregon.
n.a.- Not available.

Source: State Supervisory Reports.

TABLE A-14
Expenses of Consumer Finance Companies by States, 1958[a]
(In millions of dollars)

State	Advertising	Rent, Light, and Heat	Salaries	Taxes	Other Expenses	Total Expenses Before Interest
Arizona	0.3	0.5	2.9	1.7	3.4	8.8
California	2.7	3.1	17.8	8.1	19.5	51.2
Connecticut	0.3	0.3	1.8	1.0	2.2	5.6
Florida	1.2	1.8	8.6	4.0	10.8	26.4
Illinois	2.4	3.0	15.3	8.9	14.7	44.3
Iowa	0.5	0.5	3.1	1.0	2.6	7.7
Kansas	0.6	0.8	4.4	2.3	5.4	13.5
Kentucky	0.7	0.9	5.1	2.3	5.8	14.8
Louisiana	0.4	0.5	2.3	1.3	4.5	9.0
Maryland	0.8	0.8	5.8	2.1	7.3	16.8
Michigan	1.3	1.6	9.1	5.5	12.2	29.7
Minnesota	0.4	0.4	3.0	1.1	2.6	7.5
Missouri	0.9	1.1[b]	6.0	2.9	4.5	15.4
Nevada	0.1	0.1	0.3	0.2	0.4	1.1
New Hampshire	0.1	--	0.3	0.1	--	0.5
New Jersey	0.9	1.0	6.0	4.6	6.1	18.6
New Mexico	n.a.	n.a.	1.6	1.3	1.5	4.4
New York	2.1	2.3	13.6	11.9	11.4	41.3
Ohio	2.7	2.9	16.7	9.8	18.5	50.6
Oklahoma	0.1	0.1	0.7	0.1	0.7	1.7
Oregon	0.4	0.3	2.1	1.1	2.4	6.3
South Dakota	0.1	0.2	1.3	0.4	1.1	3.1
Vermont	0.1	--	0.3	0.2	0.2	0.8
Virginia	0.7	0.7	4.4	3.1	6.6	15.5
Washington	0.5	0.5	2.5	1.6	2.7	7.8
West Virginia	0.4	0.4	3.1	2.2	3.6	9.7
Wisconsin	0.2	0.2	1.3	0.3	1.0	3.0
Total	20.9	24.0	139.4	79.1	151.7	415.1

[a] Covers twenty-seven states for which data are available.
[b] Includes printing, stationery, and supplies.
n.a.- Not available.

Source: State Supervisory Reports.

TABLE A-15

Range of Interest Rates on Commercial Paper Sold to the Public by Two Large Companies, Including Bankers' Commissions, 1949-1958

Six Months Period Ending	90-119 Paper	120-149 Paper	150-179 Paper	180-239 Paper	240-269 Paper
6/30/49	--	--	--	1.937-2	--
12/31/49	--	--	1 5/8	1 3/4	--
6/30/50	--	--	--	1 3/4	--
12/31/50	--	--	--	1 3/4	--
6/30/51	--	2 3/8	--	2 3/8	--
12/31/51	--	--	2 1/2	2 5/8-2 3/4	--
6/30/52	--	--	--	2 1/2-2 7/8	--
12/31/52	--	--	--	2 1/2-2 5/8	--
6/30/53	--	--	--	3-3 1/4	--
12/31/53	2 3/8	--	--	2 1/2-2.6625	--
6/30/54	1 1/2	1 1/2-1 7/8	1 1/2	1 5/8-2.4625	--
12/31/54	1 1/2	--	--	1 5/8-1 7/8	1 3/4
6/30/55	2 1/8	--	2 1/4	2 1/4	2 3/8
12/31/55	2 5/8-3 1/8	3 1/8-3 3/8	3 3/8	3 1/4-3 3/8	--
6/30/56	3 1/8-3 1/2	3 1/4-3 3/8	--	3 3/8-3 5/8	--
12/31/56	3 5/8	--	--	3 3/4-4	4
6/30/57	3 3/4-4	3 7/8	4	3 7/8-4	--
12/31/57	3 3/4-4 3/8	4 3/8	3 3/4-4 1/2	3 7/8-4 5/8	4 1/8-4 5/8
6/30/58	1 5/8-2 5/8	--	3 3/4	1 3/4-4 1/4	1 7/8-4 1/4
12/31/58	3 1/4-4 3/8	4 3/8	4 3/8	3 1/2-4 3/8	3 1/2

Source: Survey made by the National Consumer Finance Association.

TABLE A-16

Range of Interest Rates on Commercial Paper Sold to the Public by Six Moderately Large Companies, Including Bankers' Commissions, 1949-1958

Six Month Period Ending	90-119 Paper	120-149 Paper	150-179 Paper	180-239 Paper	240-269 Paper
6/30/49	2 1/4	2 1/8	2 1/8-2 1/4	2 1/8	--
12/31/49	1 3/4-2	--	1 3/4-2 1/4	1 3/4	--
6/30/50	1 3/4-2	1 3/4-2 1/4	1 3/4-2 1/4	2 1/4	1 3/4
12/31/50	2-2 1/4	2-2 1/4	2-2 1/4	2-2 1/4	--
6/30/51	2 1/2	2 1/2	2 1/2-2 3/4	2 3/4	--
12/31/51	2 1/2-3	2 1/2	2 1/2-2 7/8	3	--
6/30/52	2 3/8-3	2 3/8-2 3/4	2 1/2-2 3/4	2 5/8-3	2 5/8-2 7/8
12/31/52	2 3/8-3	2 3/8-3	2 1/2-2 3/4	2 5/8-3	2 5/8-2 3/4
6/30/53	3-3 1/4	3-3 1/4	3 1/8-3 1/4	3 1/8-3 1/4	3 1/4
12/31/53	2 5/8-3	2 5/8-2 3/4	2 5/8-2 7/8	2 5/8-3	2 5/8-3
6/30/54	1 1/2-3	1 1/2-2	1 5/8-2	1 3/4-2	2-2 1/4
12/31/54	1 3/8-1 7/8	1 1/2-1 7/8	1 5/8-1 3/4	1 5/8-2	1 3/4-2
6/30/55	2 1/4-2 3/4	2 3/8-2 3/4	2 3/8-2 5/8	2 1/2-2 3/4	2 1/2-2 7/8
12/31/55	3 1/8-3 5/8	3 1/8-3 1/2	3 1/4-3 1/2	3 3/8-3 1/2	3 1/2
6/30/56	3 3/8-4	3 1/2-3 3/4	3 1/2-3 3/4	3 5/8-3 7/8	3 3/4-4
12/31/56	3 5/8-4 1/4	3 5/8-4 1/4	3 5/8-4 1/4	3 3/4-4 3/8	3 7/8-4 1/2
6/30/57	4-4 3/8	4-4 5/8	3 7/8-4 1/2	4-4 5/8	4 1/4-4 3/4
12/31/57	3 3/4-4 1/2	3 7/8-4 5/8	3 7/8-4 5/8	4-4 3/4	4 1/8-4 7/8
6/30/58	1 3/4-2 1/4	1 3/4-2 1/4	1 3/4-2 1/4	1 7/8-2 3/8	2-2 1/2
12/31/58	2 5/8-3 5/8	3 3/8-3 3/4	3 3/8-3 3/4	3 5/8-3 7/8	3 5/8-4

Source: Survey made by the National Consumer Finance Association.

TABLE A-17
Range of Interest Rates on Commercial Paper Sold to the Public by Three Medium-Size Companies, Including Bankers' Commissions, 1949-1958

Six Month Period Ending	90-119 Paper	120-149 Paper	150-179 Paper	180-239 Paper	240-269 Paper
6/30/49	$1\frac{1}{2}$	$1\frac{3}{4}$	$1\frac{3}{4}$	--	--
12/31/49	$1\frac{1}{2}$	$1\frac{3}{4}$	$1\frac{3}{4}$	--	--
6/30/50	$1\frac{1}{2}$	$1\frac{3}{4}$	$1\frac{3}{4}$	--	--
12/31/50	$1\frac{3}{4}$	2	2	--	--
6/30/51	$2\frac{1}{8}$	$2\frac{3}{8}$	$2\frac{3}{8}$	--	--
12/31/51	$2\frac{1}{4}$	$2\frac{1}{2}$	$2\frac{1}{2}$	--	--
6/30/52	$2\frac{1}{2}$	$2\frac{3}{4}$	$2\frac{3}{4}$	--	--
12/31/52	$2\frac{1}{2}$	$2\frac{3}{4}$	$2\frac{3}{4}$	--	--
6/30/53	$2\frac{1}{2}$	$2\frac{3}{4}$	$2\frac{3}{4}$	--	--
12/31/53	$2\frac{1}{4}$	$2\frac{1}{2}$	$2\frac{1}{2}$	--	--
6/30/54	2	$2\frac{1}{4}$	$2\frac{1}{4}-2\frac{1}{2}$	$2\frac{1}{4}$	--
12/31/54	$1\frac{1}{2}$	$1\frac{3}{4}$	$1\frac{3}{4}-2\frac{1}{2}$	2	--
6/30/55	$1\frac{3}{4}$	2	$2-2\frac{5}{8}$	$2\frac{3}{4}$	--
12/31/55	$3\frac{1}{4}$	$3\frac{1}{2}$	$3\frac{1}{4}-3\frac{1}{2}$	$3\frac{5}{8}$	--
6/30/56	$3\frac{5}{8}$	$3\frac{7}{8}$	$3\frac{3}{4}-3\frac{7}{8}$	$4\frac{1}{8}$	--
12/31/56	4	$4\frac{1}{4}$	$4\frac{1}{4}-4\frac{1}{2}$	$4\frac{1}{4}$	--
6/30/57	$4\frac{1}{2}$	$4\frac{3}{4}$	$4\frac{1}{4}-4\frac{3}{4}$	$4\frac{1}{4}$	--
12/31/57	$4\frac{3}{8}$	$4\frac{5}{8}$	$4\frac{5}{8}-5$	$4\frac{1}{2}$	--
6/30/58	$2\frac{5}{8}$	$2\frac{7}{8}$	$2\frac{1}{2}-2\frac{7}{8}$	$2\frac{3}{8}$	--
12/31/58	$3\frac{3}{4}$	4	4	4	--

Source: Survey made by the National Consumer Finance Association.

TABLE A-18
List of New Long-Term Senior Debt Issued, 1949-1958[a]

Period	Amount in Dollars	Effective Rate of Interest on Proceeds	Size of Company
1-1 to 12-31-49	5,000,000	3.0%	Moderately large
	5,000,000	3.0%	Moderately large
1-1 to 12-31-50	20,000,000	2.784%	Large
	15,000,000	3.0%	Moderately large
	2,000,000	3.25%	Moderately large
	13,000,000	3.2%	Moderately large
	10,000,000	3.0%	Moderately large
1-1 to 12-31-51	30,000,000	3.795%	Large
	20,000,000	3.034%	Large
	25,000,000	3.51%	Large
	20,000,000	3.875%	Moderately large
	4,000,000	3.75%	Moderately large
	750,000	4.5%	Medium
1-1 to 12-31-52	30,000,000	3.659%	Large
	25,000,000	3.64%	Large
	3,000,000	3.5%	Moderately large
	1,000,000	3.75%	Medium
	1,000,000	3.75%	Medium
	250,000	4.5%	Medium

(Continued)

182

Table A-18 (Continued)

Period	Amount in Dollars	Effective Rate of Interest on Proceeds	Size of Company
1-1 to 12-31-53	25,000,000	4.372%	Large
	25,000,000	4.12%	Large
	3,000,000	3.5%	Moderately large
	16,000,000	3.875% changed to 4.25% July 1956	Moderately large
	18,000,000	3.875% changed to 4.375% June 1956	Moderately large
1-1 to 12-31-54	25,000,000	3.421%	Large
	4,000,000	3.875% changed to 4.25% July 1956	Moderately large
	20,000,000	3.5%	Moderately large
	8,000,000	3.95%	Moderately large
1-1 to 12-31-55	30,000,000	3.41%	Large
	2,000,000	4.125%	Moderately large
	1,000,000	3.75%	Moderately large
	1,000,000	3.75%	Medium
	1,000,000	3.5%	Medium
	300,000	5.5%	Small
1-1 to 12-31-56	35,000,000	4.146%	Large
	50,000,000	4.05%	Large
	9,500,000	3.80%	Moderately large
	25,000,000	4.25%	Moderately large
	600,000	4.25%	Moderately large
	2,750,000	5.375%	Moderately large
	1,500,000	4.75%	Moderately large
	8,500,000	4.75%	Moderately large
	23,800,000	5.125%	Moderately large
	18,900,000	4.0%	Moderately large
	9,050,000	4.5%	Moderately large
	3,000,000	4.75%	Medium
	1,000,000	4.5%	Medium
	2,000,000	5.125%	Medium
	1,000,000	4.5%	Medium
	10,000,000	4.75%	Medium
	1,500,000	4.5%	Medium
1-1 to 12-31-57	50,000,000	5.353%	Large
	40,000,000	5.12%	Large
	30,000,000	4.73%	Large
	5,825,000	5.5%	Moderately large
	1,500,000	5.5%	Moderately large
	5,000,000	5.0%	Moderately large
	250,000	5.375%	Moderately large
	6,000,000	5.5%	Moderately large
	14,550,000	5.7%	Moderately large
	500,000	5.5%	Moderately large
1-1 to 12-31-58	3,000,000	5.75%	Moderately large
	2,000,000	5.375%	Moderately large
	1,000,000	5.0%	Small

[a] One small company sold varying amounts of senior debt each year during the period 1949-1958 at an unchanged rate of 6.5%.

Source: Survey made by the National Consumer Finance Association.

TABLE A-19
List of New Long-Term Subordinated Debt Issued, 1949-1958

Period	Amount in Dollars	Effective Rate of Interest on Proceeds	Size of Company
1-1 to 12-31-49	5,000,000	4.0%	Moderately large
	400,000	4.5%	Moderately large
	50,000	4.5%	Small
	75,000[a]	5.0%	Small
1-1 to 12-31-50	8,000,000	3.875%	Moderately large
	2,000,000	4.0%	Moderately large
	900,000	4.5%	Moderately large
	4,000,000	5.5%	Moderately large
	250,000	4.5%	Medium
	111,500[a]	5.0%	Small
1-1 to 12-31-51	500,000	4.25%	Moderately large
	150,000	4.5%	Medium
	455,000[b]	5.0%	Small
	130,500[a]	5.0%	Small
1-1 to 12-31-52	12,000,000	4.75%	Moderately large
	8,000,000	4.1%	Moderately large
	3,000,000	4.75%	Medium
	718,000[b]	5.0%	Small
	171,850[a]	5.0%	Small
1-1 to 12-31-53	4,250,000	4.5%	Moderately large
	441,900	5.0%	Moderately large
	3,000,000	4.5%	Moderately large
	2,750,000	5.7%	Moderately large
	400,000	6.0%	Medium
	750,000	5.0%	Small
	670,000[b]	5.0%	Small
	287,300[a]	5.0%	Small
1-1 to 12-31-54	3,200,000	3.9% changed to 4.25% April 1956	Moderately large
	12,000,000	4.0%	Moderately large
	3,500,000	4.0%	Moderately large
	962,000	5.0%	Moderately large
	8,000,000	5.25%	Moderately large
	161,000	5.0%	Medium
	82,500	5.0%	Small
	34,000[b]	6.0%	Small
	3,300,000[b]	5.0%	Small
	277,300[a]	5.0%	Small
1-1 to 12-31-55	2,000,000	4.75%	Moderately large
	613,900	5.0%	Moderately large
	2,100,000	4.25%	Moderately large
	339,000	5.0%	Medium
	2,000,000	4.25%	Medium
	700,000	4.75%	Medium
	50,000	5.0%	Small
	83,500	5.0%	Small
	990,000	5.0%	Small
	465,410	6.0%	Small
	374,150[a]	5.0%	Small
	200,000	7.0%	Small

(Continued)

184

Period	Amount in Dollars	Effective Rate of Interest on Proceeds	Size of Company
1-1 to 12-31-56	4,750,000	5.0%	Moderately large
	6,500,000	4.55%	Moderately large
	9,200,000	4.5%	Moderately large
	7,000,000	6.0%	Moderately large
	10,000,000	4.5%	Moderately large
	7,500,000	5.375%	Moderately large
	1,000,000	4.75%	Moderately large
	603,200	5.0%	Moderately large
	700,000	5.75%	Moderately large
	1,000,000	4.75%	Moderately large
	136,800	5.0%	Medium
	1,000,000	5.75%	Medium
	1,000,000	5.5%	Medium
	155,080	5.0% and 6.0%	Small
	220,000[b]	5.0%	Small
	8,090	6.0%	Small
	554,700[a]	5.0%	Small
1-1 to 12-31-57	800,000	6.0%	Moderately large
	4,200,000	6.5%	Moderately large
	2,500,000	5.875%	Moderately large
	2,800,000	5.875%	Moderately large
	987,000	5.0%	Moderately large
	454,500	4.75%	Moderately large
	3,000,000	6.25%	Moderately large
	363,000	5.0%	Medium
	2,250,000	5.375%	Medium
	100,000	6.0%	Small
	108,000[b]	6.0%	Small
	310,000[b]	5.0%	Small
	700,700[a]	5.0%	Small
1-1 to 12-31-58	10,000,000	5.0%	Moderately large
	675,500	5.0%	Moderately large
	501,900	4.75%	Moderately large
	10,000,000	5.85%	Moderately large
	1,500,000	5.25%	Medium
	500,000	5.0%	Medium
	500,000	5.5%	Small
	384,000[b]	6.0%	Small
	190,000[b]	5.0%	Small
	838,950[a]	5.5%	Small

[a] One small company reported new issues of three to five year maturity subordinated each year 1951-1958 at 5%, and new issues of ten year maturity subordinated during 1954, 1957, and 1958 at 6%.

[b] One small company reported new issues each year 1949-1957 at 5% and 1958 at 5.5%.

Source: Survey made by the National Consumer Finance Association.

COMMISSION ON MONEY AND CREDIT

Members

Frazar B. Wilde, CHAIRMAN
Chairman, Connecticut General Life Insurance Company

H. Christian Sonne, VICE CHAIRMAN
New York, New York

Adolf A. Berle, Jr.
New York, New York
(Withdrew to serve as Chairman of the U.S. State Department Latin American Task Force.)

James B. Black
Chairman of the Board, Pacific Gas & Electric Company

Joseph M. Dodge
Chairman of the Board, The Detroit Bank and Trust Company
(Resigned October 7, 1960.)

Marriner S. Eccles
Chairman of the Board, First Security Corporation

Lamar Fleming, Jr.
Chairman of the Board, Anderson, Clayton & Co.

Henry H. Fowler
Fowler, Leva, Hawes & Symington
(Resigned February 3, 1961, on his appointment as Under Secretary of the Treasury.)

Gaylord A. Freeman, Jr.
Vice Chairman, The First National Bank of Chicago
(Appointed April 29, 1960.)

Fred T. Greene
President, Federal Home Loan Bank of Indianapolis
(Died March 17, 1961.)

Philip M. Klutznick
Park Forest, Illinois
(Resigned February 8, 1961, on his appointment as United States Representative to the Economic and Social Council of the United Nations.)

Fred Lazarus, Jr.
Chairman of the Board, Federated Department Stores, Inc.

Isador Lubin
Arthur T. Vanderbilt Professor of Public Affairs, Rutgers University

J. Irwin Miller
Chairman of the Board, Cummins Engine Company

Robert R. Nathan
President, Robert R. Nathan Associates, Inc.

Emil Rieve
President Emeritus, Textile Workers of America, AFL-CIO
(Appointed May 19, 1960.)

David Rockefeller
President, The Chase Manhattan Bank

Beardsley Ruml
New York, New York
(Died April 18, 1960.)

Stanley H. Ruttenberg
Director, Department of Research, AFL-CIO

Charles Sawyer
Taft, Stettinius & Hollister

William F. Schnitzler
Secretary-Treasurer, AFL-CIO
(Resigned April 28, 1960.)

186

Earl B. Schwulst
President and Chairman of the Board, The Bowery Savings Bank

Charles B. Shuman
President, American Farm Bureau Federation

Jesse W. Tapp
Chairman of the Board, Bank of America, N.T. and S.A.

J. Cameron Thomson
Retired Chairman of the Board, Northwest Bancorporation

Willard L. Thorp
Director, Merrill Center for Economics, Amherst College

Theodore O. Yntema
Chairman, Finance Committee, Ford Motor Company

Advisory Board

Lester V. Chandler
Professor of Economics, Princeton University

Gerhard Colm
Chief Economist, National Planning Association

Gaylord A. Freeman, Jr.
Vice Chairman, The First National Bank of Chicago
(Resigned April 29, 1960, on his appointment to the Commission.)

Leo Grebler
Professor of Business Administration, University of California (Los Angeles)

Raymond W. Goldsmith
Professor of Economics, Yale University

Neil H. Jacoby
Dean, School of Business Administration, University of California (Los Angeles)

Richard A. Musgrave
Woodrow Wilson School of Public and International Affairs, Princeton University

Richard E. Neustadt
Professor of Public Law and Government, Columbia University

Paul A. Samuelson
Professor of Economics, Massachusetts Institute of Technology

Sumner H. Slichter
Lamont University Professor, Harvard University
(Died September 27, 1959.)

Edward S. Shaw
Professor of Economics, Stanford University

Alan H. Temple
New York, New York

Jacob Viner
Professor of Economics, Emeritus, Princeton University

Staff

Bertrand Fox
Research Director

Eli Shapiro
Deputy Research Director